"Buckle up, clear your schedule, and get ready for an incredible book. Phil Williams weaves sports stories and family dynamics and more, somehow merging all of it within the deeper meaning of life. His descriptive story writing will move your emotions in ways you never thought possible and open your eyes like never before. Book reader or not, athlete or not, believer or not—this book is for you. Enjoy!!!"

– ANTHONY HARGROVE, SUPER BOWL XLIV CHAMPION AND
ED BLOCK COURAGE AWARD RECIPIENT

"The best book I have ever read on the process of grief. It is a story of life, death, healing, and the search for truth. It is simultaneously gut-wrenching and inspiring. Here is one man's journey through unexpected loss and what it can teach us all when all that is familiar falls away, when there is nothing to ground you or keep you steady—not even God. As in every real journey of healing, read this book to the very end and don't stop halfway when you get to the difficult emotions. Keep going to the end, to the very last page. This book is an invitation to feel, to be vulnerable, to know what's important, to face pain that seems too intense, and most importantly: to love deeply."

– LISA NATOLI, SPIRITUAL TEACHER OF THE HEALING CURE

"As I listened to Phil's book, it felt as if I was right there with him, somehow along for the journey, and seeing and feeling it all by his side. The stories are all so clear and detailed and true, revealing someone who we can relate to and get to know—a man, a father, a husband, a friend (he was my agent for 15 years). This book is authentic—that might be the best way I could describe it—and I found myself laughing and crying throughout. Though it has its gut-wrenching moments, for sure, it has so much more."

– BRAD JOHNSON, NFL SUPER BOWL WINNING QUARTERBACK
AND TWO-TIME PRO BOWLER

"Phil Williams' life is a test and triumph of will. I love this big, beautiful, brave book."

– DON VAN NATTA JR., ESPN SENIOR WRITER AND
NEW YORK TIMES BESTSELLING AUTHOR

"There's a lot of redemption and healing written into this story of deep loss. After experiencing one of the deepest tragedies possible, Phil Williams uncovers a fundamental truth about grief, especially following the loss of a child: it burns to the ground everything you once thought important, but from the ashes, remarkable insights and gifts can emerge. His journey is striking, marked by a slow ascent to what society views as success, followed by the rapid collapse of his beliefs and values. With raw emotion and candor, Williams' once-unquestioned connection to God unravels (as the title hints) before transforming into something far more meaningful. Never could he have imagined that when he asked God to 'Do whatever it takes to wake me up,' his prayer would be answered in such a devastating way yet ultimately lead to profound spiritual growth."

– MARLA GRANT, ADVANCED GRIEF RECOVERY
METHOD™ SPECIALIST

"This book creates a window for the reader to witness the 'nightmare' of a family's loss and invites us to journey with them through the stages of their bereavement and confusion. As the jolting title of this book portends, Phil pulls no punches as he skillfully narrates this heart-rending story. For those courageous enough to take this journey, it is my hope that you, like Phil, will let your 'silent tears flow' creating a growing clarity. Through this book, may you be blessed by Hannah's 'unseen angel' sending 'new gifts' of hope, love, and transformation."

– GIL WESLEY, SPIRITUAL DIRECTOR AND FORMER PASTOR

F*CK YOU, G⊛D

F*CK YOU, GOD

One Man's Evolution from Pursuit
through Pain to Peace

PHIL WILLIAMS

AWAKEN VILLAGE

PRESS

Printed in the United States of America.

Editing by: Grace Adamarie Watson
Cover and interior design by: Andrea Gibb

To contact the author or for permission requests, visit:
www.philwilliamswrites.com.

ISBN 978-1-957408-09-5 (paperback)
ISBN 978-1-957408-10-1 (ebook)

Library of Congress Control Number: 2024917544

Published by Awaken Village Press
Sioux Falls, South Dakota, U.S.A.
www.awakenvillagepress.com

Preface

I gave this book a rather provocative title. Some of y'all probably love it. And some are probably shaking your heads, maybe even saying a prayer for me. Either way, I would ask you to give it a little space. You might be surprised at where it takes us.

Also, this memoir may be different in other ways from some you may have read before. I say that because it is different for me. Though the heart of this story comes along in its good time, that heart can best be understood by getting to know it, by getting to know me. Thus will I take you on a journey—on my journey—as you continue your own.

First of all, let me say that my story is not what I would call sweet. Yeah, it's got plenty of sweet moments, funny moments, intriguing moments. But once it gets to that instant where my world goes dark, sweet ain't the word that comes to my mind. Hell, maybe. But not sweet.

And if you didn't get to know me along the way, before that switch gets pulled, I'm not sure if you could even hang with me.

I believe you can best get to know me and, therefore, better grasp what happens later, by walking with me through the stories of my childhood and with a fairly significant dive into the world of sports, as they had their place in shaping me and my heart. If you are not a sports fan, don't worry. It is the stories of life, of insecurity and fear and hope and seeking—all within the context of sports—that reveal themselves within the realm that held such sway over me for such a large part of my life. I'm pretty sure I could merge into a tale of fingernail painting if it allowed me to experience your heart (though I don't know a damn thing about it). But it's not really about sports or fingernail painting or any other specific area that we find ourselves in; it's the story of life being worked out within our own unique substratum of existence. It's not so much about "catching the ball" as it is about why we think we need to catch it. And what happens to us after we do catch it, or even drop it.

But once you walk with me through the childhood pranks, the teenage crazies, the college trials and triumphs, and my fatherly missteps and successes, maybe then you can sit with me when I get the news that my daughter is dying. Maybe then you can hang on for dear life as hers ebbs away. Maybe then you can stagger with me as I try to find my footing after her death. And maybe then you can rise up with me and face a life that neither of us would have ever asked for and, yet, may well be what we've been searching for.

I delve into my faith, my career, and, of course, my family—and in particular, my daughter, Hannah—all to give you as clear a picture as possible of what happened when, and after, I received the call that she was dying. And when she died. Without a taste of what led me to that point, you wouldn't see the whole story. And it is a "story" that I want to share.

So yeah, maybe it's not your normal sweet, but I assure you that it's in there all along, fighting for room to breathe. It's found in Hannah, and in others along the way. Always waiting to reveal itself.

If you stay with me through it all, you might just be surprised at how it surfaces. And, oh boy, does it surface!

Let's go ...

Inspiration

MAY 4, 2022

Today I begin.

It is your birthday.

You would have been thirty-three.

Today, I feel deep within that it is time, that enough tears have been shed and enough days passed to tell the story I knew one day would be told. Today, I sense you prodding me to get on with it, to sink into the truth of the past seven years, to relive the pains and embrace their hidden promptings toward a peace that "passes all understanding." Today, I honor you, my dearest Hannah, by moving forward. I hope I can make you proud. I trust that you will guide my mind and heart as I seek for words to tell our story.

I think of you every day, of your smile, of your laughter. I see your eyes, those radiant and loving blues, as they dance for joy in my memories. I can almost touch your brown hair, so thick I could barely drag my fingers through it when you would ask me to do so during those last months. I can feel your fingers so gently upon my back as I lay facing the moon in the same bed with you during the first weeks after we found out you were dying. You, thinking I must be sleeping while, in fact, my eyes were wide open as the tears dampened my pillow. And those same fingers, so slender, gently interlaced with my own as you breathed your last breath.

Most of all, though, I can feel your heart, a heart that this world could simply not contain. So beautiful, so kind and loving, and one that always saw the best in me, that saw the best in everyone. When others chastised me or judged me, you would slip in and hold me, sometimes with your arms, but always with your beautiful heart.

Thank you for being my daughter upon this earth for twenty-six and a half years, and for eternity. You have touched me beyond any attempt to convey. So for now, I will simply hold you close in my heart and do my best to tell our story.

Today, I begin.

Prologue
NOVEMBER 24, 2018

Earlier in the day, my beloved Rottweiler had died in my arms, Tank's death taking me back to the death of my daughter, three years earlier, and into those last crippling moments with her, the grief consuming me once more. And now, as I lay down to try to go to sleep, my body was humming with agitation and fear.

My wife and I were struggling, after thirty-one and a half years of marriage, at what was perhaps the bottom rung of our relationship. The loss of our daughter had blindsided us and left us groping in the dark as we tried desperately to help each other on the road to emotional recovery. It did not seem possible that we could find healing in the early going, and if we could, it seemed more likely by the day that our journeys to doing so might be separate. We were fighting with all we had to escape from underneath the pain and guilt and grief we both carried, and that was flooding into our marriage like a torrential river through a broken levee.

The prior two nights had already been challenging. I had experienced something I never had up until then: panic attacks. They were somewhat different from most I had heard of, as I would awaken in the middle of the night, instantly enveloped in a deep state of panic, my body vibrating as if plugged into a powerful electrical socket and, worse, my mind totally gone. Every thought that entered brought doom with it. I would desperately search my mind for some harbinger of peace—anything to stem the tide of fear—but nothing worked. Each attack had to play itself out. And yet there was one thing that helped somewhat, or so it seemed.

Over the prior few months, I had begun practicing meditation and had found solace in learning how to become present. All of our hurts are in the past, no matter how recent, and our worries concern the future. Being in the moment, the present, can allow for a reprieve from those two tormentors, so each night I fought to be with my breath and escape the torture, to focus only on the breath. Both nights, it seemed to aid me, little by little softening the panic until I could relax enough to go back to sleep and, hopefully, make it until morning.

I felt a dark foreboding on this third night, fearful to even close my eyes, anxious about what awaited me. My heart ached for Tank. My body was already vibrating, and I was so exhausted. Soon my eyes became heavy. And so I drifted off.

I awoke in sheer terror in the black of night, my body shot through with adrenaline, my mind frantic. I jumped up from the bed and stumbled through the bathroom toward the front door. Where was I going? I did not know, but I felt an agonizing impulse to "get free" from this monster that had latched onto me with its black, suffocating heaviness. I opened the front door and then quickly shut it. I retraced my steps back into the bathroom and glanced nervously into the bedroom.

There is nowhere to go, Phil, a voice whispered. *You are pretty much at the end of your rope. No one really loves you; nothing really matters anymore. You've fucked everything up; your kids are better off without you; Meg will probably find her way on without you. Your future is one of utter loneliness.*

I lunged for the front door again and stepped outside onto our porch on the second floor of our jungle bungalow. Where was there to go to escape this unbearable fear? *Nowhere,* the voice suggested. *Except …*

"Oh God, no," I thought to myself.

It might be your only relief, the voice continued. *Probably is.*

I turned and staggered back into the house, fighting to keep the voice at bay, and walked back into the bedroom. Meg lay there sleeping. Because we were somewhat estranged at the moment, I hesitated to wake her up and share my predicament. But with my mind in full panic mode and fear squeezing me into a box with no good options, I nudged her awake and told her I felt suicidal.

She did not speak.

For some reason, I lay back down and grabbed her right hand, placing it over my heart. I held it firmly there, convinced that the human touch mattered. This might have been the only rational thought I had in that state. Maybe that's what allowed for another insightful thought to enter. "Breathe, Phil, breathe," I told myself. "Feel the breath in your nostrils. Just do it—it might be your only hope."

The fear I had felt when I first heard that my daughter was dying had been debilitating. The sorrow I had felt when she left this world one hundred days later had been seemingly insurmountable. The prospect of living the rest of my life without her had been severely traumatizing. All had left me with little hope.

Now, enclosed within the grip of what seemed the darkest night of the soul imaginable, a sharp, black, icy finger traced its way up my spine, and the voice broke in one more time—*breathing will do NOTHING. Give up. There is no hope. Your life is over ...*

I breathed in almost violently, if for no other reason than to stave off the voice, doing my damnedest to feel the breath as it passed through my nostrils. Then, I exhaled shakily.

"Become present, Phil," I told myself.

"Breathe!"

I did.

In ... out ... in ...

What happened next is impossible to explain with words.

And yet this story would not be complete without trying.

PART ONE

And So It Begins ...

THE CALL

"I'm so sorry."

I dug my cell phone out of the front right pocket of my blue jeans and glanced at it. There was a missed call and a voice message. I shot a quick look over at Hannah and smiled weakly.

"There's a message from Chuck," I said. Chuck Bergstrom was my personal doctor and a friend from Grace Evangelical Church, which I had attended for many years in the past. Hannah and I had visited him the day before to check out some troubling physical issues she was having, mainly associated with what seemed to be in and around her liver.

I listened to the voice message. Short and cryptic. Basically, "Call me." My heart skipped a beat. Surely he would have sounded different if the news had been good. For the first time, a wicked thought crept into my mind. Though, in that instant, I realized the thought had been there all along, one so horrid that you simply do not let it rise up to the point of contemplation. *Let it go*, I quickly reasoned with myself once more. I redialed Chuck and stared absentmindedly at the remaining chicken wings and French fries that sat in the baskets in front of us.

Hannah and I had been eating at Beef O'Brady's, barely a stone's throw away from the Outpatient Imaging Center in Peachtree City, Georgia, where Hannah had received a CT scan just an hour earlier, one that Chuck, I now realized as I waited for him to answer his cell phone, had hastily set up for us during our prior day's appointment. Hannah and I were sitting opposite each other in the booth closest to the exit door.

"What did he say?" Hannah asked as I waited for Chuck to answer. I shook my head as if to say, "Nothing, really," smiled again at her and heard Chuck pick up.

"Hello." Almost brusque, businesslike. Anybody who knows Chuck knows he is a funny dude—some might say crazy, for a doctor. In a good way. He and I'd had quite a few visits over the years, mainly just physicals, and they were all exceptionally jovial. Nutty, to be honest. Two like-minded fellows bouncing smart-ass comments off of the sterile walls where he conducted his doctoral duties and making fun of whatever little ailment I might've had. Well, except maybe for the time I had a scattering of life-threatening blood clots peppering my lungs, which reminded me that he did have his serious side. He even insisted on rolling me out to my truck via wheelchair that day, which had seemed awful silly to me, seeing how I had walked in there just fine a few moments earlier. But hadn't he seemed at peace yesterday when he had examined Hannah? He'd shown no signs while examining her that he was overly concerned, had he? Was that just a facade? Did I miss something?

"Hey, Chuck, this is Phil. I see you called."

The next words out of his mouth changed my world forever.

"I'm so sorry."

My heart froze.

"I don't know how else to say this," Chuck continued. "She has cancer. It's bad."

Hannah was reading my body language. Though I was trying to act nonchalant, either looking down at the table or at the other diners, I could peripherally see her studying me. She knew something was off. I could see *that* in *her* body language.

"Daddy, what is it?" I heard her cry from across the booth. Not loud, but fearful. There was an edge to her voice that took my heart, already reeling, and crushed it further, if that were possible.

Up until that point, I had not been looking at her, vaguely scanning the crowd of patrons at Beef's, as we called it, a bunch of people who were laughing and smiling and drinking beer and, I'm sure, discussing such mundane, frivolous things like college football and family trips to the beaches at Seaside, Florida, and other meaningless bullshit.

I couldn't answer her. I pretended not to hear, as if Chuck was still talking, but I could feel her eyes, those big beautiful eyes, from across the table, my heart throbbing in my chest, loud enough for her to hear. I shifted my own eyes from the oblivious crowd to the only person in the world who mattered to me at that moment. Oh God, why did those beautiful blue eyes of hers have to hold such fear in them? My heart sank even further, and for a second, I wondered if I had the courage to tell her.

I took a deep breath and nodded at her. I think we'd both already known but had somehow buried it inside.

"Cancer?" she asked, tears forming in her eyes.

I nodded again, almost imperceptibly, Chuck patiently waiting. The first tear spilled onto her cheek. Was it possible for my pain to get worse? Yes, it was. She scooted out of her side of the booth, asking, "Where is it, Daddy?"

While she made her way around to my side of the booth, I managed to pass the question on to Chuck. I heard his reply and asked him if I could call him back in a bit. He said yes.

By now, Hannah was sitting close to me and tears were pouring down her face, her eyes peering deep into my own. I pulled her close and whispered the answer she really didn't want to hear, my lips almost touching her left ear through her thick brown hair.

"Colon. Liver. Lungs." And I felt her body heave against mine, deep sobs convulsing her. I felt dirty. This simply could not be. This was my baby girl. How could I have allowed such a thing, not noticed, not taken better care of her? What kind of father was I? A darkness fell on me, an ungodly weight. I hugged her tight and felt her hugging me even tighter.

"Let's go outside," I suggested. We slid out of the booth and walked outside to a bench next to the restaurant.

Before we sat down, Hannah said, "I'm so sorry for you and Momma." That was Hannah, to a tee. Thinking of and hurting for others. We sat down and resumed our clutching of each other and our crying, as I had now joined in.

The mid-July day was typical for Peachtree City, hot and humid. The skies were clear enough, mainly blue with patches of clouds, but the air was thick and god-awful stifling. It had a quality to it that was like nothing I'd ever felt before, as if fissures had broken through the earth's surface, maybe all the way from hell, and released gasses from deep below with a numbing effect. Every breath I took was insufficient, unable to create room in my chest to truly breathe, to feel some kind of relief. "Not my baby," echoed in my mind again and again. Negotiations had already commenced between me and God. "Please, spare her. Take me instead. Anybody but Hannah!"

I have no idea how long we sat there before finally relaxing our grip on each other and looking into each other's tear-soaked eyes.

"I love you," I muttered, chin still quivering a little.

She nodded and even smiled a little. "I love you, too, Daddy. Maybe we should go somewhere else."

"Yeah. Let's get out of here."

We stood up from the bench and made our way toward my car, hand in hand, neither one of us with any idea where we might go, but both certain we were on a journey that would challenge every belief we had ever known.

WHO AM I?

"If you were me…"

I was born and raised in rural south Georgia by a Methodist pastor and his wife, Ben and Marilyn Williams—or as I called them, Daddy and Momma. I was their second child, thrust out into the world two years after my brother, Steve. As Momma tells it, I was close to a perfect baby. I was such a joy, happy as could be, almost too good to be true.

But that was before my sister, Kat, was born.

That, Momma says, was like God kicking me out of the Garden. My world shattered, and the once smiling, happy-go-lucky toddler became fearful, needy, and selfish for attention, all of which would be fleshed out over the coming decades.

The Methodist church moved my daddy around every few years, and it so happened that a few months after Kat's birth, they sent us to Macon, Georgia, where Daddy became the pastor at Hillcrest United Methodist Church.

On our first Sunday there, as he was preparing to deliver his inaugural sermon, Momma dropped me off at the church nursery. Shortly after she left, I surveyed the room, but I couldn't find a familiar face. A horrible feeling of abandonment came over me, and I screamed at the top of my lungs, refusing to be comforted by those awful strangers. One of them scurried off to find whichever parent they could, and soon Daddy came to the nursery with a heavy step and a scowl.

PART ONE

My normally easygoing and gentle-spirited daddy must have been extremely embarrassed because he whipped me, one of the few times he ever did (though, if whippings were "deserved," I reckon I deserved *far* more of them). Despite the physical punishment, though, I was relieved to get the confirmation that I wasn't alone in the world.

My parents knew I was "special" at a young age, that I danced to a different tune, that I saw things differently, at least in some ways. One of those ways was how my mind worked when questioned, or when I felt challenged.

One particular morning when I was rather young, my grandmother and I were alone in the living room. I was fiddling around with some contraption that had been given to me, and she evidently thought I was not doing something properly.

"Phil, if I were you, I would do it such-and-such a way," Grandmama said, bending my way to elucidate young Phil.

I twisted away from her. "If you were me," I said, eyes flashing, "You would do exactly what I am doing."

One day not long after that, at six years old, I did what a lot of six-year-olds do. I got *real* stupid. Directly next to the little parsonage where we lived sat an odd little abandoned putt-putt course. It was just a few random holes with rough concrete surfaces and a whole lot of grass around. But it was the grass that enticed me on this fine day, a strangely tempting sea of thick dry grass. There had not been a rain for a spell, nor a mowing.

Obviously, it was ripe for a Phil experiment!

The experiment and its protocols? Step one: light a match. Step two: toss the lit match onto the grass. Step three: smile and watch the fire grow. Step four: stomp it out. Step five: repeat the steps, but let it get bigger each time.

Boy, was it fun! Until about the fourth attempt, when the fire got too big and I went straight to a new, final step: run like hell to the house and hide.

Like I said, stupid.

I flew the short distance to my house, crept inside, and crawled up under the coffee table in the den. I'm not sure how long I hid there, but pretty soon I heard the sound of sirens blasting away nearby, getting closer and closer. And then I saw two very hard-looking shoes appear in front of my face up under that coffee table. Those shoes did not look happy.

"*Phillllll!*"

I do not recall what happened next, but I have not set any random fires since.

The Methodist Church must have figured that Macon had experienced enough of the Phil factor, so they shipped us off to a small south Georgia town called Dawson during the summer before I entered third grade. Shortly thereafter, I began to develop a deep love for sports, especially baseball and football. I would watch them both on television, mystically understanding the nuances of the games as if they were programmed into my DNA, and drawn deeply into the magic of it all. I would jump up and down in front of the TV, the energy, the competition, the adulation of the fans, the excitement of the players all pulsating deep within me. I just knew it was for me.

Upon arriving in Dawson, I immediately signed up to play Tee League baseball, scared as heck in my new environment but very excited. My daddy could tell pretty quickly that I was one of the more talented youngsters. But with as much success as I experienced early on, I also had some pretty rough moments along the way. The first of those times came the next year in baseball, shortly after the tees were put away and the live pitching began. For the first time in my life, I struck out in a game. This triggered something deep inside of me, as if a large neon sign had begun flashing the word "FAILURE. FAILURE. FAILURE." throughout the Little League ballpark.

I walked very slowly back toward the dugout and suddenly stopped, lunging at the chain-link fence that bordered the field, somewhere between the backstop behind home plate and the dugout, and buried my face into that fence, sobbing. I couldn't bear the thought of going back to where my fellow teammates and coaches were. The umpire even had to call timeout so my coach could trot over and coax me back to the dugout, where I sat by myself and continued to cry.

For the remaining years that I played baseball, rarely did I ever strike out again. I was a good hitter, and I likely could have been better had I not been so fearful of striking out, the bitter sting of shame seemingly so attached to such an event.

As a general rule, and maybe I didn't see it as such at the time, most things were easy for me. Or at least easier than for most kids. Part of that was probably natural, but I also seemed to have a yearning to be the best at whatever I was doing. It's not like I was super talented at everything—usually far from a savant—but I was destined to be the epitome of an overachiever. Just enough talent in my chosen endeavors, but when combined with intensity and drive, I could generally make it happen. And sometimes at a high level. Therefore, I excelled in sports and academics and pretty much most of the things I put my mind to, even if it wasn't a passion of mine.

Like band class.

In fifth grade, I tried out for the school band because a couple of my friends were in it. And maybe a cute girl or two. I surveyed the group so as to decide what instrument to play, and though it felt like the trumpet was cooler, I chose the trombone because that's what the band needed. By the time the season was over, I won Most Outstanding Band Member and went on to regionals with another band member or two. Then I quit, never to pick up a trombone again. It just wasn't cool enough for me anymore.

Honestly, you would have thought I was intent on maxing out in almost *every* area of life, as I likely would have won an award for contracting the most serious illnesses as a young fellow had there been such a thing. I, therefore, spent a fair amount of time in my early childhood visiting hospitals, sometimes even staying in them for a week or so at a time. Some of the *lesser* illnesses I experienced were mumps, chicken pox, the "big red" measles, German measles, various bouts with the flu, and severe cases of strep throat. The two I remember most are pneumonia and scarlet fever.

That scarlet fever thing seriously kicked my little ten-year-old butt. I spent almost two weeks in the local hospital, and I began to hate it when I saw the nurses walk in, usually carrying a loaded syringe. Daddy got tired of me whining, so he devised a plan to help me cope with all those needles the nurses kept sticking in me. He figured, if I knew I was getting paid for each jab, I would handle it better. Well, he was right! He gave me twenty-five cents for each *little* needle, which usually was for some type of shot, and fifty cents for each *big* one—those things seemed monstrous—which always meant a blood extraction. I didn't leave the hospital a millionaire, but I toted out a bag of change that made me feel pretty wealthy at the time.

GROWING UP

"Just shoot the ball!"

The late '60s were interesting days for a child in the South. There was still segregation in the schools back then, and prejudice oozed pretty thick, though I barely had a clue. Then, when integration hit Georgia in 1969, I was snatched right out of my comfort zone in the previously all-white public school and hauled over to Carver Junior High School across the imaginary line that divided the whites and blacks of Dawson, where I was plopped smack dab into the middle of a bunch of black kids.

At first, I was frightened about going to an "all-black" school and very unsure about my parents' decision to send me there; in hindsight, I understand their reasoning. They showed hearts of courage and compassion for doing what very few would have done back in those days—intentionally sending their children to a black public school in the Deep South in the first year of integration. I sat all alone at first, unsure if I was even safe, wondering if Daddy and Momma even loved me anymore. Probably flashing back to the nursery dropoff all those years earlier. But within a few days, and after we got used to each other, I became part of the crew, just a little different-looking one than I was used to is all.

Many years later, I learned that Daddy had been pressured by a few whites in town, including some from the church he pastored, to get his kids to the private school so as not to have to go to school with *those blacks.* Some with money were evidently even offering to provide scholarships for me and my siblings to do so. Daddy said no, he wasn't going to pay, or accept pay, to get away from *those blacks,* even if he did feel some threats lurking within the offers.

One of the obstacles I had to overcome at my new school was dealing with a kid in my grade who fancied himself the bully of the new white kid, and though he never outright challenged me, he acted awful tough, eyeing me pretty good for the first few weeks I was there. I wondered if I was going to end up in a fight, and being one of only a few white kids in the whole school—and the only white kid in some of my classes—I couldn't help but think I might be at a disadvantage if things got physical.

But it never happened.

I shared a few classes with the kid, one of which was taught by the vice principal, a fairly big fellow who occasionally swung a pretty mean razor strap across a hand or two when the notion hit him. I don't remember what the kid did, but it must have riled up the teacher because he called him up to the front of the class and began to open his desk drawer. As soon as that strap came into view, you would have thought it was a rattlesnake ready to strike because that kid began to shake and squirm and cry like a baby. And that was before the teacher even administered the whipping. Needless to say, that fellow could barely even look me in the eye after that. And I sure was thankful for not having to get into a fight at my new school.

I was never one to start a fight, but I was never one to back down, either. Such as with my big brother, Steve, who always seemed to have the time to pick on his younger brother—*me.* I, of course, never accepted that behavior, so naturally, we fought a lot. It was usually just him, but one time he and a friend of his from the neighborhood were giving me some shit, and I decided not to take it, even if it was two bigger guys against one. It got pretty rough. There was a lot of shoving going on, and a few fists thrown around, too. I went inside at some point, washed blood out of my mouth, and looked in the mirror. I did not like my predicament. I sighed a time or two, gritted my teeth, growled, and went back outside for some more.

If baseball had been my first love, football quickly became my main love. I had discovered a niche, a skill I possessed that set me apart from my peers in at least one area and made me feel *special*.

Turns out I was really good at catching footballs.

And I mean *really* good—maybe even a savant.

I began to cultivate that niche, that gift, with an intensity rarely seen. From a very young age, I had an obsession with catching footballs, such that I could be seen diving upon gravel driveways at neighbors' homes during "backyard" football games (which was always with the older boys) to ensure the ball didn't touch the ground. I was gluttonous for that ball, somehow believing even at such an early age that, as long as it was still in the air, IT WAS MINE.

I wasn't big or tall, wasn't very fast, and couldn't jump that great—average, I would say—but I did have a few redeeming traits. For one, I was blessed with excellent hand-eye coordination, a skill that helped me in most other sports as well, even games like ping pong. And then there's a gift I like to call "seeing moving things," where I could feel what the opposing team was doing. It's hard to explain; I just could visualize what the opponents were going to do as soon as there was any movement. In football, this helped me immensely, as I could "go where they weren't" with the best of them, allowing me to consistently get open. There was also one other trait I possessed: I was intense. *Intensely* intense! And so it was that these three attributes allowed me to succeed at sports.

I played tight end in football through ninth grade, and I was always the focus of the passing game for whichever team I played for. Though I would not have considered myself cocky, I guess I was. For example, my dad was transferred from Dawson to Warner Robins in the summer of 1972, and upon arriving at Warner Robins Junior High School a couple of months later, I promptly asked some of the guys on the football team who the starting tight end was from the previous season. They gave me the kid's name.

"Well, he ain't anymore," I responded matter-of-factly.

None of those guys had seen me play yet, so they sort of just raised an eyebrow or two. They didn't realize how important it was for me to be *that guy*. To be honest, I didn't either; I only knew that being successful at sports, especially football, had become almost vital to my emotional well-being.

And though I did well the next couple years while playing tight end in junior high, one of my more vivid memories is not what I would label a success. In one of our games, due to a trick play our coach had called, I found myself running all alone down the field. If ever there was an easy touchdown to be made, this was it—no one within 20 yards of me! The throw was perfect, but for some reason, instead of catching it with my hands, I cradled my arms like a basket, and the ball slid right through to the ground.

The next thing that hit the ground was me. I buried my facemask in the turf, sorely tempted to stay there for a while, crazily hoping no one would notice. Shades of Little League baseball failures rushed back into my mind like a recurring nightmare.

Robert Mills, our coach, would later say, "I thought you were about to pitch a tent out there." Which I surely thought about doing.

I don't remember dropping a pass in a game after that one, and rarely in practice. Not in junior high, high school, or college. At least not one that should have obviously been caught. That feeling, like striking out in Little League baseball, had been too unbearable.

Like many boys my age, I actually enjoyed playing basketball, too. Up until eighth grade, though, I had only played during the physical education period of my sixth and seventh grades at Carver; and let me tell you, it was a *physical* education. I was the only white kid who played in the games out on the court (a couple other white boys would shoot around on a side goal), and when you played in the *real* games out on the court, you did not go to the basket unless you were ready to be assaulted. It was as brutal as any gauntlet I ever ran through in football, including college. And, nope, it was pretty damn rare for anyone to call "foul." No one wanted to be called a "pussy," least of all me. That's just the way it was. But I'm pretty sure it helped toughen me up for the years to come.

I guess you could say I was learning to fit in, wherever I found myself. I finally played basketball in junior high, but since I'd never played *organized* basketball and my teammates had all been playing together for years, I felt insecure. In a word, I was afraid to shoot. I was the sixth man on my eighth-grade team, and one day before practice about halfway through the season, for some reason, Coach Ricky Howard announced to the squad that I had the best pure jump shot on the team and that I should be willing to take more shots. When I got home, I told my dad.

A couple of days later, we were set to play a rival from a nearby town. Daddy walked into the room with a mischievous smile.

"Phil," Daddy said. "I'll pay you fifty cents for every shot you take today." (There's my daddy with shots for money again!)

"Huh?"

"Yeah, and I don't care at all if you make them. Just shoot the ball."

Naturally, that day I led the team in scoring with 18 points, my prior high around 4 or 5. Coach Howard gave me some weird looks during the game, obviously wondering what had happened to his normally cautious player. But he liked it. The next game, I was starting.

"How much for each shot today?" I asked Daddy before the next game.

"Uh, no," he said. "Mission accomplished."

From then on, I was in the starting lineup as a forward throughout the rest of eighth grade and then ninth, though I was quite average in height for my age, maybe five foot seven or eight. But due to my intensity, toughness, quickness, and instincts, a few traits I arrived onto the planet with, Coach Howard began to make me play center on defense, which is almost always where the tallest guys play, even though we had two players well over six feet (one of whom—Scott Williams—would play basketball in college). We played man-to-man most of the time, so he would put me on the other team's biggest man, knowing I would be *very* aggressive and irritate the hell out of whomever I was guarding, almost all of them at least a half foot taller. I would lean in tight and fight for every inch, and I must have done pretty good because Coach Howard kept me there for the rest of my time on the team.

Interestingly, I'm not sure I ever scored 18 points again after that one incentive-laden outburst (though, if Daddy had offered a couple of bucks per shot, I would have probably hit 30!). I averaged around 6 to 10 or so, but at least I had established myself as a viable threat and a capable defensive player.

THE PREACHER'S KID

"I'm here to pick up my son."

It wasn't easy for me being a preacher's kid. I didn't like being thought of as a "goody two-shoes" kind of guy, so I figured I would do my best to live up to the "P.K." moniker, the abbreviation for preacher's kids, which was usually synonymous with rebellion. Yeah, I'd already torched a poor man's putt-putt course as a kid and told my grandma to leave the "how I would do it if I were you" stuff up to me, so I think I had already shown at least a slightly rebellious side—or at least a willingness to challenge a narrative or two. And, though I was generally respectful to my parents and always had a good relationship with them, I wanted to do my own thing.

So I frequently did.

My sophomore year in high school, a buddy picked me up from my house for a night out, maybe two weeks before Christmas, my mom decorating the tree as I left. There were already a couple of six-packs in the car, so he drove straight to an elementary school, pulled behind it, and began popping the tab on a cold one. We usually found an off-the-beaten-path spot to chug a couple of beers before heading out to who the hell knows where, but this seemed a bit too close to the *beaten* path to me.

"What the hell?" I said. "Don't you think the cops could cruise back here?"

"No, I've been here a few times and never seen any."

"I don't know," I said, shaking my head.

But he didn't listen, and barely after I had taken my first swallow, one of those cars with the blue lights on top snuck around behind us, and the nauseating flickering light began to brighten the dark back-side of the school. Those blues felt like they were in the car with us. A couple minutes later, we were riding in the back of a police car, headed downtown to the Warner Robins police station.

My buddy wasn't too worried about it, but I was freaking out. What would my parents say? What would they do?

The next thing I knew, I was sitting in a small room with a lieu-tenant, a desk, and a phone. My buddy was in another room. The lieutenant told me that they were going to let us off this time but I had to call my parents to come get me. He pushed the phone over in front of me and waited. I looked at him, frantically trying to think of another solution.

I sighed and picked up the phone.

"Hello," my mom said.

I realized I couldn't beat around the bush with the law sitting right there in front of me, staring bullets through me. I got right to the point.

"Mom, I'm at the police station. I've been arrested for underage drinking. Can somebody come get me, please?"

"Oh, Phil," she said nonchalantly. "What do you want?"

For some reason, I didn't expect that. She just figured it was another one of my jokes. Well, that got me. I lowered my head to the desk as tears filled my eyes. The next short sentence came out very meekly.

"I'm serious," I mumbled through the tears. I think I might have heard an ornament hit the floor.

While I was in the bathroom a few minutes later, I heard the front door to the police station open and close.

"I'm here to pick up my son."

My dad's voice sounded flat, tired, sad.

We walked out to his little red Volkswagen Beetle—damn, it felt cramped in there—and he drove me home without a word spoken, his chin quivering and a few tears falling silently down his face. His father had been an alcoholic, at times a raging and difficult one, and I think he was having flashbacks. He never even spoke about the incident; the fact that he didn't might have hurt even worse. It would be a spell before I drank again.

Not too long, though. Maybe a year later, I hosted a keg party at the house. That's right, at the *pastor's* house. Momma and Daddy were out of town for the weekend, so one of my buddies dared me to host a party at Brother Ben's (what he was affectionately called by almost everybody). So I did. The only caveat for those invited to attend—at five dollars a head, by the way—was that they could not, under any circumstances, bring any drinks of their own.

The party was a blast. I even made a little money, and evidently, no neighbors told my parents about all the cars that lined the street that night. A few days later, though, while cleaning the house, Momma walked up to me, holding a couple of beer bottle caps and giving me the eye.

"Where did these come from?"

I tried to never lie, but every now and then, I slipped. "I told Teel not to bring that into the house," I said.

Bryan Teel was one of my friends and someone my parents liked, so I made him the culprit. I don't think he was even at the party, though. I felt a little guilty. Not much, but a little.

As the years slid by, I didn't detour too far from the party scene and didn't grace too many church doors, either. Unless, of course, I was with my parents and expected to do so.

My rebel spirit—my P.K. persona—didn't normally show up in sports, but occasionally, I would succumb to its pull. Whenever I did so, it was usually because my feelings were hurt. I would make a snap decision based on that pain, and the result would usually be a bit pathetic.

One of those pathetic moments came while playing baseball for a city recreation team during the summer of my sixteenth year. I was one of the better players on the team, but I had been awful sick for a few days and had missed time leading into the championship game. But now I was healthy and ready to go.

The assistant coach's son wasn't a starter, but I reckoned that the assistant and the head coach must have figured that my missing time provided the opportunity to play his son over me, regardless of who was better.

"Phil," the head coach said before the game, looking at the ground instead of at me. "You won't be starting today, but we'll get you in before too long."

You would have thought he had told me I was being sent to Siberia. My mind was instantly ablaze with anger. And hurt. As the team walked into the dugout, I kept right on walking all the way into the stands. I stewed for maybe two innings, sick about the disrespect they had shown me. I even ordered a hot dog.

I finally decided I would stick it to them by leaving, though that decision was probably tinged a bit by the embarrassing realization of what I had already done. I just didn't have the maturity to suck it up, walk back into the dugout, and take it like a man.

I left the ballpark and never saw the coaches again.

GLORY DAYS

"Is this all there is?"

Of course, whatever else I was doing, my mind was always on football. I had been moved to wide receiver upon entering Warner Robins High School, too small to play tight end anymore, and quickly found myself a contributor on a very good team. We only had a few sophomores playing that year, and I was one of them.

We were 31-2 during my three high school seasons, including a 13-0 record as a senior in 1976, the year we won the first state championship in Warner Robins' history (we were even co-national champs).

Though I would eventually lead the region in receiving that season (not an easy thing to do on a team that ran the ball almost constantly), the initial weeks had me worried. I had pulled a groin before camp (can't remember how) and didn't participate in three-a-days—yes, three practices a day in the Deep South in August. We would travel as a team to somewhere in the bowels of south Georgia, which was a suburb of Hell, and get up way before the sun to go out and run and hit—I kid you not—without being able to see who and what we were hitting or where we were running to. Yeah, things were a little crazy back then.

I wasn't worried, though. How could a few missed practices due to injury be a problem? I had proven to the coaches over my career that nobody worked harder than me, and hell, I was the top receiver on the team by far. But Head Coach Robert Davis, a future Georgia

Hall of Famer, seemed to take every opportunity that came his way to stare at me with an eye that suggested I was a piece of shit, as if I was faking it or something. I had *lived* for this! Why on earth would I fake an injury when it was my time to shine? And yet he would just stare at me as if I were the most pitiful excuse for a pitiful athlete you could imagine.

It tore me up!

The man simply did not speak to me—for three full weeks!

I swear, it felt like I didn't exist anymore to Coach Davis. But by the first game of the season, I was close to being fully healthy, at least ready enough to play. The game started, and before I knew it, he was calling plays to me and I'd scored a couple touchdowns. He was even slapping me on the back and smiling, acting as if nothing had ever happened. Later, his wife would tell me it just hurt him so much to see me hurt. Maybe so. But I think he knew we had an opportunity to be special, and the pressure led him to stare me down … just in case I *was* faking an injury.

Our biggest challenge that year was when we played Hardaway of Columbus late in the season. The final score was decided by a touchdown—quite close, considering we'd eventually beat our three playoff opponents by an average of over forty points per game.

It also happened to be the game in which I broke a rib or two in the first half.

I ran a slant route, and Keith Soles, our quarterback, threw a bit high, such that I had to jump up to snatch the ball, all the while knowing that the safety was barreling downhill toward me. Before I had the chance to pull the ball low enough to get my arms in position to protect my side, and before my right leg landed on the turf, his helmet speared me under that arm and into my ribs, slightly on the backside. I somehow held onto the ball, but the pain was like an explosion that shot through my body and left me utterly breathless. I'm not sure how long I was on the field. I simply could not breathe.

High school medical staffs back in the '70s were more or less likely to spit in the dirt and rub it on whatever might be hurt—that, or maybe wrap a hell of a lot of tape around an injury. In my case, our team doctor, who I believe was in his eighties at the time, hobbled over to me.

"How do you feel?" he asked.

"Not good," I gasped. "I've got an awful pain in my side here. It's hard to breathe."

"Stretch it out," he said after looking at me for about a second. Seriously.

Well, that did *not* sound like the correct thing to do, but he was the doctor and I was the one desperate to get back in the game, so I started trying to lift my arm up to stretch out what I would find later to be broken ribs. The pain was excruciating. I wondered how the doctor could have advised such a thing, such a dangerous thing, even. Had he not seen the safety spear me with his helmet—*right in my ribs?* I'm guessing no. Was his eyesight failing? I'm guessing yes. Regardless, I stood there grimacing as I stretched that damned broken rib up and down.

A couple minutes into my stretching routine, Coach Stan Gann, our offensive coordinator, asked if I could play. He said he wanted to throw me a deep ball on the next possession.

What do you think I said?

A minute later, I was back in the game with a deep post called to me. I was supposed to run straight ahead for about 10 to 12 yards, fake hard outside, and then keep running up and inside toward the goalpost. That was the route called, anyway. I only made it about a yard or two. They dragged me off the field a few seconds later.

As the rest of the team boarded the bus after the game to head back to Warner Robins, Coach Davis escorted me to the hospital, where they confirmed that, yes, I did have a broken rib or two. He then positioned me in the back of his station wagon so that I could lie down as comfortably as possible—which was *not* possible—and personally drove me home.

"There ain't nothing wrong with you, Phil," he said over his shoulder from the front of the car.

"Fuck you," I muttered under my breath.

"What's that?" he shot back at me.

But we both were laughing. All was good between coach and player.

The laughing only made things worse, every movement a blade piercing into my side and twisting around.

As the pain subsided, my mind traced back to a few short weeks earlier when, at least to me, Coach Davis seemed to have questioned my integrity. My, how the tides had turned. We had survived our most difficult moment. And in so doing, we would later become very close friends, such that I called him shortly before he died a few years back to remind him that I loved him. I can still hear his raspy voice, his throat wracked by cancer, as he responded, "I love you, too, Phil."

And I could feel his warm smile as he said it.

The next week or so was miserable, but by week three, it was time for the game against our crosstown rival, Northside. Though still in pain, I was breathing well enough by then that I begged them to let me play. You always want to beat your crosstown rival, so they agreed and rigged up some kind of foam padding around my right side, which made me look a little like the Hunchback of Notre Dame—or more like the Hunch*side* of Warner Robins, I guess. Somehow, I still managed to catch a couple touchdowns, and we won 35-14.

Next stop: playoffs!

To tell the truth, we were simply unstoppable by then. Whatever hiccups had occurred, such as the close call with Hardaway, seemed to have brought our team together to a place where we felt invincible. And we were!

We beat Richmond Academy in the first game, 42-0, and Wayne County the next week by a score of 56-7. The lone score in that game was a long touchdown catch by future Georgia Bulldog star, Lyndsay Scott. It would be the last time an opponent scored a point against our 1976 Warner Robins Demons team.

PART ONE

The state championship game was played at home against Griffin, and the first quarter was scoreless. Coach Davis was naturally conservative, especially when he had such talent at running back like we did, but he was smart enough to know that it would take a little more than just pounding away when playing against such a stout opponent.

Early in the second quarter, he called my number, another post route from about 45 yards out. I faked the cornerback to the outside and took it in and up, by now a couple of steps ahead of him as I headed toward the goal line. Keith must have been a tad bit excited because the ball took off and I thought it was going to sail too long. I left my feet at about the 6- or 7-yard line and extended about as far out as I could, feeling the ball hit my fingers and stick just before I hit the ground at the two. The next play, we scored. The rout was on, 34-0. I think we threw it five times that game, and I had three catches for 60-something yards. Like I said, I took what I could get.

When the final seconds ticked off, a celebration erupted! It was the first championship in the history of Warner Robins High School football, and we didn't know how to respond. We were jumping and hollering and screaming and doing all the kinds of things you expect hyped-up athletes to do when they win *the* game.

But here's the thing—and I want to be honest about it—all the time I was jumping up and down, I was wondering, "Is this it? Is this all there is?"

I mean, I was glad, sure, but something felt slightly off. Or maybe even a *lot* off. I think I'd been expecting a state of a previously undiscovered ecstasy, or maybe a supernatural bliss of some sort, an intergalactic emotional climax, or something of the like.

Did I experience such a thing?

Nope. Barely a blip, really. Super glad to have won, of course. But, damn! There simply wasn't that longed-for ecstatic experience I thought would be there. It was all rather anticlimactic, which was revealing in an ethereal kind of way, though I couldn't piece it together at the time. I began to wonder if there was anything that could bring about that which we all long for—a transformative type of joy, if you will. If you cannot find that in winning it all, at least temporarily, I wondered, where the hell can you find it?

I woke up the next morning and realized my world was pretty much the same as it had always been. In fact, nothing had really changed, except maybe the right to brag about how I'd been part of a high school state and national championship team. But what did that really do for me? Again, not much. What I discovered was that life simply went on. It didn't seem to need to stop and celebrate my latest success with me.

It just went on.

FLORIDA STATE UNIVERSITY

"Not so fast."

The months after winning the state championship were really about one thing for me: waiting to see if I would receive a scholarship offer to play college football. Though I especially wanted to play in the Southeast, I would have likely gone anywhere for the opportunity to play NCAA Division 1 football.

I didn't know it then, but it was my way of finding validation, something to prove that I was good enough. I wanted it in the worst way.

I *needed* it.

I also felt like making it at the college level might bring along a few other perks. I, like most folks, was enamored with the potential for the notoriety I thought came from success at the collegiate level. The acceptance amongst my peers, not to mention the adoration of the fans, mattered, too. I wanted to play on television and in front of tens of thousands or more. I had already enjoyed a taste of those emotional jolts, and I had an itch that was still inflamed and needed more scratching. Certainly, college football would do that, wouldn't it? And besides, maybe—just maybe—I could increase my speed and continue on to the NFL, where the ultimate dreams come true and everything ends up "Champagne and caviar" and "happily ever after." *Right?*

It seemed as if many college coaches had a second home in Warner Robins throughout our season, as they could frequently be seen following our top three college prospects around like street dogs chasing after a meat truck. I called them "The Big Three"—James Brooks, who starred at Auburn University and would end up a future NFL Pro Bowl running back; Jimmy Womack, the starting fullback as a Georgia Bulldog (while a fellow named Hershel Walker starred at tailback); and Big Bad Ronald Simmons, or Meat, as we called him (he was benching over five hundred pounds in high school with a physique "chiseled out of granite"), who would become an All-American defensive lineman at Florida State University.

I swear, I couldn't figure out how those coaches could successfully coach their respective teams while roaming our practice fields so often. And not once did they look my way. I was starting to get a bit concerned.

And pissed! Not that that was helping anything.

Anyway, my dad was probably my biggest fan, and he got it in his head that "them college folk" just didn't have the right info, that they were probably misled, lacking some key insights. So he wrote a little something up, espousing my myriad talents, of course, and commenced upon a furious letter-sending campaign, scatter-shooting them all over the Southeast because good ole Southern football is what I'd basically been raised on. He also sent one to The University of Hawaii for good measure, partly because we had a neighbor of Hawaiian descent who supposedly knew somebody there, so we thought, "What the heck!" Besides, I figured I could forgo Southern football for another major college campus with a few swaying palm trees and a smile or two from the young Hawaiian ladies thrown in.

Upon receiving my dad's letters, I don't doubt there was a college coach or two (or maybe thirty) who called a fellow coach into his office between laughs. "Hey, Frank, look what we got here! We got us a daddy trying to tell us how good his son is."

"Haha," Frank would bust a gut, grabbing a chair for balance so as to not fall down. "That's a good one, Billy. I'll go tell the others. Oh boy, that's some good shit!"

Sadly, our mailbox continued to receive the same amount of mail as before, though Hawaii did write back fairly soon, probably because of our neighbor. "Aloha" was peppered throughout the letter, which was kind of endearing—in the way they used it, though, it seemed to mean "no thanks." And even if it didn't, that was the overall message.

I actually did receive an offer to play at The Naval Academy, but their requirements were too restrictive for my young mind to even consider—no hair to speak of, getting up with the sun (or earlier), and a five-year commitment to the Navy after college (which would have eliminated the NFL, which I still ignorantly had dreams of playing in). Life is funny, though, sometimes throwing it all back in our faces; shortly thereafter, my hair would leave of its own accord, I would end up not being able to sleep past five, and the NFL would never know my name, at least not as a player.

The only college coach who actually took the time to speak with me was Gene McDowell, linebacker coach at Florida State University, who was hot on the trail of Ronald Simmons, our beastly (the word does *not* do the man justice) middle linebacker and occasional tight end.

Our conversation went something like this: "Hey Phil, I'm Gene McDowell of Florida State. Our head coach, Bobby Bowden, wants me to invite you to walk on this fall. He feels like you can make our team and contribute quickly. We are not offering scholarships to any wide receivers this year, so in a sense, you could be our number one freshman receiver. You know, without the scholarship."

He smiled, a strange look in his eyes. "If we *were* offering a scholarship to a receiver, you would probably be it."

Well, this was not the recruiting pitch I had been hoping for.

I mumbled something like, "Thanks, Coach. It's all pretty frustrating. I know I can play, but most folks seem to think I'm too slow."

He looked at me and gave a sort of whimsical, sly smile, his eyes seeming to look two places at once. I would find out later that this was because one of his eyes was made of glass. It gave the way he looked at you an almost mystical feel.

"I played with a receiver at FSU by the name of Fred Biletnikoff who wasn't considered so fast, and he had a fair degree of success." That sly smile again. Biletnikoff was an NFL Hall of Fame wide receiver who had played with the Oakland Raiders back in their glory days, as any young wide receiver would have known.

"We are thinking you might be similar."

Hmmm.

The phrase "might be" is damned vague, and "similar" can stretch itself out pretty far, too, but this was still the first college coach who had even hinted that he wanted me.

"Thanks, Coach," I said. "I do appreciate it." I shook his hand and left, my steps a bit lighter.

A few days later, I went out to the mailbox and found a letter from Auburn University, one of the top football universities in the Southeast, and not too far down the road from Warner Robins. I think I dropped it a time or two, rushing back to the house, where I opened it amidst a few tight breaths.

The letter went something like this:

"As you know, Phil, we have recently signed your teammate, James Brooks, one of the most sought-after players in the country. Because you are not as fast as him, we cannot offer you an athletic scholarship at this time, but feel certain you can make our team while attending Auburn on academic scholarship ..."

To tell the truth, I didn't really catch the rest of it. A bunch of *blah, blah, blah.* What got me were those three little words—"not as fast." Though it was obvious that the speed issue was at the heart of my athletic scholarship dearth, I sure as hell didn't like being reminded of it. Had they just offered the academic scholarship and refrained from that gibberish, I probably would have scooted on over to The Plains of Auburn, screaming "War Eagle" all the way. But pride has a way of factoring into a young man's decisions at times, so I balled that piece of shit up and drilled it into the garbage can like I was spiking a touchdown—against Auburn! I called Coach Bowden and told him I was coming to FSU. (On a side note, Auburn has since miraculously recovered from that recruiting blunder.)

In retrospect, I realize I opted for the school that was smart enough not to mention my lack of blazing speed, even though that was exactly why they, too, didn't offer me a scholarship. The choice damn sure made sense to me at the time, or at least enough sense that I loaded up the same Volkswagen Bug my dad had used to pick me up from the police station a year or two earlier and headed down to Tallahassee in mid-August of 1977, excited to have the opportunity to be able to potentially put my name up next to that of Fred Biletnikoff's, and maybe even leapfrog him.

HOMESICK

"Don't be a quitter!"

It only took a day or two before I realized that Fred had very little to worry about. I got me a real nasty case of homesickness, and those footballs were bouncing off of my hands as if I had oven mitts on (at least that's how it felt to me). I just knew the coaches were shaking their heads and wondering why the hell they had invited me onto their team. "Did anybody watch this guy play?" they must have been wondering. I felt like the biggest loser ever and began to yearn for home.

My closest friend during that difficult week was a pay phone, and it was a damn intense relationship. The FSU football team lived at an apartment complex called Casa del Gato at that time, right across from the stadium, and there was one pay phone outside. Every morning I would trudge outside, slap the side of the phone box a time or two—out of shame, I think—and pick up the receiver. God, I hated to pick it up, so I would slap her again.

"I'd like to make a collect call, please."

I'd give out the same number over and over again, day after day, and sometimes more than once per day. "We'll accept the charges," I would hear my momma or daddy say. "How are things going, Phil? Are they getting any better?" It usually took a minute for me to respond, choking back tears and sometimes even giving in to the occasional sob. I found myself wondering whether or not they could hear the splatter of tears on the mouthpiece. "I'm not sure I belong here. I'm not even sure I like football anymore. I can't seem to catch anything. I'm embarrassing myself."

"You'll get over that," Dad said. "If there's one thing you can do, Phil, it's catch a football."

"Well, not anymore!" I snarled, slapping her once more. They were quiet on the other end. I'd worked so hard, and my parents had put the money into it; I hated the thought of telling them that I wanted to end it. Both of them had stood by me and encouraged me every step of the way.

"I'm thinking about coming home," I muttered.

I couldn't see past the next few hours, much less a few weeks or months down the road. I'd envisioned living out a masterpiece, but what I saw in front of me was more like a mess of runny watercolors.

"Well, son, we're going to be there tomorrow for your birthday. Will there be time to take you to lunch between the morning and afternoon practices? We can talk some more then."

Hell yes, there will be time, I thought, seeing how I would be packed and ready to leave. We'd have all the time in the world.

"I think so," I said and hung up. I turned and walked away from the pay phone for what I thought would be the last time.

My parents arrived in Tallahassee on my eighteenth birthday, my grandparents in tow. I met them at a downtown restaurant, miserable, barely talking or eating. Finally, I built up the courage to let them know my plans.

"I'm quitting," I said. "I don't wanna play football anymore."

My parents could tell I was done. They both nodded. My granddaddy nodded, too. By the time my eyes met my grandmama's, I could tell she wasn't going to give me another shoulder to cry on.

"Don't be a quitter!" she said, firm and strong. "You'll regret it."

Well, I had three out of four on my side, or at least responding sympathetically, so I just ignored her.

Then I called coach Bowden from a pay phone at the restaurant (a pay phone that was a bit more to my liking than the other one) and told him my decision before hopping in my already-packed car for the trip back to Warner Robins.

My grandmama was right, though. To be honest, by the time I made it back to Warner Robins, I was already feeling a bit remorseful, as if I'd looked Destiny in the face and told her to fuck off. Within a couple months, I decided to write Coach Bowden a letter and see if he would take me back. He did, mentioning that he thought I could earn a scholarship with a good spring, and I walked back on in January of 1978, this time swearing to stay away from that pay phone.

Winter workouts were brutal. They tested a man's mettle, for sure, especially with a little thing they liked to call "mat drills." Some sadistic bastard must have thought those up. They required you to get up before the sun and basically kill yourself. Big barrels were strategically placed *everywhere* so you could puke whenever it hit your fancy. Me? I never puked, but I seemed to be one of the only ones who didn't. Just wasn't my thing.

I made it through those weeks of mat drills and weights and outside workouts (including running up and down the ramps of the stadium) in pretty stellar shape. I even showed them that I was pretty strong for my size, bench-pressing more than quite a few guys who were much bigger than me. I was beginning to feel some of the old confidence creeping back in.

The day before spring practice was to start, I was in the freshman locker room by myself, organizing my stuff for the next day, when the wide receiver coach, Kent Schoolfield, happened to wander in. I had barely seen him since I arrived back in Tallahassee in January, and never alone. He had barely spoken to me. I guessed he hadn't taken too kindly to me leaving the team on my birthday the year before. But now he definitely noticed me. He glanced sideways a time or two and satisfied himself that no one else was around.

"Why don't you go back to Warner Robins?" he snarled, appearing to have put a bit of thought into his suggestion. "You know you don't have what it takes. You proved it last time. Why don't you just go back home where you belong?"

I really didn't know how to respond, so I just kept my mouth shut. He didn't wait around for a reply anyway. So there I stood, less than twenty-four hours before the first official practice of the spring, certain that my position coach hated my guts and would do whatever he could to get me out of there. Regardless, I was determined that things were going to be different this time. I felt like Cortés when he landed in Mexico, burning the ships so that there would be no leaving. *Do or die!* Or something like that.

The first day of spring training finally arrived, and I made my way down to the locker room to get dressed for practice, twenty days of grueling punishment to see who would be left standing. In fact, I was told that those who made it through all twenty days would be rewarded with a T-shirt that read, "Tough 20." Maybe it wasn't much, but that little scrap of cloth sounded better than gold to me. Upon entering the locker room, I noticed they had posted the depth chart on the wall for all to see their current value to the team. I quickly found the columns for the two wide receiver positions, X and Z, and even more quickly found my name. There were nineteen receivers suiting up for the first day of practice, nine at X and ten at Z. Guess who was number ten Z?

Practices were basically set up with a lot of position and individual stuff for the first half, then a break, followed by team activities for the second half. I must have done okay because, at the break, Coach Schoolfield came up to me and told me I would be running with the twos during the team periods. I couldn't believe it—number ten one second and two the next. Here was my chance.

A month later, I accepted my T-shirt, a gold one with garnet letters, though it really was more of a yellowish mustardy thing. Hell, it could have been bright pink with puke-green letters; I still would have put it on and strutted around campus with my chest puffed out. But there remained one detail yet to be ironed out. I still did not have a scholarship.

The Monday after the spring game, I set up an appointment to see Coach Bowden about the possibility of a scholarship. I was now running on the second team, and everybody else on the first two teams was going to school free and eating on the training table while I was paying out-of-state tuition and eating ramen noodles.

A couple days later, Miss Sue, Coach Bowden's secretary, told me to walk on into his office, so I did, a touch of sweat lining my neck. Coach Bowden looked up from something on his desk, an unlit cigar poking from his mouth.

"Philip. Come on in and have a seat."

He sat back and removed the cigar from his mouth, looked at it for a second or two and said, "What can I do for you, Philip?"

I didn't really like being called Philip, but Coach Bowden could have called me Phyllis, and I wouldn't have flinched. This man had given me my chance, and I felt like he had treated me with as much respect as the top players on our team.

I took a deep breath. "About that scholarship we talked about before. What do you think?"

He narrowed his eyes. "Well, Philip, I've been thinking about this, and I'm not sure you did quite enough during spring practice to get the scholarship. On the right track, but not quite there."

"I thought I did enough to show you what I'm capable of," I said, surprising myself with my boldness.

He gnawed on the cigar and looked at me. Maybe it was my imagination, but an idea seemed to dance behind his eyes for a second. He shifted in his seat and smiled almost imperceptibly.

"Here's what I'm thinking, Philip. As you know, we have signed three wide receivers who will be coming in here as freshmen."

I sunk a little lower in my seat.

"I will hold a scholarship available for you, and if you come back in August and take up where you left off, I feel certain you will hold those freshmen at bay. I'll give you the scholarship then, in time for the fall quarter. How does that sound?"

To this day, I don't know whether the next couple of minutes was a negotiation by me or simply the result of having almost no time to contemplate his offer, or both, but at any rate, I took a long hard look at the carpet in front of me before I responded. I was eighteen years old and sitting face to face with a future legend, a man who had earned my respect and who I did not want to disappoint. I raised my head and locked eyes with Coach Bowden, nibbling on my bottom lip. I'll never forget what I did next, dropping my head again and studying that dadgum carpet as if it held all the answers in its threads. I shook my head slowly.

"I don't know, Coach. I don't know. I don't know what my daddy is gonna say. The out-of-state tuition has already been a strain on my parents. I'm not sure they can even think about the possibility of more." Deep inside, I felt like my parents could and would make it happen, but I wasn't about to mention that. Besides, I hated the thought of being a burden to them any longer. How long could they be expected to fund Phil's Dream? And I would still have to carry that despicable moniker around with me—"*walk-on*"—for a few more months, at least.

With my head still shaking, I muttered, "I just don't know."

Coach Bowden slapped his desk with a pop like a firecracker, and my head shot up. He was smiling. He got up and walked around the desk and shook my hand.

"Come back and see me in two weeks, Philip."

And with that, he jammed that cigar back in his mouth and slapped me on the back, right on the kidneys, a painful little habit of his that I later learned to avoid. I headed for the door and kept on walking, wondering what the heck had just happened.

I showed back up at Coach Bowden's office at the scheduled time, two weeks to the day, and, once again, Miss Sue said to go on in. Coach Bowden was engrossed with some papers in his hands, sitting cockeyed with his feet propped on his desk. An unlit cigar, possibly the same one, hung from his mouth. He didn't seem to notice me, so I just stood there.

He shot me a quick glance and then looked back at his papers. "Sue has your scholarship on her desk. You can go sign it now."

I swallowed hard and just stared at him, my mouth falling open. He kept staring at his papers. It was difficult to be certain, but I thought I noticed a slight smile lurking on Coach Bowden's face as his lips twisted around that old cigar.

"Thanks, Coach. You won't regret it."

And with that, I became the newest signee of the Florida State Seminoles. I was willing to bet the farm *and* the reservation that none of the others were as excited as I was when they signed their scholarships. No cameras, no newspapers, no parents, no nothing. Just me and Miss Sue. And, of course, that little man with the unlit cigar just a few feet away, the one destined to be one of the top coaches in college football history, probably with a sly smile still on his face.

CONTROL ISSUES

"Think again, son!"

Now that I'd made it, everything was destined to be hunky-dory. Perhaps even sublime. Right?

Erm, no. Not even close.

Though the great pain—the one that would find me prodding God to go fuck Himself—was on the distant horizon, my time at Florida State was essential, you might say, in preparing me for that coming period of pain and the subsequent searching it precipitated. In fact, there was a play in each of my four seasons as a football player that, when pieced together, would define this coming reality.

And what better time and place for these lessons to begin to reveal themselves than game number one of my freshman season, right?

On September 10, 1978, we traveled up to Syracuse University to play the Orangemen on the same hallowed grounds upon which former Hall of Fame great Jim Brown had mercilessly trucked many a would-be tackler. That field still bore remnants of those battles, it seemed, probably more divots and uneven spots than on any field I had played on since backyard football as a kid.

I was a wide-eyed eighteen-year-old freshman (by a couple of weeks) who was actually running second team and, therefore, expected to get some game action. I could hardly believe my ears when a pass was called to me down near the goal line in the first half,

I think around the 12-yard line. It was a curl, a route designed to be run to a depth of 16 yards and then break back at an angle directly toward the quarterback.

There was one problem. Actually two.

As I lined up, I realized I hadn't really practiced running the route into the end zone—not much, at least. Part of the reason such routes were effective was the notion that the defensive back had to respect the possibility that the receiver might keep going deep, which obviously was not going to happen in the end zone. So I instantly realized that I had to be creative.

My instincts kicked in, and I faked out the cornerback with a little move, getting enough separation to begin the second part of the route—back toward the quarterback. To be honest, I sort of expected the ball to already be in the air, but it wasn't. Maybe Jimmy Jordan had looked the other way first, I don't know.

This is where the second—and main—problem surfaced.

I was always somewhat of a literalist—and a rule follower, you might say (though I admit that depended on what the subject was)—doing my damnedest to perfect whatever the specifics of a route called for. If I could diagram the actual route, it would pretty much end on the chalkboard after planting the outside foot and bringing it back about 3 yards. Go 16 and come back 3. I swear, that's how it was drawn up. And every time we ran it in practice, the ball had been in the air before the 3-yard return had been fulfilled. Bang-bang, more or less.

This time, since it wasn't in the air yet, even after coming back toward the quarterback the requisite 3 yards, and because that would have brought me out of the end zone, which somehow made no sense to me in that split second, I guess you could say I hunkered down. However, it might help to consider that all of this was happening rather quickly.

For whatever reason, Jimmy finally decided to let 'er rip. My eyes got big, I'm sure, as I waited to pluck that thing from the air for my first collegiate catch *and* touchdown. But just as I was about to snatch it out of the air, their safety broke in front of me, intercepted it, and ran it back a ways out into the field of play.

That was my last play of the day.

It was also my last play until later in the season.

George Haffner, our offensive coordinator that season, literally jumped on my back as we were leaving practice the following Monday.

"You think you've got it made, rookie? You think you're all that? You think you're ready for big-time college football?"

Hell if I knew what to say, so I kept my mouth shut as he dragged me toward the ground.

"Think again, son!"

Well, I felt like shit. I wondered if those first few snaps in the first game of my freshman year would be the last of my college career, scared to death that my personal moment in the spotlight had been nothing more than a puny flash of lightning far off in the distance, barely even noticed. But I went back to work with all I had.

It took a few weeks of quality practice before Coach Haffner developed enough trust in me to put me back out there. But the first game I was allowed back onto the field, I caught four passes for 45 yards against Southern Miss in Hattiesburg, an array of quick outs and slants, at least a couple of them caught against a future All-Pro cornerback by the name of Hanford Dixon. I was never less than second team after that game.

Against Virginia Tech the following week, I only got the chance to catch one pass—another shot at a curl route, the first called to me since the debacle at Syracuse. Wally Woodham, the other part of the famous two-headed quarterback at FSU of the late '70s, looked elsewhere to go with the ball and, finding no one open, looked back my way. This time, I was ready. Having met my 16-yard depth before he even saw me, I was blazing a trail back to Wally, and by the time I caught it, I was tackled for a 7-yard completion, maybe the shortest curl in FSU history. If he had waited much longer, I might have run over him. I had learned my lesson well from Coach Haffner!

What was that lesson? Don't cut things short, or something like that ...

However, there was another lesson buried in there, as well. A much deeper one, in fact. I mean, I did what I was taught. Go 16, come back 3. Do what you are supposed to do to perfection. *Control* the situation. I did all that, but I found that no matter how you follow the protocols, sometimes you just can't control everything. This truth would stab me in the heart a few decades later when I would come to realize that no matter what you do, no matter how closely you follow whatever mandates you believe to be true, you just can't control everything.

As far as that lesson at Syracuse, I was on the verge of learning another version in the classroom. So far, I had made nothing but A's. But that was before this preacher's kid took Religion 101.

The grades for that class were entirely based on two essays, one at the midterm and one for the final. I was pretty relaxed about the final, as I had been awarded a high A on the midterm, which had required us to write an essay-type response to our choice of three out of five questions. The professor had stated that the final would have a similar format, so I made sure I was well-versed in the first eighty percent or so of the material, figuring I wouldn't need to know it all. He'd even mentioned that the questions would be spread from throughout the text material.

What he didn't tell us was that, this time, the questions would be grouped into pairs and that the last two pairs would be on the final forty percent of the study material.

If ever there was an essay or two of total bullshit spewed out on a Religion exam, it was from this preacher's kid. I cursed under my breath during that damn exam at least a hundred times and sweated as if in hell from the start of class until the end. Yeah, I ended up with an overall B in a class that should have been an easy A for me had I not thought I could control the process on my terms.

At least I was able to appreciate the professor's sense of humor as he scribbled a note on my paper in reference to those two particular essays: "How beautifully and creatively written. Too bad it's meaning-less bullshit!"

That hit my funny bone.

"Bullshit," the *religion professor* had said. I was beginning to wonder if maybe all religion was bullshit, if God was real, if Heaven existed. Not that it was on my mind all that much, what with football and par-tying and school taking up so much of my time. In fact, it really *wasn't* on my mind all that much.

But it would be. It damn sure would be.

PRESSURE

"Don't Drop It!"

Nobody worked harder than me, probably because nobody had to work as hard as I did to even have a chance to succeed at playing major college football. I did the best I could at controlling the things that I could, doing all within my power to instill confidence in Coach Bowden that I could do the job when called upon. It was already obvious to me that the man didn't play favorites, per se, but that he went with his gut and with what he saw on the practice field. He would prove this to me frequently as my career unfolded, though perhaps no more so than our game against Cincinnati in 1979.

I was a sophomore for that season, and it was shaping up to be the best in Florida State history by the time Coach Bowden took our team, with a 7-0 record and No. 6 ranking, up to play lowly Cincinnati; 8-0 was a cinch, or so we thought.

But with a little over eleven minutes left to play, we found ourselves on the wrong end of a 21-7 score. We also faced a fourth and 5 from somewhere around midfield, and Riverboat Gambler, as coach Bowden would later be called by some, was busy dialing up a "do or die" play in his mind.

I was standing beside him, ready to run the play in. He grabbed my facemask and looked me in the eyes.

"Okay," he said, and then rambled off the formation and the basics of the play, finishing with "X Drag."

"Well, I'll be damned!" I thought. "*I'm* X."

For those who don't know, the drag route is possibly the scariest thing any football player is called to execute and sometimes ends up feeling like an execution (get it?). Simple, yes. But dangerous. It requires darting up the field for about 5 yards, planting the outside foot, and then sneaking across the middle of the field where the linebackers lie in wait, drooling to bone-crunch whoever comes their way. The pass, the hopeful catch, the hit—all usually happening within the blink of an eye. I thought about suggesting, "Hey, Coach, do you mind changing that to an out route or something?"

Did it flitter across my mind that perhaps Coach Bowden was resting his hopes of an undefeated season on my shoulders by calling the pass to me? Why, yes, it did, so all I wanted to do was sprint to the huddle, call the play, run out to my spot, and get this thing over without thinking about it. Just do it.

But perhaps he was having second thoughts. Maybe he was wondering the same thing. Was he out of his mind, calling such an important play to a former walk-on who had only made a dozen or so catches so far in his fledgling career? If I were him, I would have questioned myself, too.

As it so happened, I literally turned my body to run the play in to Wally Woodham, our quarterback, who was anxiously awaiting the play call, the clock ticking away, but Coach Bowden couldn't seem to let go of my facemask. He jerked my head back around. I ain't kidding, he *jerked* my head back around and just about stuck his head inside my helmet with me.

Eyes bulging and spit flying. "Don't drop it!"

And then he released my facemask.

To be clear, most folks think it's not a great idea for a coach to tell a basketball player "not to miss" the free throw that might win or lose a game, or a pitcher "not to throw a ball" on a pitch where a strike is imperative, but hey, pressure does strange things to all of us. And like I said, Bobby Bowden was human, whether folks realized it or not.

I remember thinking, "Geez, really?" before hauling my ass in there, giving Wally the play, sprinting out wide to the left, sneaking inside the hash marks, somehow eluding the bloodthirsty linebacker, and, finally, making the catch for a first down. It was all lightning fast, which is what I wanted so I didn't have time to think "Don't drop it!"

About ten minutes later, with a little over a minute left, we scored the go-ahead points and escaped Cincinnati with our record still unblemished.

Looking back, I was so very thankful that Coach Bowden had the faith in me to make that call. Even if he freaked out a little. And yeah, at times the coolest and calmest of us can get their cages rattled and lose it a bit. Like Coach did.

Many years later, I was fortunate enough to visit with Coach Bowden at his home about a year before he died. We reminisced about our time together and revisited a few of the bigger plays we'd both been a part of, like the Cincinnati call and catch. Coach was ninety at the time but still as sharp as ever.

"Coach," I said. "I always wanted to ask you about that play in Cincinnati, when it was fourth down and we were down 21-7 in the fourth quarter, and you called that drag route to me. Do you remember what you did?"

"What did I do?" he asked, his head cocked.

"Remember, you kept ahold of my facemask and sort of yelled at me not to drop it?"

"I did?" he asked. "Well, I'll be darned." And he laughed away, shaking his head happily. "Sorry about that." And then, "Did you catch it?"

He winked.

I smiled. "You know I did!" And we laughed.

As I look back on my time at Florida State, it even feels like Coach Bowden actually favored little ole me. I mean, I'm not sure many NCAA coaches would have even allowed such a small and slowish receiver out onto the field, much less put him in the starting lineup. But he did, even starting me a game or two late in my freshman year and then on and off my sophomore year. He saw past my limitations—physically and emotionally—and embraced who I truly was as a young man and athlete, giving back to me as a coach what I fought to give to him and the team as a player. He was always there when I needed him, as I tried to be for him.

I loved him.

He had given me—the little guy—a chance to make the play and rise above the circumstances. I did so that time, but there would be far more challenging times in the distant future that would prove I didn't always handle the extreme pressure with confidence and grace.

Times when I *did* drop the ball.

SCRATCHING THAT ITCH

"Something was missing."

W̶e finished the 1979 season with an 11-1 record and ranked sixth in the final Associated Press poll, both milestones for Florida State football at that time. We returned an excellent and very experienced defense for the following season, and though we may not have been what some would call "explosive" on offense, we played well as a team.

After a 3-0 start in 1980, my junior season, we went down to Miami to play the Hurricanes and entered into a dogfight against future NFL Hall of Fame quarterback Jim Kelly and crew. Prior to the game, we were ranked ninth in the AP poll.

Down 10-3, we scored a touchdown with a few seconds left, and Coach Bowden decided to go for two rather than accepting a tie. He called a pass to me, but it never made it to me, bouncing off of a lineman's head and out of the end zone. And with that, our hopes of an undefeated season bounced right out of there with that damn ball.

That was a tough one. Brutal.

But to me, it was perhaps one of the most defining moments in Florida State football history. When we hit the practice field on Monday in preparation for playing No. 3-ranked Nebraska for our next game, there was something in the air. I'm telling you, I could feel something. It was as if that loss down in Miami had jarred something out of our collective energy field that needed to be jarred out. As a team—and, it seemed, every single player—we were simply born anew, confident, feeling it. In other words, perhaps the loss had even helped us in some strange, ethereal way. We had an awesome week of practice, probably the most focused one I can remember.

And we were absolutely ready for the Nebraska Cornhuskers!

I knew I was, anyway, so I treated that week like any other week as far as extracurricular activities were concerned. Which meant I was ready to hit the town, as usual, regardless of whatever else was happening.

On that note, Coach Bowden was under the assumption that it was difficult for players to sleep the night before games, especially one as important as the Nebraska game, so he would almost always have a curfew for Thursday nights. He figured that would help those who didn't sleep so well on Friday nights. Well, I slept quite fine on Friday nights, thank you, and wasn't overly fond of having to be in my apartment by midnight on Thursdays (and now I can barely stay awake past eight!).

So here we were, two nights before an extremely big game, and I wanted to hit the town. Hence, shortly after one of the assistant coaches, Jim Gladden, had made the rounds at our apartment complex, making sure we were all in, I went out.

I stumbled back through my door at just about the same time the sun was peeking over the trees to the east and crashed for a few hours. Had they caught me, I likely would not have played that week and would've missed out on one of the highlights of my life until that point.

As it was, nobody ever even knew, I don't think.

We boarded the plane for Nebraska a few short hours later.

Late in the second quarter in Lincoln, Nebraska, it might not have appeared that we were as ready as I had thought, though, as Nebraska led by a score of 14-0. Bill Capece kicked a field goal before halftime to at least get us on the board. I have no recollection of anyone panicking as we gathered ourselves at halftime, again—to a man—each of us somehow expecting that the day was ours.

Our defense continued its stout play, and after a couple more field goals by Capece and a touchdown run by Sam Platt, we crept into the fourth quarter with a 15-14 lead. We had a third and 13 from our own 28-yard line with maybe four minutes left. Coach Bowden had installed a new wrinkle that week, a play designed to go to me, a deep out and up. In other words: take the route to a depth of 16 yards, stutter step as if heading toward the sideline on an angle, back toward the line of scrimmage, and then burst up the field on a go route. Everything needed to click on all cylinders—enough protection from the offensive line, a clean release by me so that I could get into the route quickly, and a perfect throw down the sideline.

Truthfully, I did not sell the out as much as I normally would have because the safety was playing a bit deep and I could tell I needed to get on up the sideline as fast as I could. The cornerback bit enough on the move, though, which allowed me to stay far enough ahead of him on the route so that he could not make a play on the ball. It was the safety that concerned me, pretty much running side by side with me.

Rick Stockstill threw the absolute perfect pass under the circumstances, slightly behind me, such that I sort of twisted my body back around to grab it while shielding the safety so he could not reach it. Okay, perhaps I did nudge him a little with my elbow to help the cause, but evidently not enough to draw a flag. It cleared the cornerback and fell gently into my arms as I cradled it and fell out of bounds at the Nebraska 32-yard line.

A couple minutes later, Capece kicked his fourth field goal of the game, and we were up by 4 with 2:37 left. Now Nebraska had to score a touchdown; a field goal wouldn't be good enough. The rest is basically Florida State football lore, as Nebraska drove the length of the field and snapped the ball from our 3-yard line with less than thirty seconds to go. Their quarterback scrambled left, linebacker Paul Piurowski blitzed and knocked the ball from his hands, defensive tackle Garry Futch jumped on the ball, and the entire Seminole nation went berserk. Folks, back then, you just did not go into Nebraska and beat them there.

But we did, and Coach Bowden would forever call that game perhaps the most important victory in FSU football history. I kind of liked that, especially since I felt like my 40-yard, third-down catch, coupled with Bill Capece's fourth field goal of the day, had been such a big part of it. I had also caught a ball in the third quarter down at the Nebraska 6-yard line that had set up our only touchdown. I truly felt as if this former walk-on that nobody had wanted had finally arrived.

To be honest, this felt closer to the feeling I had expected after we won the high school state championship, perhaps because it was on a much grander scale. I felt like I was floating in the clouds while walking into the locker room after beating the mighty Cornhuskers. At Nebraska! And to see my daddy in the locker room—how the hell did he get in there!—and watch him and Coach Schoolfield (the one who called me a quitter) hugging each other, well, that was next-level stuff for me at that time.

But it still didn't fully scratch my itch. It just didn't. In fact, it even hurt a little bit (or a lot), though, because the newspapers and other media outlets barely even mentioned the big catch I had made, a play that was essential to the victory. They seemed content instead to use up all their ink recounting the defensive play made by Piurowski and Futch. It felt that no matter what I did, the little former walk-on would never get his due.

Notwithstanding that, it was all quite a remarkable sequence to my way of thinking—a super close loss to a heated rival, a complete abuse of team rules by *this* Academic All-American, and, of course, maybe the most important win in FSU history.

Still, I felt like something was missing.

TIME STOOD STILL

"I caught a fucking shadow!"

The 1981 season—my senior year—is perhaps best known for a series of games that would be called "Oktoberfest," probably as tough a stretch as any ever played by a collegiate team. It started in late September, actually—but why quibble over semantics? Here was the schedule: a game at Nebraska, then at Ohio State, then at Notre Dame, then at Pitt, then at LSU.

The most important thing to notice is that little word "at" preceding each game. That's right. Five games. In a row. *Away.* All at five of the toughest places in the country to play, and against five of the most storied programs in college football history. The final rankings of the Coaches Poll had Pitt at second (we lost), Nebraska at ninth (we lost), and Ohio State at twelfth (we won). We also won at both Notre Dame and LSU. In other words, regardless of the rest of our schedule (which was tough!), Coach Bowden had displayed his cajones for all to see by negotiating such a difficult schedule. He preferred leading us through a field of landmines than escorting us to a picnic—something about putting Florida State on the football map. And the Seminoles have more or less been on that map ever since.

It was the Pittsburgh game that stood out to me, though, for a different reason or two than one might think. First of all, on Tuesday of game week, I had a case of strep throat that combined chills, nausea, a touch of delirium, and a fever hovering around 103, all into a nasty little package. We must have been tougher back then because I was not allowed to go to my room to sleep it off. I guess they figured sitting in the Florida sunshine was more medicinal, so that's what I did, watching the Wednesday and Thursday practices from the sideline of the practice field, staving off nausea and freezing my ass off in mid-80-degree temperatures.

Somehow, the coaches snuck a play into our game plan for Pittsburgh that featured me and one of our young wide receivers, Cedric Jones. As they practiced it on Wednesday with another player in my position, I imagine them glancing over at me retching on the sideline and questioning their sanity. They had no idea that the reverse pass from Cedric to me that Coach Bowden had no doubt conjured up in his laboratory would result in a play that would ultimately define my career. At least to me.

Still weak from the lingering effects of the strep throat, I traveled to Pittsburgh with the team and wondered if I would be able to make it through the first quarter, much less the entire game. I weighed in at around 166 pounds, a half a dozen less than my normal playing weight. With a few minutes left in the first half, Coach Bowden decided I was sufficiently recovered and called the play. We were on our own 8-yard line and down 21-0. Backed up and desperate.

It was surreal. I lined up wide to the right with Cedric wide left. The ball was snapped, and I drifted downfield as if preparing to block the safety. When he bolted toward the line of scrimmage, I took off deep up the right hash marks. I couldn't believe that everybody on Pittsburgh's defense bought into the reverse. I'm not exaggerating when I say that absolutely no one in the entire stadium was more alone than I was. I could have run 20 yards in any direction with my eyes closed and zero threat of running into anything.

It's amazing how many thoughts can run through your mind when you're on an island alone. The next few seconds took more than a minute, I'm pretty sure. As I drifted on down the field and everyone else ran the other way, I looked back into our backfield and picked Cedric out of the mass of bodies, the ball still in his hands.

"Throw it! Throw it! Hurry up and throw the ball!"

It seemed to take forever. Sooner or later, those other guys, the Pittsburgh defenders, were going to see what was really happening and turn around and come after me. Thankfully, even with my limited speed, I felt I had enough of a head start to make the catch and glide into the end-zone for a 92-yard touchdown, which would stun the crowd. But what was taking so long? Surely he's not going to run with it!

Finally, Cedric slowed down abruptly, raised the ball, stopped, planted his back foot, took a step forward, and let the ball fly in my general direction. By now, I was standing on the 50-yard line, twiddling my thumbs, humming a tune, and watching the game like everyone else. As the ball left his hand, I did what every receiver is trained to do. I was determined to follow the path of the ball and would continue to do so until it had been gathered into my hands. Simple enough: "Catch it with your eyes," we called it. I could see what looked like the entire Pittsburgh defense do a 180 and begin the long journey toward me. But they did not bother me. I was focused.

Once that ball was in the air, it was mine. And nothing could distract me from the mission. Nothing could make me lose focus. Nothing!

Except the sun.

As I said, it's funny how many things can run through your mind when the adrenaline jumpstarts. I once watched a movie where a man lived a lifetime in his mind, from the time he stepped off the plank of a pirate ship until he hit the water and was devoured by sharks. A second after the football left Cedric's hand, I suddenly remembered the description of the Pittsburgh stadium. East-west. The astute football fans know that running backs are always encouraged to run north-south, toward the end-zone. But not at Pittsburgh. As Saturday afternoon was drifting toward evening, the cursed decision by past University of Pittsburgh officials haunted me. Didn't they know that the sun traveled from east to west? Didn't they know that this might cause problems for receivers? Maybe they did.

PART ONE

As the ball disappeared into the sun and stayed buried deep within its blinding aura, a few other thoughts danced in my head. This game is on TV, right? Yes, I think so. At least back home, where everyone who knows me can see it. Had I ever seen a player get hit smack-dab in the face by a football as if he wanted to? Not to my recollection. What would my coaches think? They are probably staring at me right now, just 15 to 20 yards over to my left, giddy with excitement. And how about my teammates? How would they feel when they watched me grope about for the ball like a blind man reaching for a beach ball? And my dad, wasn't he sitting up over to my left somewhere, spilling his popcorn and soda on his pants while leaping to his feet to celebrate what looked like would be a certain 92-yard touchdown?

For a second, I considered throwing my arms over my face and dropping my head toward the ground in obvious surrender. People would have felt pity, maybe. *Poor guy.* Such an opportunity, but that's what the sun will do to you. At least they might understand, I thought. The embarrassment otherwise was sure to be even greater. I could hear it already.

"What?!"

"I've never seen anything like that!"

"How pathetic!"

"It hit the guy right in the face! With nobody around him!"

"How does that guy get to be out on the field?"

And then the laughter.

No, something deep inside stirred me to ditch that course of action and pursue another course of action. *You can't just give up. At least try,* a small voice seemed to say. So I decided instead to stare slightly off to the side of the sun and see if there was any way to pick the ball up before it impaled me. My retinas felt as if they were burnt to a crisp, probably useless for at least long enough for me to head back to my bench with my head hung low. I narrowed my eyes to slits and managed to make out a bluish background, the autumn sky in all its beauty. I focused on that alone. I didn't know what else to do.

And then it happened. A dark, blurry, moving object popped out of nowhere into my periphery, to my left, seemingly a foot or two in front of me, and was making a rapid descent, possibly toward the ground a couple of feet from my left hip, or somewhere in that general area. I couldn't be sure. I took a wild guess and figured it must be the ball. In the millisecond that I noticed the racing dark object, I stabbed at whatever it was with both hands while lunging toward where I thought it might be headed. Instinctively my hands formed the basket they had been trained to form, with fingers outstretched and ready. There was not even time to hope.

Something hit my fingers. And stuck. Right before my left knee, and then hip, hit the ground.

I snatched it upwards and cradled it next to my chest. I had just made probably the most difficult catch of my life, perhaps anyone's life, for that matter, as I had somehow pulled in a football thrown 50 yards in the air without seeing anything other than a peripheral view of a dark speeding blob, like trying to catch a shadow. And all with the tips of my fingers. A miracle!

Basically, I caught a fucking shadow.

Was I excited? Yes, sort of, but also stunned. What the hell had just happened? As I sat on the ground—on my ass—and looked toward the sideline, I realized how it must have looked. If I could, I would have grabbed a microphone and explained to my team and the crowd what they had just witnessed. *A feat never seen before! Feel free to leave a tip.* As it was, I just sat there for a second or two with my arms in the air and off to each side, the football in one hand, suggesting to my team that things were not as they appeared (there is a photo of this to prove it).

As I rose to my feet and headed toward the FSU sideline, I did not see anyone jumping up and down, no beaming smiles of pride. The coaches had crazy expressions on their faces, as if they had expected to watch a classic and, unfortunately, been stuck with a B movie, fully unaware of the magic trick I had just performed.

I felt helpless.

PART ONE

Such a deep life lesson was being presented to me, though I was far too sensitive to see it at that time. I would never, ever, under any circumstances, be able to find or feel full acceptance from a world outside of me—one, I was slowly learning, that could never fill my void.

PART TWO

Life after Football

THE "REAL WORLD"

"The most despicable profession."

When I first made my way down to Tallahassee to play football at Florida State, I was rather undersized and what some would call *slow*. In fact, after thoroughly embarrassing myself running a slow forty-yard dash for the FSU coaches my freshman year (I ain't saying what my time was!), I steadfastly refused to run another one. From then on, every time they pulled those irritating stopwatches from their shorts, I would grab my hamstring and begin to wince, rubbing it furiously. They would more or less smirk and run the rest of our team while I stood over in the shade.

Yet I did still have a faint dream of playing in the NFL. And that was not going to happen unless I ran the damn forty.

So in early 1981, when the professional scouts came to campus one day before my senior season to check out each of our teams' upcoming seniors—to watch a little film, to get our measurements, and to see how fast we were—I put on my workout gear and got stretched out.

I was not excited.

But I said, "What the hell!" knowing I would have zero chance to play in the NFL if I didn't. And since I'd trained my ass off the three years prior without being timed in the forty, I wondered if maybe, just maybe, I had gotten faster.

After watching several of my teammates run the forty, one of the scouts called my name. I stuck my hand in the grass in the middle of the playing field at Doak Campbell Stadium and gave it my all. I swear, it felt like I was running into a hurricane. When I passed those scouts, with their damn stopwatches, and saw them looking at those things in disbelief—*and* Coach Bowden standing there beside them laughing—I knew that was all she wrote.

I never even asked what my time was. By their expressions, and Coach Bowden's laughs, I knew that if it had improved since my freshman year, it must not have been by much. My NFL dreams ended, right then and there. At five feet eight and three-quarters inches, 175 pounds, and not a whole lot faster than most of our linemen, I knew I was cooked.

Well, I guess there was always the *real* world. And to that point, I had double-majored in Finance and Accounting at Florida State, not because I was into self-flagellation but because of my belief that understanding the world of money might very well help me in whatever career I chose.

I, therefore, began the interview process with a few of what were then called the Big Eight international accounting firms. They were all hot on my trail due to my grades and, I guess, my football success, so I was pretty much able to pick where I wanted to go. I chose a company called Coopers & Lybrand in Fort Lauderdale, Florida, and trekked down there to begin work in early January of 1982, just a few short weeks after my football career ended.

The summer before, I had met a young lady named Melanie Tomlin, who still had two or three years of school left. We hit it off and were dating pretty steadily by the time I graduated and headed to South Florida. I was feeling my oats, soaking in the new world of making money while not tearing up my body anymore, and she was still at FSU, working a nighttime waitressing job to make it through.

She would call me almost every night after her job, usually near midnight, and I was always out cold with a wake-up time of around five in the morning. I liked her a lot, but after a few of those late-night calls, I decided I had to have my sleep.

"Melanie," I mumbled, half asleep. "I can't take this anymore. You've gotta stop calling at this time of night."

She stopped.

And not just the late-night calls.

She had been lonely without me, but after my insistence that she stop calling so late, she found another boyfriend, which made it easy for her to fulfill my request. Once I realized what was going on, I got hit hard by depression. It's funny how that works. I probably would have been okay if I had been the one ending the relationship, but since it was *her* idea, I fell into a downward spiral of grief with deep feelings of rejection. I went from about 180 pounds (yeah, I was already on my way up after graduating from college!) down to 155 in barely over a month. I simply couldn't eat. I didn't know how much longer I could make it.

I called home a few times, hoping for some kind of help from Momma and Daddy.

"Momma, I feel so bad. I don't know what to do."

"Phil," Momma said. "I don't know what to say. You've always been the strong one in the family." It seemed she had forgotten my spat of homesickness when I first arrived at FSU as a freshman.

"Well I ain't now."

She passed the phone to Daddy, who didn't really say anything. I heard him groan a little, though. I *felt* his compassion through that old landline phone, an energy of understanding and knowing love coming through. It didn't do much for me, but I was greedy for any type of comfort I could get. Even if it was just a knowing grunt.

About five or six weeks into my heartbreak, I decided I had to do *something*. I had a talk with God, or who I thought was God at that time, and told Him I was handing my life over, that I needed some help getting out of the pit I was in. I didn't hear anything in return, but I made the decision to start going to a church in West Palm Beach.

I barely stepped into a church during my time at Florida State, so it felt a bit strange at first. But I really didn't know what else to do or where to turn. Church had obviously been a big part of the life of my family when I was growing up, so it at least seemed worth a shot, and a few months later I was more or less okay. Filling my mind with affirmations of a loving God, and being around others who bolstered that concept, was a definite boost to my emotional well-being.

Soon, I was attending church regularly, which led to other changes in my life. Of course, I approached my newfound faith like many things in my life—with intensity. Therefore, a few short years later, I was a church deacon and eventually led multiple spiritual book and Bible studies, and even a mission trip or two, all the while studying my Bible rather furiously. Though I had been withering away from the loss of my girlfriend, I still managed to maintain my job at Coopers & Lybrand. Nonetheless, it barely lasted longer than my first stint at Florida State, as I soon realized that sitting behind a desk all day ranked right up there with going to the dentist and eating Brussels sprouts. No offense to the Brussels sprouts.

At that point, the thought of becoming an NFL agent had never even crossed my mind, maybe because it wasn't thought of as such a big deal back in the '70s. But there are a couple other reasons as to why I never gave it any thought, too. First, whenever there was an article in the newspaper that mentioned agents, I got the distinct feeling that the journalists writing the articles would most certainly not be inviting agents to any of their parties. Second, and more influential, was the vibe I got from Coach Bowden, my head coach at FSU, when he spoke to the team every year about agents.

"Men," he would say, his eyebrows falling down heavy and his voice edging a bit deeper, "some of you are going to have the opportunity to play professionally, which means you will hear from agents."

What he would say after that was his way of cussing but not cussing—you could *feel* the cuss words hidden within such scowling terms as *"dadgum scum"* and *"leeches"* and such as he spat them out of his mouth. When you trusted someone as much as I did Coach Bowden, how could that not turn your mind away from the thought of becoming an agent?

So after I left the accounting world, I went solo into various financial endeavors until 1985, when a former FSU player, who had been a freshman when I was a senior, asked for my help choosing an agent. I took his request seriously, looked closely, and decided that becoming an agent was right up my alley, *"dadgum scum"* be damned. It had much of what I was looking for, allowing me to be my own boss, remaining heavily involved in football, relying on personal communication and relationship, and providing the potential for gobs of money.

It also included one other element that I didn't give much consideration to at the time but which would be a bit of a thorn in my side throughout my career: it is very hard to be successful as an agent without selling your soul, or at least without compromising your integrity, neither of which I intended to do.

Once I made the decision to become an agent, I naturally went to see Coach Bowden. I was twenty-six at the time and looking for all the help I could get in starting my business. And I figured Coach Bowden might even put in a good word for me if a player asked about me.

"Coach," I started, feeling slightly queasy, wondering if he might run me out of the house once I told him what I was doing. I fidgeted for a second or two, then looked him in the eyes.

"I'm becoming an NFL agent."

He sort of chuckled, sort of sneered, sort of smiled. Anybody who knew Coach Bowden knows that he rarely skipped a beat. "Well, Philip, you are entering the most despicable profession."

Seriously, that was the word he used. *Despicable.*

"Let me know whatever I can do to help you."

I sat there with an interesting mix of emotions. He had affirmed his feelings toward the general occupation of agenting, which he had shown so clearly all those years earlier, but at the same time, made me feel welcome and supported. He was the master!

Through the years, though, I never asked for his help. I just couldn't bring myself to do it. But back in the day, when the rules were far more lax, he did something that would fill my heart with gratefulness and pride whenever I thought of it. During my early years of agenting, I was pretty much broke, if even that. On at least two recruiting road trips—one to Gainesville, Florida, where FSU was to play the Gators, our most hated rival, and another to Ann Arbor, Michigan, where FSU was to play the Wolverines of Michigan—I showed up at the team hotel the night before the game and ran into Coach Bowden.

What happened each time might be difficult for some to believe.

"Hey, Philip, good to see you."

"You, too, Coach."

"You got a ticket?" he asked.

"No," I mumbled, not even sure if I would go to the game. I always tried to save a buck wherever I could and reckoned I could watch it at a sports bar nearby and then hustle over after to meet and greet a few of the players.

Coach nodded.

"Come over to the hotel tomorrow morning, before we leave for the game. We'll see what we can do."

I did, and without batting an eye, he slid his own sideline pass from his waist and handed it to me. For both games! I roamed the sidelines during those two intense games, taking me back into the energy and adrenaline of it all.

So yeah, Coach Bowden continued to be there for me.

MEETING MEG

"Hey, what's your name?"

The first years of agenting were particularly choppy, but around the time I thought the ship might be sinking, I met Meg Rinard, a beautiful brunette from the beaches of South Florida.

I saw her at church on a Sunday morning, my sister-in-law pointing at her and exclaiming she had *picked her out* for me. I thought to myself, "Hmm. Yes. Interesting." The next day, I saw her pushing her shopping cart across the steamy asphalt outside of a Publix Supermarket off of West Pensacola Street, just a few blocks from where I had lived while playing football at Florida State. I felt the synchronicity kicking in, and my heart skipped a beat. *Surely, this had to be a sign?* I quickly surmised that if I missed the opportunity to meet her now, my destiny might very well need to be reset, for I had determined the day before that I had fallen for her.

Being the suave wordsmith that I am—or, rather, desperate I would miss my chance—I opened my mouth before she could escape into her car and drive away. She was at least fifty feet away, and I had no clue what was about to come out as she began to open her door.

"Hey," I said—safe so far!—and then, because nothing else came to me, "What's your name?"

Seriously. That was it. That was my line. She gave me a "Who the hell are you?" look and began to open her car door.

I was calling to her from across the parking lot while straddling the doorway to my Mercury Grand Marquis, a now-defunct car the size of the FSU football stadium I had leased for business purposes (though it wasn't helping much). I also had a pretty thick beard at that time, which was not exactly in vogue in the mid-'80s.

Meg, on the other hand, was all of twenty years old, trying to finish up her senior year at Florida State, just shopping for a little food. She was most definitely not looking to meet some older dude in a parking lot.

"I saw you at church yesterday," I managed to spit out before she landed in her seat. I almost threw in a *"Praise the Lord"* for effect but decided against it. She smiled.

"Is it okay if I drive over there to speak for a moment?"

She nodded yes and was leaning in my passenger window a minute later, sweating bullets in the sweltering Florida heat but smiling and talking with me.

Somehow, I got her phone number that day.

On our second date, we stopped at some fast-food place on Tennessee Street (I don't remember the name of that spot, but I do remember they had awesome shakes). We were more or less just getting to know each other, and I was kind of excited.

"You wouldn't be going out with me if you weren't thinking you might marry me," I blurted out, pretty much out of the blue. For me *and* her.

A mouthful of milkshake spewed from her mouth onto the table, and her eyes got big. But she didn't say no.

We dated for a few months, kind of just going through the motions. I think I was in a pretty weird spot—definitely interested but not really sure what was going on. She would soon be graduating with plans for her life, while I was twenty-eight and trying to build my agent business. Notwithstanding my aggressive comment at the milkshake spot, I remained cautious.

One Saturday night after a few dates, we decided to go to my apartment to watch a rental movie and found ourselves lying on the couch. I hadn't kissed her yet and was a bit nervous about doing so.

But there we were, so I gave it a shot. She kissed me back, and we were off to the races, probably spending a whole hour just kissing and hugging.

I don't remember what movie we watched. Perhaps we didn't watch one at all.

The next morning, I saw her at the church where I'd first seen her, and we greeted each other as if we barely knew each other.

"Hey, how are you doing?"

"Fine, thank you. How are you?"

"Fine, thanks."

That was it. Talk about awkward. We moved on past each other as if we hadn't been all kissy-face just a few hours earlier.

Then came December—time for Meg to go back to Clearwater, Florida, for the Christmas Holidays. I was falling for her, though not yet certain she was "the one."

The day she was supposed to head home, I heard a knock on my apartment door. It was her. My heart skipped a beat.

"Hey," I said.

She held out a small envelope, shifted her feet a time or two, and twitched her lips as if she wanted to say something but couldn't figure out exactly what. Then she spun around, jumped in her car, and took off.

What the hell?

I opened the envelope and quickly read the short note. It basically went something like this:

"I don't think we should see each other anymore. I've got plans after college in a few months. Maybe we can be friends."

All I heard was *Goodbye! You're not what I'm looking for!*

Heartbroken, I waited a couple days before contacting her. I had been cautious up until that point, maybe not wanting to give my heart away, afraid of getting hurt, so I really hadn't let myself realize how much I had grown to like her. But once she gave me that *terrible* note, I knew I had better think about her a bit deeper, to let some of my reservations go, even if it hurt to do so. As I did so, I decided she may very well be "the one," and I wanted to at least find out whether there was something else behind her seemingly abrupt decision. So I called her and asked if I could come to Clearwater to have "one last talk."

She said okay. A few days later, I drove down. And when I got there at night, she came out of her parents' house and sat with me in that same Grand Marquis I had met her in a few months earlier. We chatted for at least an hour, Meg affirming her decision that she had a plan for after college, which did not include me. We agreed to be friends.

There really weren't any hotels nearby, and it was approaching midnight, so Meg asked if I wanted to sleep on the couch. I really didn't want to—I felt rejected and just wanted to get the hell out of there. But before she stepped out of the car, I was hit by a tidal wave of fatigue so powerful that I could barely move. I wasn't sure I could even push the gas pedal. So I accepted.

The next day, she invited me to go out to eat with her and a couple of friends, so I did. While out, we stopped in Harbor Island, an eclectic area of Tampa, and somehow found ourselves in a recording booth singing *Grandma Got Run Over By A Reindeer*. Who knew that song was such an aphrodisiac? Meg and I were all of a sudden googly-eyed for one another. After the note from a few days earlier and the talk in the car from the night before, I'm quite sure neither of us had expected such a thing to happen so rapidly and with such intensity, and yet there we were, staring into each other's eyes and holding hands. Far more romantic than even our evening of kissing those couple of months earlier.

Less than a month later, after Meg had returned to Tallahassee for her last semester of college, we were alone in her room in a house she shared with a couple of other girls. She was giving me a foot massage, and I got to thinking she must like me pretty good if she was doing *that*. We were dating far more seriously than before, and though I was beginning to like the idea of marriage, I wasn't about to bring it up. Plus, I was certain she would say no.

Then, another crazy Phil moment happened.

"What do you wanna name our children?" just seemed to slip out of my mouth.

If she had some milkshake in her mouth that time, I might have been sprayed again! But she didn't, and she kept on digging her fingers into my feet, looking at me as if thinking of an answer. Finally, she gave a couple of names.

This gave me an idea.

"You're thinking you're gonna marry me, aren't you?" I asked.

She looked startled, and then like she was trying to think of an answer to a very difficult exam question, took a big gulp.

"I guess so," she finally said, seemingly surprised by herself.

I didn't skip a beat.

"Then why don't we?" I blurted out.

I could almost see the wheels turning in her mind. She was staring straight ahead and thinking.

"We couldn't tell anybody," she finally responded.

I was stunned! I had just proposed without the slightest clue that I had been about to do so, and with a rather unorthodox delivery—*then why don't we?* Not exactly a marriage proposal Hall of Fame candidate!

And though her acceptance—*we couldn't tell anybody*—was less than what most men would have wanted, I was thrilled. I latched onto it with all I had, and we went out to get pizza to celebrate our engagement.

I was way above cloud nine.

The reason Meg didn't want to tell anyone was that she was scared as to what her mother would say. At only twenty-one, with her life in front of her, she felt like her mother would probably freak out a little, especially since she had barely met me over the holidays. So we agreed to keep our engagement a secret for the time being.

That only lasted a couple days.

Meg began to feel more comfortable with everything, and after perhaps a bit of coaxing from me (I was a very excited boy!), we decided to tell her parents that week. Meg called her sister Amy, and a plan was devised. We drove down on a Wednesday evening, and when we were just a few miles away, Meg used a payphone to call Amy, who made some excuse to get her mother to go for a night walk. I dropped Meg off at the planned spot so that she could meet her mom and break the news while I drove the remaining block or two to the house and knocked on the door.

Pat Rinard, Meg's father, opened the door. I felt like he kind of liked me already. He was an FSU football fan and knew who I was as a player before I had met him a month earlier.

"Hey," he said, a slight look of confusion in his eyes.

I took a few tight, quick breaths and reached out to shake his hand.

"I'm here because I've asked Meg to marry me, and she has said yes. I would like your approval. Meg is down the road meeting with Mary."

He looked at me for a second.

"Do you want a glass of wine?" he asked, opening the door wider.

"Yes." He had offered me wine a couple times on my earlier trip down, and I had declined both times. I wasn't declining this time.

Four months later, Meg and I were married.

LIFE AS AN NFL AGENT

"It hasn't hit me yet."

As noted, those early years of agenting were difficult, notwithstanding the support of people like Coach Bowden. It was really hard to walk into a recruiting interview as a twenty-something without clients and convince players I could do the job. Plus, the top players were all being offered money and cars and women and such, and I wasn't doing any of that. One, it went against my beliefs, and two, I didn't have any of that stuff to offer, anyway.

Interestingly, and perhaps beneficial to my career, one effect from fitting in at Carver Junior High all those years earlier surfaced early on in my time as an NFL agent. It happened while attempting to recruit an athlete from Jackson State University in Jackson, Mississippi, a historically black university. I had spoken to him on the phone a few times, and though I was not aware of it, I evidently must have used the way of speaking I had picked up from my time at Carver. I flew him to Atlanta on a recruiting trip after Jackson State's last game, and as soon as he walked off the plane and saw me, he stopped in his tracks.

"You ain't Phil Williams." He stood there shaking his head. "Phil Williams is a black man."

I laughed and laughed.

PART TWO

Fortunately, I landed a six-round draft choice in 1986, my first recruiting cycle, and my career was at least set in motion. Orson Mobley had been a freshman tight end at FSU when I was a senior, though he had transferred to a small school in West Virginia called Salem. From our time together at FSU, he trusted me, and this gave me my start in the agent business and the tad bit of experience that was needed to begin to recruit more successfully.

A couple years later, I landed a high draft choice in the 1988 NFL draft and a later pick by the name of Martin Mayhew, a cornerback from FSU who would go on to have a very successful NFL career (which included winning a Super Bowl with the Washington Redskins while playing against the Buffalo Bills, the team that had drafted him) and eventually be named General Manager for two NFL franchises.

So by 1989, I was off and running—far from having secured a spot in the NFL agent Hall of Fame, I had at least stuck my foot in the door with every intention of squeezing my whole body through.

While Martin had played at FSU, Deion Sanders had been the *other* starting cornerback, though he was one year behind Martin. He was scheduled to play his last collegiate season in 1988 and then hit the NFL draft in 1989.

From the moment Deion stepped on campus, it was clear that he was destined for superstardom. I saw it instantly, perhaps before almost anyone else. It was also clear that he was cut from a different cloth. He had a natural-born instinct for business and self-promotion. It was uncanny (still is).

It was also absolutely 100 percent clear to me that Deion Sanders was not going to give simple, little ole Phil Williams even a cursory glance as his possible agent. He seemed to walk on a different plane of existence from me. Hence, even though a former teammate of mine at FSU by the name of Eric Riley was working with me at that time (he knew Deion well, and they were from the same area of Florida), I made zero effort to recruit him. Even though he was in my backyard.

Imagine my surprise, then, when Eric told me Deion wanted to meet with me. I had no expectations whatsoever but agreed to meet with him at Bennigan's, a now-defunct restaurant off of Apalachee Parkway in Tallahassee, on a cool autumn evening near the close of 1988. Deion bought *me* coffee, and we chatted for maybe an hour.

It was obviously just a minor look-see for him—maybe an attempt to satiate a curiosity as to what the local agent was like (I was the only NFL agent who lived in Tallahassee). Or maybe it was simply a gesture of common courtesy to his homeboy, Eric. But it was clear from the get-go that we were just there to shoot the shit.

So I shot.

"Deion," I said between sips of a cup of very so-so black coffee, "I've got a proposal for you."

He raised an eyebrow.

"How about we go out onto the field at Doak Campbell (FSU's home stadium). I'll run one route. Just one. You cover me. It can't be a hitch; it's gotta be at least 10 yards. I catch it, you sign with me. I don't, you do what you're gonna do anyway."

I'll never forget his response, his Jheri curl shaking side to side.

"Hell, no. Anything can happen on one play."

I think I may have called him a pussy, or something to that effect, both of us laughing.

Here he was, perhaps the most dominant coverage dude ever to play the game, speaking a truth that few would dare to utter. Though I was thirty years old, obviously not remotely in the same shape as him, or as skilled, he realized that life always has an arsenal of flukes ready to pop out at any second. And he wasn't about to let me be his fluke.

He pulled his wallet out and a few hundred dollar bills fell to the floor. He obviously had more money than me, wherever it came from! He kindly took care of the small bill, we shook hands, and I've barely spoken to him since.

But I look back on that strange but telling meeting with a half-smile on my face. The *greatest ever*, shying away from a challenge—or at least not wanting to tempt fate. I didn't blame him. In fact, I figured I could have pulled it off. Probably not, but hell, one can dream!

Nonetheless, I ended up representing six or seven guys in the 1989 NFL draft (Deion went fifth overall) and continued inching my body in through the doorway.

A couple years later, I received a call from Martin. Back in the day, players from some of the NFL teams would cobble together a basketball team from their football roster and play other teams (this would be disallowed shortly thereafter due to risk of injury). Martin played for the Washington team, and during one of their games against Minnesota, he ran into a former teammate of his from FSU, quarterback Brad Johnson, whom I had recruited but who had chosen a different agent when leaving Florida State after the 1991 season. In fact, he had signed with the same agent who represented Coach Bowden, trusting that if Coach Bowden worked with him, he must be good. Whether good or not, Brad found himself to be the low man on the totem pole, and after a discussion with Martin at that basketball game, Martin let me know that Brad was interested in signing with me.

A few weeks later, Brad was a new client of mine.

Though there are a slew of stories I could share about Brad and our adventure together, I'll offer only a couple.

Brad became the starting quarterback for the Vikings in the mid-1990s and signed a contract that was to pay him approximately seventeen million dollars over a four-year period, substantial enough at the time for Al Michaels, renowned broadcaster, to state on Monday Night Football that Brad had just signed a "mammoth contract."

Twenty-five or so years later, that "mammoth contract" would equate to peanuts for most nickelbacks and third receivers!

But as it so happened, that same night, after the ink had barely dried on the contract, Brad woke up with a significant twinge in his throwing arm. And just like that, he was in surgery and out for the season. Eventually, he was traded to the Washington Redskins, where he made the Pro Bowl in 1999.

Two years later, he signed with the Tampa Bay Buccaneers. There had been five or six teams offering contracts to make him their starting quarterback, but he chose Tampa Bay because we believed he had the best chance to win a Super Bowl there.

"I don't care about the money, Phil," he said. "I've made more than I'll ever need. Just get me somewhere I can win a Super Bowl."

That was about it, verbatim. Refreshing as hell, to be honest. A player that realized he had enough money. Go figure.

At any rate, we agreed to a contract with Tampa Bay, although we could have gotten more elsewhere, and in his second season there, they brought home the first-ever Super Bowl trophy for the Buccaneers. I'm pretty sure he would say it was worth it.

Representing NFL players had its benefits, for sure. But it also had its downside. Watching young players chase their dreams and then finding out that those dreams were often hollow began to wear on me. I never once saw a player whose life was truly fulfilled by making it, no matter how successful they were—not mine, after making the crucial catch at Nebraska, nor anyone else, when cornered and pushed for honesty.

I've been to several Super Bowls through the years, always courtesy of clients who were playing in them, and I've watched a bunch more. I'm always amused when the players are standing on the podium after the game, a lot of the world watching, and the television reporter sticks a microphone in their face after asking that one question they can't seem to avoid asking: "How does it feel?"

It is as if it all gets broken down into a *feeling*. I mean, it's got to be a state of ecstasy, right? Like the bliss I had expected from winning the state championship back in my own glory days, right?

But what do they usually say?

"Uh, umm, uh … I don't know. It hasn't hit me yet."

To be honest, I'm not so sure it ever will.

BEHIND THE SCENES

"They just don't know you ... "

In early 2003, a client of mine from Georgia Tech came to visit me at our house outside of Atlanta, Georgia. When I went to open the door, I saw that another guy was with him. They walked in.

"This is Tony Hargrove," my client said. I recognized the name.

Tony reached out his hand and smiled a smile I will never forget. I shook his hand.

I soon learned he was only nineteen years old and what sports folk call a "freak." In a good way. He could run and jump with the most athletic of the wide receivers and cornerbacks, and he was as strong as Hercules. But it was his smile, his demeanor, his one-of-a-kind energy that attracted your attention the most.

I barely spoke to him on that first meeting—pretty much just hello and goodbye—but he had already entered our hearts. There was just something about him. A few months later, he called me after flunking out of Georgia Tech (several Georgia Tech players flunked out at that time, a strange anomaly), looking for advice and help. Folks, this is a smart dude. Things are not always as they seem. In fact, in reality, they almost never are. But that is another story.

It was soon discovered that his options were limited, and based on his extreme potential—and a call or two to a couple of NFL scouts who verified that he was on the NFL radar in a fairly substantial way—he chose to hire me as his agent and begin the process of preparing for the 2004 NFL draft after only two seasons of college ball.

Tony spent a fair amount of time at our house in Peachtree City, helping me with an assortment of odd jobs, like putting together a basketball goal for our kids (we'll get to them in a bit). But mainly I think he was there to clean out our pantry and refrigerator. That young man could eat! One time, Meg made enchiladas, at least two days' worth, but by the time we got up from the table, they were gone! He even licked the casserole dish they were cooked in! To this day, she still makes them. The name on her recipe card? Tony's Enchiladas.

Those times of odd jobs and meals began to open a door into Tony's life that shook me a bit. Through all of our talking, having fun, laughing, and getting to know each other, his story began to leak out little by little. I saw a young man with very deep pains—no father to speak of, a loving mother who died when he was around nine, homelessness on the streets of Brooklyn, just to get started—masked by his effervescent smile and cheerfulness. At nineteen years old, with a life of heartbreak and struggle supposedly behind him, a personality that oozed charisma and charm and warmth, and a future deemed bright by those who create the narratives, I wondered what lay in store for him.

Tony's ebullient personality may have papered over some pretty deep scars, but it wouldn't be too long before the wounds beneath those scars would manifest and then rupture, subsequently spewing out enough poisonous residue to bog down his NFL career.

He finished the 2005 season with a flurry of quarterback sacks, a sign that this very young developing defensive end (he had been a quarterback in high school and was barely even comfortable with his new position) might very well be on the precipice of NFL superstardom, a force to be reckoned with. Behind the scenes, though, Tony was being pulled by another force, as he had unwittingly stumbled into a multi-year battle with drugs and alcohol.

Gabor Mate, a world-renowned addiction expert, says that addiction is always a response to suffering and that any outside relief is always temporary. In other words, the addict's choice of medication *almost* works, so he keeps going back for more. He also says that the issues that precipitate addiction go back to childhood trauma—sometimes severe, sometimes simply a lack of nurturing, and often by a parent who's under a lot of stress. From this comes shame, and it is this—the shame—that comes before addiction. And it is not lack of willpower, or moral failure, or any of these negative things that society usually judges, that causes it.

Tony's childhood and subsequent addiction issues would likely serve as a litmus test for Mate's observations. And render them accurate.

Due to a prior series of positive drug tests, Tony spent a month in a rehab facility before the 2006 season. Nonetheless, four weeks into the season, I received a phone call from the Rams.

"Phil, do you know where Tony is?"

I thought for a second. Uh-oh.

"No," I said. "I'm guessing he ain't at work?"

"That's correct."

"Let me see if I can find him."

I got off the phone, sighed a time or two, and called Tony. He didn't answer.

After two or three quick redials, I left a message. *Please call. We need to talk.*

Eventually, he did. It was not easy to talk him into going in. Tony had spent the night snorting coke in someone's basement, and now that he had missed work, he was embarrassed and very ashamed. But he finally went and met with the head coach. And shortly thereafter, he was traded to the Buffalo Bills to finish out the 2006 NFL season.

Looking back, it was easy to see that the drug and alcohol issues were just getting started, that he was on a fast train, headed straight out over a canyon that was just waiting to swallow him up. Sure enough, after more positive tests, he was called into the League office to meet with NFL Commissioner Roger Goodell and League Attorney Jeff Pash.

I flew to New York for the meeting and entered the waiting room a little before Tony got there. When he walked in, he barely looked my way, almost as if I wasn't even there, and instead made his way over to the corner where there was a coffee pot and some water. He stood in that corner and cried. Silently. He kept his back to the room, but you could see this big, sweet fellow reaching up time and again to wipe his whole face. He stood that way for a while.

When Jeff and Roger heard Tony's childhood story and looked him in the eye, I'm pretty sure they saw what I had always seen: a good guy who had been through a lot in his life. They decided not to suspend him at that time. They warned him, though, that they did not want to see him in there again.

But after the 2007 season, they sent him to a drug rehab facility in Charleston, South Carolina, to spend another month or so working on his issues. Tony walked into the facility ... and right back out. Against their orders. That was all the NFL could take, and they quickly issued a one-year suspension.

The shame that Gabor Mate describes kicked in pretty good then, and Tony basically became incognito. Hell, I couldn't even find him; no matter how hard I tried, all my calls and messages were ignored. A couple weeks later, we reconnected, and after a few discussions with me and a couple of other folks, he decided that if he ever wanted to play football again, he would have to face his devils. So off to rehab he went ... again. I visited him a couple months after he entered the hospital in Charleston, and then again a few months later at the facility they sent him to in Miami to continue his healing journey. His issues ran pretty deep; he spent almost a full year straight dealing with his shit. But when he came out in early 2009, he had a new lease on life.

The problem was that the NFL could deal pretty harshly with

those who have flaunted their rules. It soon became painfully obvious that teams were afraid to sign a player with such a checkered past, either concerned that the fan base would react hysterically to their team signing a recovering addict or worried that Tony's history of usage would put him at too much of a risk for relapse. Either way, Tony and I knew we had to come up with a unique strategy if he was ever going to play in the NFL again.

Tony flew to Atlanta in late February to stay with me and the family for a few days and do a bit of brainstorming. I was genuinely perplexed that no teams were calling, expecting the amazing potential that Tony had exhibited before the drug problems surfaced would trump the suspension and its accompanying issues. After all, there are only so many six-foot-four, 290-pounders on earth who can run like the wind, jump out of a building, bench press the same building, and get after NFL quarterbacks—almost none, in fact. Surely, that would have been enough to allow the team personnel departments to look beyond a little ole *past* addiction problem.

"What are we gonna do?" Tony asked as I dumped a mess of bacon and eggs onto the table on his first morning after flying in from Miami.

"I'm thinking on it," I said.

"Well, I feel a lot better."

"Shut up. We'll figure it out."

Not much else was said during breakfast, and afterwards we made our way into the living room and sat down.

"You know," I began. "The way I see it, they just don't know you." I leaned forward, a smile forming on my lips. "I think I've got a plan."

Within a few days, we had mailed out a letter reminding everyone we could think of—from each NFL team's general manager to personnel directors, from position coaches to a few head coaches and even a couple of owners—that Tony was not only a fantastic athlete, as they already knew, but a gosh-darn, real-life human being who had changed his life. A great story of redemption, in fact. We even threw in a bonus video—free of charge—of the two of us having a nice little fireside chat so folks could actually hear from Tony himself how he now viewed life and what they could expect from him as a person if they would please take a step out of their glass houses for a second.

It worked! A little, anyway; three or four of the teams responded. Philadelphia even offered a contract, which was rescinded once they learned of a long-forgotten, somewhat irritating little warrant for Tony's arrest in Upper New York for an incident during training camp with the Buffalo Bills back in 2007 (which itself was later "rescinded"). The deflation that came with the offer being pulled was offset by a call from Pro Personnel Director Ryan Pace of the New Orleans Saints, who said they liked what they saw in the letter and video. Would Tony like to come in for a workout? *Well, hell yes!* A few weeks later, he was a New Orleans Saint.

Tony hit New Orleans like a man released from a long stint in the joint. He remained focused on staying off the streets and working through his newly learned twelve steps, a few affirmations, and anything else that would keep him living his "one day at a time" mantra. When he walked into the Saints facility, everyone there soon knew that the building had a little more juice in it. Had someone fiddled with the wiring or something? This dude was bouncing off walls with excitement, and before you knew it, it was rubbing off on others. There was, to coin an old phrase, electricity in the air, and it would later prove an integral part in helping the Saints win their first-ever Super Bowl.

One moment in particular gave the Saints a preview of who Tony was and the magic that was actually in their midst. It happened on the final day before players were released for the summer before reporting back in late July for training camp. The Saints had a conditioning test that each player had to do. It was pretty damn exhausting and gave an indication of the type of shape they were in. Normally, the test consisted of three 300-yard shuttle runs that had to be done in under a minute, actual time requirement depending on the position of the player.

Charles Grant, a starting defensive end, said to Tony, "I bet you can't run six of them in under a minute."

This was basically considered impossible. No one had ever tried, at least to their knowledge, and nobody wanted to! Even the thought was grueling.

"I bet I can," Tony responded.

And before you knew it, the bets were flowing between teammates, almost all against him, though a few wanted him to succeed so badly that they took the underdog and his rebel spirit. He almost died on the last one but somehow crossed the finish line within the allotted time to a more raucous, cheering crowd of teammates, coaches, and others than was sometimes heard after a Drew Brees touchdown pass in the Superdome on Sunday afternoons.

Why did he do it? It was an inspiration, really—an opportunity for him to show those who had taken a chance on him that he would do all that was humanly possible to live up to their hopes for him. He stood up in a defensive meeting afterwards and said, "The point wasn't to show off. The point is this: If I tell you I'm going to do something, I'm going to do it. That's what I tell myself every day—that I'm going to do this."

Seven months later, Tony was drowning in confetti while hoisting high the Lombardi Trophy in the middle of Joe Robbie Stadium in Miami Gardens with his teammates, just a stone's throw away from where he had been in drug rehab less than a year earlier. The irony brought tears to his eyes and joy to his heart. He found himself lying in the middle of a sea of people and crying, all the while performing what from the stands most likely appeared to be the biggest and clumsiest snow angels in history, more aptly called confetti angels. I stood nearby watching it all, so very proud. And laughing!

What a rags-to-riches story, huh? And a damn good one. Hollywood worthy. However, those rags were pretty difficult to get rid of. The NFL would soon seize upon a narrative that it hoped would make them look like the compassionate entity of which they have proven through the years that they most definitely were not. And, in so doing, drag Tony back through the mud of their creation.

That narrative? A not-so-little thing that would eventually be called Bountygate, a moniker for a monstrous NFL story that eventually prompted my decision to leave the world of agenting for good. And challenge much of what I believed in.

From my experience, the National Football League had never been overly concerned about the health of their depreciable assets— the players—as long as enough of the players could suit up and bring in the fans and, therefore, the money. They ran commercials that made fun of the concussions and other injuries experienced by the players, and the resulting cognitive issues, until concussion lawsuits began popping up. From 2002 to 2006, ESPN even ran a segment called *Jacked Up!* on Monday Night Football, where the hosts would celebrate the biggest hits from the prior week's games (as the lawsuits rolled in, *Jacked Up!* was quietly canceled).

And then came Bountygate, an incredible story that played itself out over the second half of 2012, which had a profound impact not only upon Tony's life but also upon my own.

At some point after being fired, a disgruntled, former New Orleans Saints employee went to the NFL with news about a "bounty program" that Coach Gregg Williams had implemented in an attempt to encourage his defense to play *aggressively*. According to the reports, the players were to be paid small sums of money (tiny, in relation to their normal pay, and out of the players' own pockets— already extracted *from* the players due to fines and such) for certain categories of plays.

There were at least two issues with this: first, many teams through the years had similar programs, and second, after a careful viewing of the film, no one would have accused the Saints of even having such a program, as they probably set a record for the least amount of injuries ever caused by an NFL team. In other words, if they did have a program crafted by the coach that was meant to injure opponents, it seemingly wasn't followed by the players out on the field.

But this presented an opportunity for the NFL owners and the league office to look as if they cared about player health and safety and hopefully curb the inevitable outflow of funds from the lurking lawsuits.

The NFL seized upon the narrative and went about the business of concocting an indictment against the Saints that had more holes in it than a cheese grater. They told the world their version of what the players had done wrong, vilifying them every step of the way, and pitted the rest of the teams against them. Most importantly, they controlled the narrative, many in the media frightened to truly challenge the power structure, afraid that their credentials would be taken from them or, worse, that they would lose their jobs. Almost none were willing to cast a leery eye at the hand that fed them, much less bite it!

And somehow Tony found himself at the center of the controversy, along with three other players and a couple of the coaches. The NFL lied about him from the beginning, ostensibly because he was already damaged goods. More than likely, they saw him as an easy target, someone they could throw under the bus without much fanfare. Hence, they accused him of saying things he did not say. Proof didn't matter in the least to the NFL brass, so they lied whenever it fit the narrative that implied they were looking out for the safety of their collective assets—again, something they had proven over time was categorically false.

My entire family was saddened by how the NFL publicly lied about Tony. Especially me. I couldn't help but involve myself in the controversy; Tony was more than just a client to me—he was part of our family.

In September, while the players were appealing various suspensions imposed by the commissioner, the NFL called each player in for "interviews," which were actually "grillings" that involved the hired counsel for the NFL mercilessly trying to extract something—anything!—that would help their indictments of the players appear more legitimate in the public eye.

I went with Tony and witnessed the malevolent circus, held below Manhattan in some underground room that felt like a dungeon, and watched them tear into Tony, trying to get him to slip up and give them some damning fodder. But he did not. At the conclusion of the charade, I asked one question and watched them fall all over themselves with lies. I sensed evil in that cold, dismal room, as if there was a very large serpent slithering around throughout the interrogation.

Upon being released back into the world up above, I meandered the streets of Manhattan by myself for quite a while, my worldview shifting with each moment of contemplation. I realized that up until that morning, I had been sheltered, unaware of how certain things worked. But now, I had witnessed a powerful organization—an entity made up of some of the world's wealthiest individuals—use its mouthpiece, the NFL Office, as a *shield* to protect them and their money. It was clear to me that they would do whatever it took to do so. They were obviously willing to lie and scheme and drag an innocent person through the mud, absolutely uncaring about Tony as a human being, to further their pathetic wants and needs.

The whole charade sickened me.

FATHERHOOD

"I knew I was changed forever."

Ａnd while all the crazy business of football and negotiations and NFL shenanigans was going on, Meg and I had started a family.

Less than a year into our marriage, I got home from a business trip, and Meg told me she wanted to show me something, shoving a little white stick in my face with what looked like a plus sign on it.

"What is that?" I asked.

"Pregnancy test."

I looked at it again. "Plus means positive, right?" I was an Academic All-American, remember!

"Yes," she said, smiling and giving me a big hug. "Looks like you're going to be a daddy."

Well, this had not been planned. "I thought you said we were safe that time?"

She shrugged her shoulders.

Within seconds, I started getting super excited—maybe a little scared, too, but dancing around the kitchen seemed the right thing to do, so we laughed and cried, and I stepped on her feet a time or two. Less than three months later, we were in the hospital for what they called a D&C, removing the fetus that had died sometime earlier within Meg's womb. The excitement was gone, replaced by a sense of loss that is tough to explain. I remember Meg asking the doctor several times after the procedure, while still under anesthesia, whether it was a boy or girl. It seemed very important. He gave no answer.

While we were leaving the hospital, though, the doctor had told Meg something I didn't hear. I didn't find out until a couple weeks later when Meg threw the little tidbit of information out at me, casual-like. "You need to wait at least three months to get pregnant after having a D&C," she said and then waited for some type of response.

"Huh?"

What was she telling me that for? I mean, the first time had been a slip-up, and look how that turned out. I figured she was still reeling from the pain a little is all. Just give her some time.

"I really liked the thought of being a mother. It was growing on me."

"Uh-huh," I muttered, working on a batch of letters I was intending to send out to potential clients for the upcoming 1988 football season. Back then, I wrote them all by hand, a personal touch I hoped would matter to somebody—plus, I didn't have a typewriter (this was before personal computers were the rage), and I couldn't type anyway.

Meg was still only twenty-two at the time. And beautiful. She smiled at me. Uh-oh.

"When the three months are up, I want to try. I want to get pregnant again."

"Are you sure?" I asked. "I mean, aren't you a little, you know, scared? Don't you want to give it some time?"

"Yes, I'm scared, but I can't explain it. I got excited about being a mother, and I don't want to let fear control me. I feel like I'm ready, and this is the right thing to do. What do you think?"

I thought for a quick second. "As long as we can practice a lot beforehand, to make sure we get it right."

So we did what Meg desired. We waited the requisite three months before we took another chance, with not quite enough practice along the way (is there ever?), and, before we knew it, Meg displayed that little white stick with the plus sign again sometime in late August of 1988. This time, I was not so surprised.

PART TWO

The due date was late April, but Hannah decided to delay her arrival, an interesting anomaly because that might have been the last time she was late for anything. She had a penchant for respecting others to a fault and hated to make people wait. But she was evidently enjoying her nice, warm temporary home and was in no rush to break out of her watery environs, so the doctor scheduled the delivery for May 3, 1989, with an induction in store if Hannah insisted on remaining contrary. Which she did.

In the wee hours of May 3, Meg rolled out of our waterbed, which sent a small wave my way, and I grunted. I heard her feet slowly patter downstairs and through a squinted eye saw a light flicker on. Before I knew it, Meg had become a whirling dervish of spraying and wiping and cleaning just about anything she could reach, bending over her swollen stomach, if need be. By now, I had crawled out of bed and walked to our door at the top of the stairway.

Still half asleep, I asked, "Umm, what are you doing?"

"Cleaning," she replied, taking a few steps up the stairs and wiping down the handrails as she did.

"Thank God you're cleaning those things," I said. "I was about to get up myself and clean 'em."

She smiled.

"Seriously, what are you doing?"

"I couldn't sleep. I'm excited and nervous. Just felt like cleaning a little."

"I guess so," I said.

"I think they call it 'nesting,'" she said. Unbeknownst to me, or maybe both of us, a new tradition had been established in the Williams household. The evening before a birth was Meg's nesting time.

Soon, we were out the door and headed to the hospital, still unsure if the baby was going to be a boy or girl. Meg said she was going to go as natural as possible—no pain-relief drugs, please—but that was before the pain. This particular hospital had a waiting suite connected to the birthing room, and I was enjoying a pizza with some other family members when I heard my name called.

"*Phiiiiilllll!*"

My head jolted up and I stopped chewing. Uh-oh.

"Get in here now."

I did, choking the bite of pizza down as I went in.

"Get the doctor now. I want an epidural."

We still had only been married less than two years, and I had not yet learned the appropriate way to respond to a woman in pain.

"Didn't you say you wanted to go natural, no drugs?"

Her eyebrows fell down heavy and bunched up over her eyes—those same eyes, hours earlier so alive and radiant, were now barely visible and had turned a crimson red, somewhat reminiscent of a scene from *The Exorcist*. "Get ... her ... now," she snarled, rolling her "n." Well, this was a new look and way of communicating that I was not accustomed to. I disappeared instantly from her sight and shot down the hall on my mission.

Meg was soon at peace again, as the doctor's needle and special serum did the trick, but Hannah still insisted on taking her time. The epidural came early in the afternoon, but Hannah waited until early the next morning on the 4th. I had never witnessed a birth, turning away and slamming my eyes shut the only time a video had been shown in my presence depicting a live birth with full visuals. But this ... *this* was different. When I saw the crown of the head, I was riveted. I stood there like a kid watching the circus, all wide-eyed and amazed. Popcorn would have been nice. The next thing you know, Hannah slid on out into the hands of the doctor, who somehow managed to thrust a pair of scissors into my hands and yell, "Snip!"

I did not recall the rehearsal for this part of the show, but instincts kicked in, and I evidently aimed for the right spot. Blood splattered onto the doctor's glasses, and then she looked up at me and exclaimed, "It's a girl."

If I were to be honest, I think I had been hoping for a boy, but instantly, my heart melted, and I knew that this was right. Nothing could have been more right, in fact, and Meg and I both loved our Hannah with all we were capable of from that moment on.

There was another moment, though, that somehow held more magic for me. After spending only one more night at the hospital (Meg was always anxious to get out of those places), we rolled baby Hannah out of there and took her home on the morning of the 5th. Upon arriving and walking up the freshly cleaned, pristine stairway, I promptly and gently scooped Hannah up from the car seat and snuggled her against my chest, settling down into the waterbed.

As I lay on my back, holding her firmly and tenderly, something mystical was happening to me. *This* was the bliss, the ecstasy, the unexplainable joy that winning the state championship all those years earlier had not produced—nor had anything else, up until this moment. Good God, I was amazed! I can see it so clearly now, over three decades later, gazing at her as she burrowed deep into my heart. I started to cry, not like I usually do, in big, great sobs, but with tears forming in the corners of my eyes and gently slipping out to make their way down into my ears. It probably sounds crazy, but I can almost feel those tears like it was yesterday.

I knew I was changed forever. I became instantly aware that I had never truly felt love the way it was intended to be. Just by being herself, the beautiful bundle we now called Hannah was teaching me the most tender and painful and beautiful form of unconditional love a man can experience. I was a spellbound daddy, all in. Little did I know how that same love, twenty-six years later, would rip me out of my so-called comfortable life, hurl me into a pit of despair, and force me to grapple with everything I had ever believed.

DADDY'S GIRL

"Where did Daddy go?"

Hannah was different.

It's not that she was eccentric, nor was she a rebel or an against-the-grain kind of person. She just didn't fully fit in, at least as a child.

She had an old soul type of persona, as if she had already been around the block a time or two and knew where all the potholes were. She wasn't as interested in many of the things her peers clamored for, though she tried to be at times. She wanted to have friends, to be part of the crowd, but she just didn't seem to know how.

Raising Hannah was such a joy, though. We would take her on outings and see other parents with seemingly uncontrollable kids and hold our chins a little higher. She was so easy that Meg and I figured we had the whole parenting thing down, no problem.

Of course, that was before the boys came along.

Hannah wasn't perfect, though (or perhaps it was just that she was a child), and at fifteen or sixteen months old, she decided to defy me. That's how I took it, at least. She started to lift herself up onto a glass coffee table behind the sofa, looking at me as she did so. She knew not to do it, but somehow she couldn't help herself.

I saw her right leg move slowly up and over the edge of the table.

"Hannah, no," I said.

That little right leg froze for a second or two and then kept on going.

"Don't you do it," I said, Meg watching and waiting nearby to see what would happen. Hannah's eyes were glued to me the whole time.

"You don't want a spanking, do you?" I added.

She shook her little head from side to side, everything in slow motion. But that leg had a mind of its own. It landed on the table and then pulled her body right along with it until she was up on top of it.

Meg and I had been gleaning some of our parenting skills from a program called Focus on the Family, and we had heard the founder state that by fifteen months old, most children were old enough to be spanked, that they could understand what was happening and be corrected that way. We were advocates of the "spare the rod, spoil the child" meme we had learned from the churches we had attended, so I was ready to "help her learn."

I snatched her up and popped her leg. Her eyes swelled up fast, big and full of tears, the first one spilling out in no time flat and many more following quickly after. I kept my eyes on hers the whole time, perhaps expecting an "I'm sorry, Daddy" look, but it was clear to see that she was simply stunned her daddy would do such a thing.

All of it happened and was over within a few seconds, and I cried right along with her, my first tear probably falling within a heartbeat of hers and my heart thumping me good, suggesting that I screwed up. I pulled her tight and told her how much I loved her.

Whether right or wrong in my actions, Hannah rarely ever disobeyed again.

When Hannah was three and Kyle, our second child, was one, we moved from Tallahassee, Florida, to Jonesboro, a suburb of Atlanta, Georgia. Part of the reason for the move was thinking Atlanta would be a better location from which to operate my agent business. It would be easier and less expensive to fly in and out of than Tallahassee—for myself and for potential clients—and it also gave the appearance of a metropolitan business, perhaps adding the stamp of validity that a smaller city might not provide. In addition, the move allowed us to be a good bit closer to my parents (who lived in Columbus, Georgia, at that time), which had become an emotional matter to us because we had learned only a few months earlier that my father had prostate cancer.

We arrived in the summer of 1992 and settled in rather quickly. One of the attractions of our new neighborhood was a community pool in the front of the subdivision. The pool had been closed for repairs, but as soon as it was open, we took the kids. Meg stayed busy with Kyle while I was playing with Hannah on the steps leading into the shallow end of the pool. There were a couple of neighbors there, as well, so I told Hannah to hold onto the railing and walked over to introduce myself. After a few seconds of chit-chat, I looked back to check on my little girl. My heart leapt into my throat—she had evidently stepped down one step and was now underwater, just standing there holding that rail like Daddy had told her to do, but with her head under and obviously clueless as to what to do. I could see her eyes under the water, wide and full of fear. A rush of panic swept over me, and I'm pretty sure I flew the few feet that it took to land by her in the water and thrust her up into the air.

Her eyes were so big as she cried and shook. She clutched me, and I held her close, my heart exploding in my chest as I squeezed her tightly, sick to my stomach at the thought of possibly losing my baby. I was so very thankful that I had turned around in time, but I was also extremely angry with myself for allowing such a potential tragedy to have almost occurred. My heart ached.

A few weeks later, in the fall of that same year, my alma mater, Florida State, played a big football game against one of our two most heated rivals, the Miami Hurricanes. It was a tight battle throughout, with Miami coming out on top by a field goal at the end. I was devastated.

I told Meg that I needed to go for a ride, to get out of the house and clear my head. Upon returning, maybe thirty minutes later,

Meg told me what happened in my absence. Evidently, Hannah had noticed my dismay.

"Where did Daddy go?" she asked her mom.

"Well," Meg told her, "Daddy went out for a drive because his team lost."

Hannah thought for a second. "Did he go to find them?"

Meg laughed.

And so did I, once I walked in the door and heard the story. I picked Hannah up and smiled, thankful that her concern and her innocence could have such a healing effect on me.

Another couple of years passed by, and Hannah turned six. We bought a home in a new development just outside of Peachtree City, Georgia. Meg had begun homeschooling Hannah and signed her up for a homeschool activity called "American Girl," which was all about dolls and books and games and such. I'm not sure I even knew about it until one day when Meg needed my help.

"Phil," she said. "Could you please take Hannah to an outing today? It's an American Girl get-together."

"Huh?"

"Yeah, she's very excited. She's been planning on going for weeks and is hoping to make new friends."

I was between a rock and a hard place. I did not want to let Hannah down, but American Girl? On my Saturday?

"I don't feel well," Meg continued. "Don't you think you can handle it?"

I thought about saying I wasn't feeling so well now, either.

I was also not feeling absolutely sure I could handle an outing that centered around dolls, but I looked over at Hannah, who was studying me, and heard myself say, "Okay."

Hannah and I arrived at the home where the festivities were taking place, and within a minute or two, I realized Meg had left out a very important tidbit of information. This was obviously a mother-daughter event, and I was the only father there. Most of the mothers, none of whom I knew, smiled pleasantly enough at me, but a couple of them didn't appear overly happy to see a man there. One even said as much.

Hannah, though, was so very happy that I was with her. She smiled brightly, grabbed my hand, and tugged me along. She perhaps was oblivious to the protocols, but I'm not sure about that. I think it was more so that she was proud I was willing to be with her, even if I wasn't supposed to be, according to the American Girl guidelines.

I don't remember a thing about that event, other than those couple of ladies looking down their noses at me and Hannah beaming from ear to ear.

I quite enjoyed myself.

As we pulled out of the driveway and headed home, I looked over at Hannah. Her eyes were bright, and a big smile lit her face. I could tell she was happy.

Still, I was beginning to notice that making friends was not easy for her. And though this tugged at my heart, how could I feel bad when she seemed so content? Especially since her contentment was at least partly because of being with me.

Hannah continued to grow up, and by the next summer, she went to a church camp for kids that was to last the whole week. I had no idea it would be so hard for me to be without her for that week, so when the day came that camp ended, I was rather excited to go pick her up.

It was a family affair, with Meg, Kyle, Luke (our third child), Rebekah, whom we have always called Beka (our fourth child), and me, all making the short trek over to get her. I'm an early bird, always early or on time for whatever is happening, an attribute of mine that Hannah was already exhibiting, so we arrived before schedule and meandered about, saying hello to others who were also anxious to see their children. When the kids were finally released to their families, a few began to spill out of the building. There was one and then another, and then, whoosh, like a sprinter out of the blocks, Hannah was shooting towards us. She ran as fast as she could the whole way and made a beeline straight for me, jumping up and into my arms. She wanted her daddy!

We clung tightly to each other, perhaps both of us surprised at how much we missed each other. She didn't have to say anything, as her extremely tight squeeze said all I could have ever wanted to hear.

"You big softy," Meg said, as tears were beginning to fill my eyes.

That was one of the best feelings I ever had.

Not long after that, we signed Hannah up to play softball. She had indicated an interest in sports, and since a lot of the little girls were signing up for softball, she wanted to give it a shot. I don't remember if they had any practices before their first game or not, but when we went to watch that game, and after watching her bat, I was mortified. I internally scolded myself for not taking the time to practice with her and do my best to ensure she at least had a few fundamentals down. And now, watching her first game, it was clear that she had no seeming capacity to swing at the ball with fluidity. In fact, she basically chopped downward at the ball each time it came her way. And she missed it every time, strike after strike, strikeout after strikeout. It was hard for me to watch.

Her team was losing, and Hannah was far down in the batting order heading into the last inning, but somehow they gained an unlikely momentum, and I began nervously counting how many batters remained before it would be Hannah's turn again. I was practically on my knees begging God to let some other players get out ahead of her so that she would not have the chance to bat, cringing at the thought of her striking out again to lose the game.

Mercifully, the last out was made with Hannah in the on-deck circle.

"I'm not very good," she said as we drove home.

She didn't seem too upset, though. I, on the other hand, was embarrassed. I hate to say it, but as a former college football player and all-around good athlete, I didn't think it reflected well on me, a thought that later got me pissed off at myself.

What a pathetic prick!

We got home from the game, and Hannah wanted to practice hitting, even suggesting it herself. We went onto the driveway, and I tossed her a few, but she kept chopping downward, no matter what I said or how hard she tried. Perplexed, I thought for a second.

"Why don't you turn around," I said. "Try it from the other side."

"Left-handed?" she asked.

"Why not? You never know." I was not optimistic.

She changed her stance and her hand placement on the bat so that she now stood before me, ready to hit left-handed (though she was right-handed in everything she did). I tossed an easy one up there.

She swung. To anyone else, it wouldn't have been considered a thing of beauty, but to me, it was! Her stroke was smooth and level as the bat made contact with the ball, and her eyes almost popped out of her head.

"Who'd a thunk it?" I said.

She smiled.

"Throw some more, Daddy!"

Now, at least I knew she had a fighting chance. She was never great after that, as hand-eye coordination sports were not her thing, but she did connect with the ball far more frequently.

I grew to love groundouts!

THE KIDS

"If you keep talking ..."

By the time I married Meg, I had morphed into what many would call a strong Christian. I attended church regularly, devoured my Bible, and was even a deacon by age thirty.

I was deeply committed to my faith.

Shortly after Hannah's birth in May of 1989, Meg and I sat in the back of the movie theater where our church met at that time, Hannah sleeping and occasionally cooing in her car seat between us. The pastor launched into a sermon on the great love affairs of history—biblical ones.

Except for the last one.

"And, of course," he said, "Perhaps the greatest of these is Phil and baby Hannah."

All the heads in front of us swiveled to look back and smile, a few people even clapping. It was obvious that I was smitten, drinking deep from a new type of love, one laced with unconditionality, with purity, and, to be honest, with confusion. I simply did not grasp how love could be so encompassing, so seemingly total.

The days and weeks and months rolled by until, a little over two years later, Meg went back into labor. This time, we knew it was going to be a boy. What I doubted, though, was whether it was possible to love any other child as I loved Hannah. It seemed like an impossibility. Of course, the instant I held Kyle in my arms, that concern flew out the window, and he nestled into my heart as Hannah had, just by being my son.

Kyle would prove to be a deep thinker, quite the contemplative one, even as a young child. He hated to hurt anyone's feelings, as can be seen through the way he handled one of my fatherly lessons, or, as he would later call them, lectures (which still stings a little—I never liked being lectured to myself!).

When Kyle was around five, I made him sit on the sofa as I stood before him, trying to drive home what I am sure was a very important point, something sure to help him grow up "properly." Meg was behind him, working on something in the kitchen. To this day, I have no idea what I was going on about, but I do remember with perfect clarity what he said after I had rambled on for a bit.

"Dad," he interrupted, his little face as serious as could be. "If you keep talking, I'm gonna have to stop listening."

Meg immediately threw her head around and was grinning from ear to ear. Though I was temporarily thrown off balance, I quickly gained my wits and realized how brilliant and, quite frankly, *kind* he was being, not wanting me to continue on without his attention. I put my hand over my face so that he wouldn't be able to see my own smile, but I couldn't contain myself and began laughing. Though the success of my talk was likely nil, the end result was a great memory and another example of how thoughtful Kyle could be.

Over a year after Kyle was born, as Meg and I were capping off a date night, she assured me there was very little chance of anything happening. But it did, and Benjamin Luke was born nine months later. Apparently, we were sticking to an unseen schedule that added to the Williams clan every couple of years, a ritual of sorts. It was a very difficult labor, but Luke eventually snuck on out, all twenty-three gangly inches of him. Though he weighed over nine pounds, he was skinny as a rail due to his length.

Even as a child, Luke always had a flair for life and generally was (and still is) willing to push the envelope, as well as push us to the limits. His energy was of the non-stop variety, and he displayed it whenever and wherever he got the chance.

PART TWO

On one such occasion, when Luke was five years old, our family was being given a tour of the FBI building. It would eventually become a private tour—one of the perks of representing Brad Johnson, the quarterback for the Washington Redskins that year—but we started with a larger group of sightseers. Perhaps because we were in the FBI building (what could happen to us there?), we lost track of where Luke was. About the time we noticed him missing and started scrambling about, walking along in the rear of our group, many of the people ahead of us started clapping.

Meg and I looked at each other. Call us crazy, but we knew what they were clapping at. Because we knew Luke! Sure enough, our suspicions were correct; the little fellow had slipped ahead of the crowd, turned to face everybody, and commenced performing a series of splits. He was, and still is, exceedingly flexible and simply enjoyed entertaining whoever might be around, regardless of where he was, including such a seemingly stoic venue as the FBI headquarters. I could only shake my head, feeling pride and a deep love within, and yet, at the same time, inclined to thump him a good one. It would not be the last time this strange combination of emotions would settle within me due to his actions.

Luke's attention span was less than that of Kyle's, but both were severely tested as youngsters due to a "brilliant" idea Meg had. She and I had seen *Les Misérables* in New York City years earlier—second row middle—and had love, love, loved it. The show was coming to the Fox Theater in Atlanta, and Meg somehow decided it would be a great thing for the whole family to go. I had my doubts but pretty much kept my mouth shut.

This time, our tickets were very near the back row, which I guess in hindsight was a blessing. Meg must have had a premonition because she had the boys positioned next to me, away from her. Those two boys were out-of-their-minds bored, and when Luke got bored—watch out! I sat next to Luke, with Kyle on the other side of him, and I might have been even more miserable than they were as I tried to keep them occupied and quiet and under some modicum of control. I'm pretty sure I pinched Luke a few times, which didn't help and only added to the mayhem.

In English, *Les Misérables* means "the miserable ones," and we most definitely were! I think all three of us were on the verge of a serious breakdown when, all of a sudden, the crew up on stage took a bow, and the crowd stood up and began applauding. Luke and Kyle looked at each other as if they'd just woken up on Christmas morning, their eyes enormous and their mouths wide open in astonished glee. They both jumped up on their seats and began hooting and hollering. You would have thought they'd just witnessed the most triumphant play imaginable, high-fiving and dancing and clapping louder than anyone else. But I knew. They were just so excited it was over. And so was I! I must admit, though, it was one of those moments that one treasures forever. Watching them play it up was hilarious, so I ratcheted up my applause to join in.

Meg had learned her lesson. Next time, and for the foreseeable future, she would think long and hard about taking those boys out to anything that might require silence and patience.

As fate would have it, two years after Luke's birth, Meg and I sat in a doctor's office (yep, another date night with Meg where there was supposed to be "very little chance of anything") and were told that our fourth child would be a girl and that she had a very serious heart issue they called congenital heart disease. They hinted pretty strongly at an abortion, but that was never a consideration for us. We were informed she would definitely need open heart surgery early on in her life to repair an assortment of life-threatening problems.

If I were to be honest, I think perhaps I held Beka a tad loosely in my heart, terribly afraid I might lose her, the thought of which terrified me. There was a part of me that tried not to let myself fall madly in love with her, of course, to no avail. How silly! When I first held her, it was as if I was holding Hannah all over again, the mystery and the beauty overwhelming.

We had been told by the doctors to keep Beka as content as we could, to stave off fits of crying if at all possible, as the heart works harder when babies are screaming and holding their breath before the next outburst. The calmer she could be, the better. We needed to make it to six months so that her heart would be bigger and give the doctor a better chance for what promised to be a very complicated surgery. Meg gave stern warnings to the other three kids—in particular the boys, now four and a half and two and a half years old—to stay out of her room when she was sleeping, "or else!"

"Or else" it was when one afternoon we heard Beka scream bloody murder from upstairs, where she was napping in her crib. Meg burst up the stairs, and then I heard a most hideous sound, that of Meg screeching out death threats at those two boys. By the time I made it up to check out what was going on, I saw the boys running over each other down the hallway to their room as steam was flying off of Meg. She was hyperventilating while sitting down to nurse Beka, hoping to calm her down.

"Those little snots!" she hissed. "They were IN the crib with her!" The thought tickled me on some level. What nerve they had! Sneaking into her room to agitate Beka, no doubt.

I didn't know what to do to help calm Meg down, but I reacted to the first thought that came to my mind, and said, "You've gotta let some steam off or you might have a heart attack."

Then, without really considering the consequences, I bent over and brought my face in close to hers as she sat nursing Beka, and said, "Why don't you just slap me. It might make you feel—"

BAM! Her hand came up and popped my face about as quick and hard as she could muster, and it stung me pretty good. I stood straight up, we looked at each other, and then we both broke out into hilarious laughter.

Later on, we dealt with the boys, and they never disobeyed their mother in that way again. And I never stuck my face within slapping range from that day forward if Meg happened to be teetering on the edge of maniacal anger. I guess all three of us boys learned a lesson that day.

A couple months later, Beka now six months old, they performed the surgery—repairing this, rebuilding that, and rerouting a thing or two. It was confirmed as a success, but there remained the tricky issue of waiting for the heart to start beating on its own again. They said if it did not do so within twelve days, they would put a pacemaker in, and if so, she would live with it for the rest of her life.

Meg and I slept at the hospital with Beka almost every night, finding any place we could to get a few hours of ragged sleep. And each morning we would head to the nurses' station to find out if her beautiful little heart had finally kicked in on its own.

After what we had been told was her last night before she was to receive a pacemaker, we walked down to the nurses' station once more, not expecting anything different from the other mornings. I noted how many more medical personnel were hanging out than on the other days we'd been there, wiping a little sleep out of my eye as I waited. That's when I noticed that they were all looking at Meg and me, one by one starting to smile. Yep, her heart had started beating on its own during the night, and we discovered it is fairly common for hospital folk to gather around to witness the faces of the parents when good news is forthcoming. We did not disappoint! I'm pretty sure I hugged every single one of them at least once!

Twenty-two years later, Beka would begin her work as a neonatal nurse at that very same hospital, where her heart was so beautifully and wonderfully repaired by a doctor Meg and I knew we would always love, even if we never saw him again, Dr. Kirk Kanter. Meg and I were so proud, and a bit nostalgic, especially when Beka texted us both a photo of her standing in an elevator next to Dr. Kanter. She had entered the elevator, noticed his name tag, and because she had heard us mention his name several times, had introduced herself and told him how he had performed surgery on her all those years earlier. How beautifully synchronistic!

PART TWO

The years of raising the kids, we affectionately dubbed "The Blur," a period where it seemed we barely had time to think. You look up one day and go, "What the hell just happened?"

I spent much of my time developing my agent business while simultaneously trying to juggle kid duties and church activities and family vacations and more. Business was good, everyone was healthy, and we were known by some as a model family. I was frequently asked by parents with younger children, "How do you do it? Your kids are so awesome!" To which I generally responded something like, "Thanks, they are wonderful. But you don't see them all the time, and I really don't have a clue. I just love them the best I can and let God do the rest."

But that was the thing; I had invested so much of my time in pursuing God, praying, meditating, journaling, attending churches and conferences and such, and yet I was becoming more and more frustrated. Where was this inner peace I had been seeking? That I felt God had promised for those of us who sought Him as diligently as I thought I had? Why was I not feeling with more absoluteness the joy the scriptures espoused?

I couldn't really complain. My life appeared on the outside to be comparatively rosy, and it probably did on the inside, too, based on what I heard and saw from others. But my journal progressively became a venue for crying out, my pen digging deeper into the paper, with far more capital letters and exclamation points peppering the pages. My inner world simply did not match up with what I was longing for, the elusive "peace that passeth all understanding" concept and "the life more abundant" passage often grating at me.

Was it all just a sham? No, I could not let myself think that way. What else was there to turn to if I was wrong? Was I simply not doing it right, not good enough, not praying as I should, not loving my neighbor "as myself"? The questions tormented me. And yet I trudged onward in my journey of faith, hoping that one day the answers to my questions would be answered.

In 2007 or so, I wrote in my journal more than once that I was okay with God doing whatever it took to "wake me up"; in fact, I was almost begging Him to do so. But I also remember thinking that I needed to be careful what I asked for. Surely, He would not do something as drastic as taking a child from me, a horror that crossed my mind during those contemplative moments. Would He dare do such a thing? Surely not! How could there be love in that?

I confess, though, I was not sure.

KIDNEY STONES

"God sure has a sense of humor."

Notwithstanding all of my confusion as it related to God, there was one moment from my past that lurked within my mind. From then on, I knew it was at least *possible* God could actually be heard by His children.

And it was a pretty crazy moment.

Luke was born a little over two years after Kyle, but not without an interesting twist. Meg was in a great deal of pain at the hospital—if she'd had a weapon in her hand, someone would have been hurt. In response, the attending nurse mentioned to me in a "just so you know" kind of way that she only knew one type of pain worse than childbirth—kidney stones. She said she had a couple of friends who'd experienced both, and they both said the stones were more painful.

Whatever, I thought. *Who cares?*

In less than seventy-two hours, I cared!

Three days after Luke popped out, I awoke to a piercing pain in my lower back. Before I knew it, I was on my knees, deliriously begging Meg to get the car ready and get me to the emergency room. Whatever illness it was that had latched on to me hurt enough that I thought I might be dying. All I remember on the car ride to the hospital was kneeling in the front seat of our Jeep Cherokee.

"Run the lights, baby! Help me, Jesus. Oh God, help me, Jesus. Run 'em, baby! Please!"

Kidney stones have a stunning capacity to limit one's vocabulary. And besides, she didn't run a damn light, and my prayers seemed to fall on deaf ears.

Upon arriving at the hospital, they took one look at me and smiled at each other, nodding as they said, "Kidney stones."

It was the most physically painful day of my life.

Though they had suggested kidney stones before both feet even hit the pavement outside of the emergency room, I still had no real clue. They loaded me up onto a cold slab of table to do some X-rays for confirmation and soon had me on morphine, which, as far as I could tell, did nothing for my pain. It apparently added to the confusion and desperation, though, as I was now begging God to either heal me or let me die—and *soon*, please.

I began to wonder if I might be going to hell. Was I secure enough in my salvation? Was I good enough? I figured I would be willing to take that chance if the pain didn't die down soon.

By late afternoon, after maybe six or seven hours of what seemed worse than hell could possibly be, the pain somehow subsided enough to allow me to go home, with instructions to pee through a strainer they gave me as a parting gift.

"See if you can catch something," the doctor said. "If not, we'll see you in a week to blast that little rock out of you."

The next morning, as I sat on my sofa reading my Bible, I had what might have been my first "true" connection with the one I called God. As clear as day, I heard a voice within my mind tell me that He—God—was going to do something for me at the last second as it related to the kidney stone. I was certain of it, so much so that I called Meg in and told her about the voice and its message.

"God just told me He was going to do something at the last second," I said.

She smiled and said, "Nice," probably thinking there was a bit of morphine residue in my system.

As prone to do, I promptly forgot that little revelation and dutifully peed again and again into that useless strainer. Seven days

later, we went in for the lithotripsy procedure, the stone still somewhere inside of my urethra, though not causing the pain from a
week earlier.

I sat in the little waiting room with an IV in my arm, bored. They
had told me the procedure worked best with an empty bladder, and
though I had urinated an hour earlier, I didn't want there to be any
problems. So I stood up and began rolling my IV contraption down
the hallway toward the bathroom. Just as I was about to open the
door, the nurse turned the corner and said, "It's time."

I took my hand off of the door handle and started to walk with
her but thought, what the heck, I'm standing right here.

"I'm gonna use the restroom one last time to be sure," I said.

"That's not necessary," the nurse responded.

"Well, I'm already here. Just give me a second."

I walked into the restroom, lifted the toilet seat, and could barely
manage a pathetic little dribble. I was looking down just in case.
When it seemed the final drop had fallen out, I lifted my head and
looked at the wall in front of me, just in time to feel a strange sensation down there. I quickly looked back down and saw a tiny splash,
and a small dark object hurtling toward the bottom of the toilet.

That's when the memory of the revelation came flooding back in.

I pushed open the door. "Meg. Meg!" I called. "Come check
this out."

Both Meg and the nurse came running, and sure enough, that
small stone, the cause of so much pain, sat at the bottom of the
toilet. It had come out the instant before I was about to head down
the hall for the procedure.

"God sure has a sense of humor," Meg laughed, recalling what I
had told her six mornings earlier.

I left the hospital that day in early July of 1993, knowing
that there was something crazy about what had just happened.
Coincidence? Hardly. I somehow knew it could not be such, that
voice so clear days earlier. Perhaps it was just a hint of things to

come—of something not of this world, even. All I knew was that I had heard an inner voice which, after declaring that It was God, had promised something, and delivered, in an interesting and humorous way.

It would be a long time before I heard the voice of God again. Or recognized it as such. Though the next time it happened, it would change my world forever.

PEACHTREE CITY

"Girls can be bitches."

We never could seem to stay put, moving from one house to another almost as frequently as some folks go on vacation. I'm not really sure why we did it, but we did. The craziest move, and a very short-lived one, happened in the summer of 1998. My father had recently retired, approximately six years into his battle against prostate cancer, and he and my mother had decided to move back to Warner Robins, where they had made more friends and where I had played my high school football. The cancer was now progressing, albeit little by little at that point, so Meg and I decided to give living there a shot. That lasted about six months. Now, away from the life we had cultivated at our previous home, and without any friends nearby, Meg was depressed and missing the suburbs of Atlanta.

"Can we move back to the Atlanta area?" she said one afternoon out of the blue. "Maybe Peachtree City?"

I knew she was having a hard time, and if Mama ain't happy ...

"Okay," I said in about three seconds, simple as that. So we loaded up a U-Haul for the fifth time in our marriage and headed north.

We landed in Peachtree City, Georgia, in early spring of 1999 and put the kids in public school for the first time. Hannah was extremely excited to plug into her new school and meet other kids. In fact, the house we purchased was in a neighborhood that included at least two girls she was hoping to be friends with, one in fourth grade with her and the other in fifth grade, who happened to live right next door. Hannah was counting the days until the move.

I walked her hand in hand to the bus stop in our cul-de-sac on the morning after we moved in and watched her ride away, my heart a lump in my chest. I expected her first day to be wonderful, but I was one naive man. When the bus stopped in front of our house that afternoon, Hannah spilled out of it, staring straight ahead, and continued rapidly into the house, erupting into tears the second she crossed the threshold to our front door. Evidently, the little girl that lived down our street, the one in Hannah's grade, had spent the day, and particularly the bus ride home, protecting her turf from the new girl in the neighborhood. She had somehow convinced the other little girl who lived next door to give Hannah the cold shoulder, as well. Hannah's heart was broken, and, to some degree, so was her dad's.

"Girls can be bitches," Meg said matter-of-factly.

But there was nothing matter-of-fact about it to me. This was my little girl, and I was upset. I felt much of her pain, at least in my own way, and subsequently spent years trying to control the pains that would enter into her and her siblings' lives. This, of course, proved to be a futile strategy and one that I would now never recommend to other parents.

Hannah eventually settled in at her new school and neighbor-hood, though that first stinging rejection would be far from an isolated occurrence. She just did not understand the world of cliques. And she never would.

Not long after settling into our new home in Peachtree City, Meg and I were having a disagreement of sorts. It started in the boys' room, but to avoid their innocent little ears from hearing us fuss, we stepped out into the hallway. I perceived Meg to be living up to her "girls can be bitches" meme, so I gently nudged her into Hannah's room at the end of the hall so no one could hear (we both thought Hannah was downstairs) and said, "You're acting like a bitch."

The sentence came out as we were entering Hannah's room, just in time to notice she was sitting on the floor in front of her closet as the last word slithered out. She looked at me with eyebrows raised, I looked at Meg, Meg and I both looked back at Hannah, and Hannah burst out laughing. Our argument was over, saved by our ten-year-old daughter's laughter, her capacity to see through our silliness and through her daddy's penchant for saying things he shouldn't say in the heat of the moment. We all ended up having a gut-busting laugh that quickly dissolved the conflict.

We lived for three years at that first home in the Peachtree City cul-de-sac until it was time to call U-Haul again. I was actually doing quite well, bringing in enough quality clients and resulting income to afford a 7,000-square-foot house that sat on a lake in probably the most exclusive neighborhood in town. I told myself it was worth the investment, a sign of success for potential clients, perhaps, and hopefully an appreciable asset, as well. So we moved across town in the spring of 2002.

In early September of that year, I lay down on a sofa in the basement to watch a college football game, mainly lying on my left side, and by the time I got up, my left shoulder was aching pretty bad. By bedtime, I was in a lot of pain, and by the middle of the night, I wanted to shoot myself. All I could think about was getting in to see the doctor as soon as his office opened, if I could make it until then.

I busted the doors down as his receptionist was unlocking them. The wait after that seemed like hours, the pain agonizing. It was probably five minutes.

I was a bit embarrassed when he asked me what happened.

"How did you hurt it?" he asked.

"Lying on the sofa," I said, shaking my head.

He raised an eyebrow.

"An old football injury flaring up," I felt compelled to explain. "Tore up both shoulders playing college football. I can't believe this happened while watching college football."

He grabbed a syringe and dug the needle into my shoulder socket and seemed to enjoy watching me wince in pain. He then gave me a prescription for some pain pills and said that the cortisone shot would wear off in a bit. He didn't seem overly worried—nonchalant, even. By the time I got home and settled in, I wanted to shoot him, too!

I've experienced tremendous pain in my life—kidney stones, shredded ligaments, and more—but I swear, my left shoulder felt like it had a million tiny razor blades pistoning up and down, getting faster and meaner by the second. I sat on the sofa in the den and began to cry like a baby.

"Meg," I managed through the sobs. "Please go get the prescription! Oh God, please go now!"

All of the family had been in the room when the cortisone wore off. Most had remained when I had begun to cry. I had closed my eyes by the time the pain had ratcheted up to a twelve on a scale of one to ten, and I wailed and moaned without the slightest pride for a moment or two. In the midst of one of my sobs, I opened my eyes, only to see that everyone had scattered, clearly unable to handle Dad's extreme exhibition of pain. Except for one.

Hannah was a step away, simply holding space and being there with and for me. The rest had left the room, probably huddled in a closet somewhere (and I did not blame them!), but my oldest stood nearby, doing all she could to shoulder a little of my pain. She simply looked into my eyes with a compassion that most of us do not know we have within us. And she stayed there with me until Meg returned with the painkillers and the agony had subsided. To this day, I still remember those moments.

I can still feel it.

Twelve years later, that very memory would return to me and inspire me to navigate the most difficult thing I ever had to do.

A WIN IN THE HEART

"She's got a gift, Phil!"

My daddy was my best friend. As he continued his battle with prostate cancer and as it seemed that his time on earth was nearing its end, I would call him almost every day. He was my buddy, my confidant, the one who I felt could meet me where I needed to be met when things were difficult, the one I turned to for advice.

The kids all adored him and his fun-loving nature. He was always smiling and laughing and occasionally breaking out into a silly dance. And he loved to take them to what he called "the bubble gum store," a moniker from his own childhood that basically meant any store where he could take them to get candy. Of course, the kids loved *that*, and he did, too. The kids would all come home with big ole bags of candy, chewing on something as they entered the door, but I'm not sure his bag wasn't even bigger!

The truth is, Daddy was special. It seemed he was born with an innate capacity to realize that any problem anyone has with anyone else is something inside *their* heads, in *their* minds. Therefore, he simply did not take offense when criticized or put down. He saw it as the other person struggling, not realizing the truth of who they were and how much they were ultimately loved. More than most, he knew who he was and loved himself, which allowed him to look past the stuff of others and love and accept them, too.

126

He was a much-loved man.

By October, just a few short weeks after my shoulder flare-up, he couldn't answer the phone anymore. The reality of it all hit me … I was about to lose my daddy.

He died October 26, 2002, and I instantly knew I had lost an anchor in my life.

He and Hannah were remarkably similar in ways that defy description. They both knew how to *be*, in particular, to be with one who is hurting. My daddy had done so more than once for me through the years, including that time when I was heartbroken over Melanie and he comforted me without saying anything. And, now, Hannah was showing the same tender ability to be with those who are hurting.

They put others above themselves.

Perhaps it was one of those generation-skipping things because, at least at that point in time, I had seemed to miss out on what they had—the ability to just *be*, and to love others in exactly the way they needed.

They were both teaching me a type of capacity to love that I would not begin to understand until much later in my life.

Though Daddy was no longer around to model this for me, Hannah would continue to do so in many different ways, even in the realm of competitive sports.

She may have been a bit behind her peers when playing sports that required hand-eye coordination (remember her softball issues, which ended up lasting for just that one season?), but Hannah was quite good at swimming, especially excelling at the butterfly stroke. All of the kids would end up being competitive swimmers at the youth level, but Hannah may have been the best of them all.

At one swim meet, with a good chance to win her heat and progress onward, she noticeably slowed down for some reason. I had no idea why, wondering if she was sick or had injured herself. But no, she had evidently realized that she was way ahead of a depressed friend and that her friend was going to finish a distant last and, therefore, slowed down until her friend caught up with her. They went the last bit together, Hannah waiting to reach her hand up and touch the wall until her friend had done so.

A loss at the meet. A win in the heart.

At seventeen years old, before her senior year of high school, Hannah volunteered to work for two weeks at Camp Sunshine on beautiful Sebago Lake in Casco, Maine. She had spent a great deal of time researching options on how to spend her summer and stumbled upon Camp Sunshine. It grabbed her heart as soon as she read about it. The camp is a place for children with severe illnesses, mainly types of cancer, to come and enjoy a free week filled with fun activities for the kids and their families. They also provide counselors and group sessions and more for the parents, a truly beautiful respite from the day-to-day grind that many of these families endure.

When Hannah returned home from Camp Sunshine, she was aglow. She couldn't stop talking about it, even writing a compelling story about her trip in her high school's newspaper. She had been deeply touched by many of the children that she spent time with, especially one little girl with a very serious brain tumor. She fell in love with her and her mother, and they would remain in touch long after the week ended.

As our family considered our summer vacation for the following year, guess where we went? That's right, we took the whole family up to see what had impacted her so deeply and to offer our help with the kids and their families.

Several months before we were scheduled to depart for Camp Sunshine, I had a conversation with one of my former clients, Martin Mayhew, who was an Assistant General Manager for the Detroit Lions at the time (he went on to become their GM, as well as the GM of the Washington Football Team years later). Martin and I had remained close (and still are) after his playing days. He had won a Super Bowl (XXVI) as a starting cornerback for Washington after the 1991 season and later left for Tampa Bay as part of the first year of free agency in the NFL. He started for the Buccaneers for several more years before retiring to become an attorney.

During our conversation in early 2008, I mentioned our upcoming vacation to Martin, as well as the effect it had had on Hannah. Martin thought about it, said something about his kids needing an experience like that (though they were much younger), and a few weeks later, he and his family were signed up to go with us. It was an incredibly special week for both of our families, which wouldn't have occurred without Hannah's great big heart for hurting children.

In February of 2010, I set up a mission trip of sorts to Swaziland, Africa, a country decimated by poverty and AIDS, and asked three of my current NFL clients to go: George Foster, Anthony Hargrove, and Cornell Green. The average size of these three guys was about six foot five and 330 pounds, with Hargrove being the baby, at not quite six foot four and 305 pounds (he still gets mad at me when I don't give him the full six-four). Cornell arrived in Peachtree City early and came by the house for a bit of relaxation, only to find himself alone with Hannah for a few minutes.

Cornell had been a client of mine for about a decade, so I knew him pretty well. He was not in a good mood when he stepped into our home; in fact, he was ornery. Trust me, I know ornery when I see it because, well, I'm pretty familiar with the feeling. He was wearing it on his sleeve, though, which wasn't abnormal. Don't get me wrong— Cornell is one of my favorite people in the world, and I love him dearly. He has a heart of gold. He likes to keep it real, though, and most folks are a bit intimidated by massive fellows when they furrow their brows and their eyes darken and their tone of voice gets that edge to it. I had learned over the years when to keep my distance.

This was one of those times.

Cornell had one of those times, too, one that would forever be etched in his memory. He sat down on the porch by himself, just to clear his mind, if possible, or at least to spend some time alone before the long flight ahead. He had a scowl on his face. I knew not to try to engage him too deeply. He took a few deep breaths, hoping to make it through an hour or so, I think, without being interrupted from his quiet introspection.

I was sitting only a few feet away from him, a screen door separating us, when Hannah walked right past me, out the screen door, and plopped down in a chair across from him.

"So, Cornell." She smiled, nodded, and squinted her eyes at him. "You look like you are in a funk."

"Hey, Hannah." He stood up and hugged her. "Yeah, I've got a lot on my mind," Cornell said as he sat back down, and yet, somehow, just like that, the scowl seemed to soften.

"You know, Hannah," he said, "You can make lemonade out of piss."

Hannah laughed, her eyes suggesting that Big C might be exaggerating a little but not flinching at the language. She had been around her dad enough to hear a lot of colorful ramblings.

Cornell smiled, a peaceful look in his eyes. He turned toward me.

"She's got a gift, Phil!" He would later say that her capacity to see past his bullshit, knock his walls down without causing a fuss, and have zero judgment (he could tell that in her tone of voice) was the therapy he needed. He thought, *how does she do it?* and chalked it up to the fact that she simply had a genuine, hard-to-find, God-given gift. I just nodded.

This memory would come back to him furiously a few years later when he heard of her illness.

NOMADS

"Let's sell the house."

Even years later, the effects of the Bountygate saga affected me more than I realized. Slowly but surely, they seemed to be metastasizing into the final nail in the coffin for me as an NFL agent. The whole thing had sickened me to the world of glamor and glitz and money and fame, and I began divesting myself of all dealings with the NFL. I began to go deeper into myself and into the things of God (though still far from certain what that truly meant), wondering what the hell my future was going to look like without the career I had been involved in for over two and a half decades.

In mid-December of 2012, shortly after the Bountygate saga was purportedly resolved, my youngest son, Luke (nineteen years old at the time), sat me down at the kitchen table with a serious "Got news for you, Dad!" look in his eyes. He cleared his throat and narrowed his already serious eyes a bit more, the Christmas tree lights flickering behind him.

"I'm heading to Guatemala in January," he started. "I'm an adult now, and you can't stop me from going. I've got my own money."

I almost blurted out a joyful, "Thank you, Jesus!" but I felt that might be inappropriate. Instead, I tilted my head back for a second and took him in. He had always loved adventure and exploring, and this sounded exciting to me right off the bat, both for him and for me! It instantly stirred something within my gut that I interpreted as jealousy—not a bad type, mind you, but a slight yearning to just be able to take off wherever I wanted to for myself. I continued to study him while he awaited my response.

Finally, I spoke.

"Why would I stop you? It sounds great to me." I thought for a second about his "my own money" comment, which I figured meant about $1,000, and wondered how long that would last him. "How long do you intend to travel?"

"I'll start in Guatemala and do a few weeks of Spanish school and make my way to Peru a few months later." He smiled, a very disarming trait of his. "And, don't worry—I know what you're thinking. If I need to, I can work on the road. Lots of people do it. I've been reading up on it."

I kept an air of caution alive, mainly because ever since Luke was a little fellow, his free spirit and accompanying laissez-faire attitude had us convinced he would need all kinds of help, perhaps even crossing roads and such, as he grew into an adult—and maybe even for the rest of his life. To be more succinct, he made the term free spirit look a bit docile.

"I've already bought my plane ticket," he said.

Mm-hmm, I thought, nodding. I was pretty sure I knew what was coming.

"Six a.m. on New Year's morning," he said.

I furrowed my brow.

He smiled. "Sorry about that. It was the cheapest rate out there."

That figures!

By the time he left, Hannah had already accepted a nursing job in Gainesville, Florida, that was set to begin in February of 2013. She had a few weeks to kill.

"I was thinking about flying down to Guatemala to check on Luke," I said to her. "You wanna come with me?"

She smiled. "Of course. And why don't we do a week of Spanish school with him while we're down there?" She winked. "That way, he won't realize we're mainly there to check up on him."

"Sounds great," I said. And we both laughed.

So in late January of 2013, Hannah and I traveled to Guatemala to make sure Luke was still alive, join him for a week of Spanish school, and, of course, enjoy the country. Both Hannah and I became a bit enamored with the place, mainly because the people were so kind and the living expenses so minimal. A simple life was not only possible, it seemed, but perhaps even required.

We returned home from Guatemala the day after Super Bowl XLVII to find Meg deeply immersed in a book that had come in the mail while we were away. She got up to give me a hug and sank back down into the book before I could ask what was for dinner. I glanced at the cover. *The Crash Course*. Meg raised her index finger high in the air, her eyes still glued to the book. I waited patiently.

She sighed and looked at me. "You need to read this as soon as I'm through."

"What's it about?"

"You'll see when you read it. But I think it might be very important."

"Okay," I said. "Where did you get it?"

"It came while you were gone. I figured you ordered it."

Ah, yes. I now vaguely remembered that a free book was included with a free trial on some financial internet website I had signed up for, the name of which escaped me at the moment. Before leaving for Guatemala, I had been doing research on alternative investment strategies, with no real idea what I was doing or why. With a background in finance and well over a quarter of a century as an NFL agent negotiating contracts and studying money, I simply had an uneasy feeling about the financial future of the USA. Things felt wrong, but I couldn't say why for sure. I just knew I had to start exploring and learning beyond what the mainstream was advocating.

Within a day or two, Meg had finished the book, and less than twenty-four hours later, I had, too. It contained in-depth and fascinating information about the course our country and, in fact, the entire world was on, one where the economy and energy and environment are all heading towards a "crash" point at some time in the coming decades. When I put it down, we stared at each other for a few minutes. She spoke first.

"Let's sell the house," she said.

If I had not just read *The Crash Course,* I probably would have said something like, "What the hell are you talking about?" Instead, I said, "Okay." We were both excited about the possibility of exploring what we hoped would be a simpler way of life. And less expensive.

Just like that. I think we agreed on a price before we stood up.

A couple of weeks later, we helped Hannah pack her car for her trip down to Gainesville, Florida, to begin her new nursing job. It all seemed a bit mundane as I took things to the car and organized them for her. Having packed for a few moves myself—what was it, like a hundred times now?—I was what one might call an *expert*. I just did my duty, enjoying the father-daughter banter we were so used to, but as the last piece of luggage was stuffed in there and I turned around to see her with keys in hand, it all hit me.

My baby is leaving.

I got a lump in my throat and felt the strangest sensation, as if I was losing her for good. It hurt. But I didn't want her to feel any more anxious than she already did, so I hid my sadness as best I could.

"Call me as soon as you get there," I said.

She stifled a cry and then hugged me.

"I love you, Daddy."

As her car pulled away, I realized I had not been prepared for this part of life. There was a hole in my heart. But this one was tiny compared to the one that was coming.

Over the following weeks and months and even years, I began to do a lot of research into global issues, going down a few proverbial rabbit holes, learning things that were unpleasant yet I felt might be important. Once the door opened up, I stepped through it and found that I was in a room where deep secrets are hidden, where the narrative being told by the power structure comes under a great deal of scrutiny, to say the least.

It was a little like that famous scene from the blockbuster movie *The Matrix*, where Morpheus offers Neo an opportunity to take the blue pill or the red pill. *Remember?* Take the blue, and you remain naive and go on about your life. Take the red, "and I'll show you how deep the rabbit hole goes." Neo took the red. Well, so did I, and I found that hole to be pretty damn deep—so much so, in fact, that almost all the beliefs I had previously held dear began to be shattered, one after the other.

With Hannah now working in Florida and both boys in college (when Luke wasn't traveling, that is), that left Beka as the only child still under our roof.

Hmmm. Beka, still in high school?

Maybe we hadn't thought everything through as well as we should have. Meg and I discussed our hasty decision to sell the house and uproot our lives and quickly figured we could talk Beka into tagging along with us on our vagabond journey throughout Central America, and perhaps even Southeast Asia, signing her up for dual enrollment (high school and college courses online at the same time). What high school senior wouldn't want that?

That's what I figured, anyway.

"You aren't taking my senior year away from me," Beka blurted out when presented with the opportunity of a lifetime.

I looked both ways, as if she might be speaking to somebody else.

"Uh," I responded. "That's not how I saw it."

"Well, you saw it wrong," she said.

I mumbled a few words about excitement and adventure, but she wasn't in a buying mood. She walked out of the room with a quick turn, leaving a "no way" hanging in the air.

A few weeks later, without any prodding, she informed us she would do it after all. She never really explained the change of heart, at least not to me, but I was overjoyed. By the time we listed our house in late April of 2013, our plans were set. Central America and Mexico in the fall, then on to Southeast Asia after the new year began.

Did I mention that we loved our home? That Meg, in particular, loved her home? Well, both were true, but we had decided that the adventure before us was too enticing to pass on (and we fully expected to live abroad in the near future), so we cleaned and painted and repaired every day, such that sleep came easily when our heads hit the pillows each night.

Selling most of our stuff was a bit of a challenge, though. When you see strangers hauling off your $1,800 leather sofas for a couple hundred bucks, reality has a way of yanking your chain. Meg had hung in there until one of the garage sales, most likely operating on automatic, when, during the middle of a transaction, I noticed her eyes glaze over. She simply pivoted on a dime, slid out to the back yard, slinked down into a lawn chair, and stared at the trees, several potential customers still loitering about in and around the garage and driveway. Since she was in charge of the sale and much better at it than me, I went into near-panic mode. Our daughters continued to bicker with the customers (Hannah was home for the weekend) while I went out back to check on Meg.

What I saw reminded me of a scene from the movie *The Firm*, when an attorney sat in a lawn chair staring into space, a stiff drink in hand, as a water sprinkler pummeled him again and again, oblivious to the fact that his expensive suit was getting soaked as he sat there. No sprinkler was on in our yard, but if it had been, she wouldn't have cared. Tears streamed down her face. She didn't seem to notice me.

"Are you okay?" I asked.

Without looking at me, she said, "I may need to go to the hospital."

I began to realize that this life change was more of a delicate maneuver than I had expected. We somehow made it through that morning, and the day we put the house on the market, we had two full-price offers. We accepted one of them and set the close for the middle of June.

A few days after the closing, Meg and I were on a flight to Panama. Beka stayed with a friend for the time being.

Our adventure had begun.

It began with a caveat, though—I was no longer working as an NFL agent. Which just sort of happened. Turns out, if you don't recruit clients, you can't negotiate contracts, and voila!—no more income. All of the clients I had represented were now retired. So there was *that* to chew on as we considered our future.

Nevertheless, for the four weeks that followed, Meg and I zigzagged through Panama, Costa Rica, and Nicaragua, joined by Luke and Beka for the second half. We were fairly clueless, mainly trying to take in the cultures of Central America and feel things out. Enjoy ourselves, experience new places and traditions, relax, and learn.

By the time we flew back to Georgia, the reality sank in that we did not have a home. Until then, we didn't have to think much about it—on extended vacation and all—but as the tires of the 747 dug in and spun up smoke off of the Hartsfield International Airport tarmac in Atlanta, we realized that we were now nomads. The next couple of months would find us bouncing around from Meg's parents' home near Clearwater, Florida, to my mother's in Warner Robins, Georgia, and a couple of other places thrown in for good measure. Not exactly homeless, but never sure how long we would be in any one place, either. The good part was that we didn't really have any of the set-in-stone monthly expenses that come with owning or renting a home.

After maybe a couple of months of hoboing between Florida and Georgia, we decided to go back to Central America and Mexico for a more extensive look, so Meg, Beka, and I flew down to Guatemala in September of 2013 to take a couple of weeks of Spanish school in Antigua. By then, we were starting to feel like Latin America might serve as our future home, and honing our Spanish-speaking skills might be helpful.

We made our way up through Guatemala and on into southern Mexico before taking a left and hitting the Pacific coast of southwestern Mexico. On our earlier trip, Meg and I had ratcheted up our adventure meter and started testing out staying in hostels versus hotels and the like. We had been thrilled, enjoying the adventurous free spirits of the younger generation, who naturally preferred hostels for their cheaper accommodation. We found that the camaraderie alone was worth the price of admission to the hostels, engaging in amazing conversations and learning about the places we were headed to next. Besides, the beds were comfortable enough, and how much time do you spend in your room anyway? We were hooked. So throughout Guatemala and Mexico, we always sought out a good hostel before even considering fancier digs.

About five weeks into the trip, while hunkering down for several days in Puerto Escondido, Mexico, Beka crashed and burned as she started yearning for her friends and, well, familiarity. A few crying sessions led to a few calls, a quick flight to a temporary new home for her back in Peachtree City, and a continued adventure for Meg and me across to the Yucatan of Mexico, down to Belize, back through Guatemala, and on to El Salvador and Nicaragua. All the while, we were asking ourselves whether or not moving to Central America made sense. We finally flew back to Georgia in mid-December.

Beka had had enough, so she informed Meg and me that she would no longer chaperone us and would be remaining in Peachtree City. *"Thanks for the experience."* We weren't sure what to do, but Beka assured us that she would be okay and would even appreciate the independence. How could we say no? She had options regarding where to live back in Peachtree City, so Meg and I decided to continue our journey. We felt like it was important to give Mexico and Central America a bit more time to see if either felt right as a future home. We made another trip to Panama and Costa Rica after the new year and then returned to the States in February, leaning toward putting our Latin America experiment on the back burner. We loved it, but being near extended family and, of course, Beka tilted the scales a bit, at least for the moment.

So much so that in June of 2014, we made the decision to purchase a 69-acre farm in rural Tennessee. Perhaps our nomad days were behind us?

Erm, no.

As I said before, we just couldn't seem to stay put.

Well, we did for a year, but that year was packed with explosives. I had insisted that we invite various family members to come and join us up in the beautiful hills of Tennessee, somehow oblivious to the relational dynamics, and it was only a matter of weeks before my homestead fairytale began to unravel. By Christmas, we were already back to exploring Central America, and by June, we had sold the farm. Meg, Kyle, and Hannah (yes, we convinced her to join the crazy adventure) boarded a flight for Costa Rica, before the ink even dried on the sales contract, to see how they liked the possibility of living there.

I had chosen to stay behind for an indeterminate amount of time—as little as a few weeks, or up to a few months—mainly because I did not want to leave Beka behind again, and, to be honest, I was very confused. I wanted to be near my youngest child—that was the most important thing. Whatever the future held for my family, at least for the moment, I wanted to be near her. Luke was still in the States, too, bouncing here and there like the hobo he was becoming. He had hiked a few hundred miles of the Appalachian Trail shortly after we sold the farm and then came down to Peachtree City to hang with me for a few days. So I stayed with a good friend, Terry Borsare, and his wife, Linda, who had graciously invited me to live out of the large room above their garage, which was generously furnished.

Almost a month into the Costa Rica experiment, Hannah called me.

"Daddy, can I come stay with you for a little while?"

"Of course, that would be wonderful!"

I was very excited to be able to spend some alone time with her.

"And can you set up an appointment with Dr. Bergstrom?" she said. "Hopefully for the day after I get there?"

"Yes," I said.

I knew she had mentioned a couple of physical issues she was dealing with, so seeing a doctor made sense. I just had no idea how serious it was.

A PREMONITION

"You never know..."

N ow we move to that part of the story that becomes quite difficult to tell, a story that, even as I type out each word, has me feeling the echo of pain as my fingers hit each key.

To tell it true, though, or to share as close a glimpse as possible of the miracles that would later reveal themselves, perhaps here is the place to note an unlikely premonition, a story within the story that asks us to listen more closely to our hearts, and a hint for us to allow that we simply do not know all that we think we do.

As noted earlier, Hannah had begun work in mid-February of 2013 at UF Health in Gainesville, Florida. Upon arriving, she had met Mary Oliver-Marney, who was assigned to be her preceptor, or mentor.

There was an instant bond between them, Mary later saying that she had never met anyone like Hannah, her inner beauty and light obvious.

As her preceptor, Mary spent a lot of time with and around Hannah, and they shared many beautiful moments and, obviously, quite a few harrowing ones, as well, since they worked in the Trauma Unit at UF Health and dealt with some excruciatingly painful cases. One such case was that of an elderly woman who was dying, and who felt ready to die, and yet whose family was fighting over what could be done to medically keep her alive. The woman had determined that she wanted to go to her home and die and that all she wanted was a bath. Could Mary please give her a last bath?

The next morning, before she left, Hannah told Mary that she would be happy to help with the bathing of the woman. It was obvious to both Mary and Hannah, who had observed some of the family nuances, that the woman was feeling a great deal of stress from the interactions with her relatives. Mary brought in some nice lotions and body wash with the intent of pampering the sweet lady. But first, Mary had to deal with one of the more distraught family members, her daughter, who did not want to accept the lady's wishes. After a tense moment between Mary and this family member, Mary offered her a hug, and the agitated woman fell into Mary's arms, sobbing.

They bathed the sweet little lady, who thanked Hannah and Mary constantly as they ushered her down the long hospital corridor and into the elevator. They gave her hugs and kisses galore, as if she was their own mother. Then, Hannah and Mary embraced each other, the emotions of the event and of the sweet lady fresh in their hearts.

Later that same day, Hannah came to Mary and asked her how she was doing. Mary relayed how she had mixed emotions, of course, but that she felt great about the special bath they had given to the lady. She thanked Hannah once again for her help and told her what a great nurse she was.

The next words out of Hannah's mouth would jolt Mary, though Mary would quickly dismiss them as nonsense.

"When I'm getting ready to die," Hannah said, "I want you there with me and my family."

"Are you crazy?" Mary replied.

Another co-worker, who was standing there with Mary and Hannah, asked what the heck was going on. The way Hannah had said it sounded too *knowing*.

Hannah gave some response about Mary diffusing a fragile situation between family members before they had sent a lady home to die and how they had both given that lady a spa treatment before she left.

Mary, old enough to be Hannah's mother, still felt uneasy. "I'll be gone from this world long before you, Hannah."

"You never know," Hannah replied and added, "My family will need your caring and gentle correction, like this lady's family."

The three of them laughed together. Hannah then spoke lovingly of how wonderful her family was, but Mary was still nagged a bit in her spirit at what Hannah had said about "getting ready to die."

"Little did I know," Mary would later whisper while softly crying when she shared this all with me as I prepared to write this book.

PART THREE

The 100 Days

AFTER THE CALL

"How bad is it?

My life has its own *before* and *after*, that tiny instant when time seemingly split in two for me.

It was because of that damn return call I made to Dr. Chuck Bergstrom as Hannah and I sat eating wings and fries at Beef O'Brady's in Peachtree City, Georgia, on that mid-July day in 2015.

It was because of the words that came out of his mouth that day, words that fell heavy upon me, that suffocated me, that assured me that life was over as I had known it to be and happiness was now a forever illusion.

"I'm so sorry," he had said.

"She has cancer. It's bad," he had said.

"Colon. Liver. Lungs." he had said.

God, I hated him.

But I hated God worse.

After we left Beef O'Brady's on that fateful day, we ended up driving about a mile away to the Borsares' home, where I had been staying for the last month. We pulled into the Borsares' driveway and scaled the stairs to the bedroom. I opened the door and stepped in, Hannah following closely. Luke was there waiting for the news, sitting at the far end of the room. When he stood up and looked into our eyes, I shook my head and looked down at the carpet in front of me.

He sighed and moved towards us. One glance at Luke's face and

I realized he had been expecting bad news. Hannah and I had held back emotions on the ride over, broaching the subject of how we were going to defeat this unbeatable monster, but the tide rolled back in like a furious hurricane, flooding each of us in a heavy deluge of grief. The thickness that enveloped me at the restaurant had dissipated ever so slightly on the way over, yet now it was reinvigorated to a fever pitch as Hannah, Luke, and I joined together in a group hug, each of us dazed and brokenhearted.

Luke, ever the loving brother, waited patiently for one of us to speak. Finally, I breathed deeply and said, "Cancer." Once again, the word snuck begrudgingly from my lips.

"What type?" Luke finally asked, possibly hoping for something bland.

"Colon," Hannah said. "But it's spread to the liver and lungs."

Luke sighed again and reached for Hannah, tears now streaming down his face. She fell into her younger brother's arms and buried her head in his chest as he squeezed her with tender, loving arms. They remained that way for a while.

I slipped outside onto the stairwell and took the opportunity to try and call Meg, which I was dreading doing. No answer. I inhaled a deep breath of hot, thick air and then dialed my mother. I heard her cry on the phone in front of her friends, out to lunch in her hometown.

"I couldn't get Mom," I said to Hannah as I stepped back in.

She nodded.

"I'm not sure how to reach her," I added. "Any ideas?" Meg had a cheap phone with paltry coverage and was probably scouring the jungle for a finca (Spanish for a small farm) to start a sustainable living venture for our family.

"Try Charlie," Hannah suggested. "He seems to be easy to reach and might know how to find her." Charlie, an expat from the USA living in the Puerto Viejo area where Mom and Kyle were, was also a realtor who seemed to know everybody and how to get things done. Hannah gave me his number, and I left a message on his phone. A couple of hours later, Meg called.

"Hey, baby," I started. I think I groaned next.

"Oh my gosh, Phil, what is it?" she whimpered, sensing that if I had reached her through Charlie, a man she knew I had never even spoken with, then it had to be serious.

"She has cancer."

"Noooooo. Noooooo," she cried, her voice cracking. "Not Hannah. Not my baby girl."

I could barely hold the phone to my ear, her pain adding to mine. Meg somehow formed words through the high-pitched moans escaping from her throat.

"How bad is it?" she managed to ask, her voice shaking.

I hated the fucking questions.

"Pretty bad," I said, and then filled her in on the rest.

Meg wept.

We then made plans for her to return to the States, leaving Kyle behind to manage affairs in what we had been hoping was our new country. With Meg, Luke, and Beka (who was now living in an apartment in Newnan, Georgia, while attending nursing school at Georgia State University in Atlanta) alongside Hannah and me, I was hoping we might be able to lock hands with God Almighty Himself and witness a miracle.

Though I tried to be calm and reassuring, on the inside, I was anything but. After the conversation with Meg, the rest of the afternoon saw Hannah and me racing all over Fayette County and parts of Coweta County, searching for the freshest organic produce I could find to get Hannah on a healthy, nutrient-intake regimen. If Meg had been a whirling dervish the night before Hannah's birth, I was more like a Tasmanian Devil on speed, darting from farm to farm.

I did not tell Hannah what I had heard in Chuck's voice. Hell, every time it slid into my mind, I thrust it away. But it kept knocking. Menacingly. *Death Sentence*, I heard. It ate into my being like a hungry, mocking parasite. I'm not sure how many times I looked over at my baby girl during this time, but it was a lot.

PART THREE

We had relaxed a little by the evening, exhausted enough to sleep. Terry's apartment contained one single bed, one double, and a sofa. Hannah had been sleeping in the single, me in the double, and Luke on the sofa. However, that night I had the inclination to ask Hannah something I never thought I would ask again.

"Hannah, you wanna sleep next to me?"

"Yes."

For the next one hundred days, this is how it would be. I would place my hand gently upon her belly, now starting to swell by the day, and pray. When I would wake up in the middle of the night, and only if I felt that it wouldn't disturb her, I would slide my hand ever so delicately onto her belly again, next to her liver, and pray as I would fall back to sleep. I would ask God to make a transfer, *do the right thing*, let it be me and not her. I'm guessing that's normal.

Meg arrived from Costa Rica a little after 1 p.m. on Friday, the 17th of July, approximately twenty-four hours after I had given her the news. I picked her up curbside at Hartsfield International Airport in Atlanta. She was a mess. Shaking and weeping. We hugged for a minute as I tried to assure her that we were going to beat this thing, and then we headed back down to Terry's place in Peachtree City. After arriving and giving Meg and Hannah time to catch up, we made a final decision to move out into the country to stay with friends Buddy and Dina Dennis, who had offered us the use of two of their bedrooms for as long as we needed them.

As I considered the road before us, I was confused as hell, clueless as to what steps to take. I didn't have a script to work from. I found myself walking down a slippery path, a treacherous one where I felt that any slight misstep could lead to horrific consequences. And even if everything did go perfectly, did we truly have a chance? The world of traditional medicine didn't offer any options for lasting healing, only the potential to extend her life by a small margin via extremely debilitating measures. Hannah had nixed that route immediately and affirmed her decision whenever discussed. She was at peace with whatever lay ahead. Hence, Meg and I immediately and frantically began a mad search for information about the latest alternative/natural options that might be available.

One of the problems we discovered was that there were so many natural treatment remedies and aids out there that our heads began to spin. The medical industrial complex of government, Big Pharma, and the hospital establishment barely give the holistic realm a glance, for obvious reasons, which made it hard to get a concise game plan going. We were winging it. Of course, we talked to a few people with some degree of knowledge in the area, but most of them sounded rather pessimistic when alerted to Hannah's status, even if they were trying to hide their feelings.

Before the first evening rolled around, less than five hours after receiving the news, I was already wheeling and dealing and ordering different types of healing implements and supplements. This would go on throughout the one hundred days, dollars flowing out as if there were an endless supply of them. *A chance it could help? A few thousand bucks? I'll take it.* I'm sure any parent would have done the same.

By the time we arrived at the Dennises' home, we were on day three. I was so thankful when they opened their door and said, "This is *your* home."

The reality was that we didn't have a home in the USA anymore—or anywhere, for that matter. We were nomads with a dying daughter and, therefore, at the mercy of kind hearts. And taking a very sick woman into your house along with her anxiety-ridden parents is not on the top of most folks' to-do lists. To adequately express my gratitude to those brave, loving souls would be impossible.

The first day at the Dennises' home, Hannah and I were sitting in the living area. She looked at me and said, "Daddy, could you do me a favor?"

"Of course. Anything."

"Well," she said. "There are a few friends I'd like you to call and let them know what's happening. I feel they should know."

"Okay. Sure."

So I did. I can't remember who all was on the list, but Hannah felt that certain friends should know for reasons only she knew. As I recall, the first couple of calls were to Sarah Flynn, a close friend she had met in Spain seven years earlier, and Mary Oliver-Marney, her preceptor from her job in Gainesville, Florida, whom she dearly loved.

Both calls were pretty similar.

"Hey, this is Phil. I'm calling for Hannah. I've got rough news. Hannah has a very aggressive cancer, and she wanted me to call and let you know."

Mary moaned and Sarah mumbled. I swear, I don't know if I heard a word out of Mary's mouth, her moans and whimpers dragging her words into an undecipherable place. I had never met Mary, but the picture I got on that call was of a deeply emotional lady who had just received the worst news of her life.

Sarah, on the other hand, spoke somewhat intelligibly but in pathetic little fragments, almost every other word "um" or "uh." You could hear the tears trickling down her cheeks.

I took a lot of deep breaths during both conversations and tried to speak with confidence—*we're gonna beat this thing*—but it didn't seem either of them was hearing it.

Both of these wonderful souls would be there for Hannah, especially during her last month.

Sarah had just had her first baby in June and yet told me on the phone that she would be down, with baby in tow, within a couple of weeks to stay and love on Hannah. This cheered Hannah up.

We stayed maybe a week with Buddy and Dina. I slept with Hannah each night in a wonderful king-sized bed in the room that had previously belonged to their son. Meg tried it out one night, and would a couple times more over the course of Hannah's illness, but she got very little sleep on that attempt, so I assumed the role for most of the one hundred days.

I felt it was my job to do so. Besides, my heart ached so bad that if I did try to sleep in the other room, I slept even less.

Though Buddy and Dina made it clear we could stay as long as we wanted, another option opened up that would allow us to stay in our own house, so to speak, without invading someone else's space. It was actually a renovated barn, up in the foothills of the North Georgia mountains outside of Big Canoe, owned by friends of ours from way back in our Tallahassee, Florida, days. Doug and Linda Tatum occupied the cute white house, farther up the hill by a couple hundred yards, and warmly invited us to stay in the barn house, which was also part of their property. It was rather nice, offering all we could have hoped for.

Sure, I had been a mess ever since calling Chuck—Dr. Bergstrom—from Beef O'Brady's, but I sensed as I canvassed the hills of North Georgia that I was in the early days of a journey that, unless a miracle came, might very well destroy me. I honestly had no idea how I would survive if she didn't make it. But there was something serene about the hills and the woods and the blue skies of mid-summer. The barn wasn't up especially high, but you could still see off into the distance from its slight perch on the hill. I would sit and stare, sit and stare. It seemed to give me a very slight reprieve from the constant emotional stress. Not much, but a little; it was maybe one of the small things that would carry me through. So I sat outside and stared off into the blue.

Within a week, the Tatums were preparing to make their annual pilgrimage to Tallahassee, Florida, where Doug taught a class at Florida State University during the fall semester. They graciously invited us to move from the barn into the white house, as it had a queen-sized bed on the ground floor. So we did, moving in the day they left, with me back in the same bed as Hannah for the duration of our time there. The three of us had been sleeping in the same room in twin beds while in the barn. And to be honest, my mind was so attached to the moment, and more specifically to the constant swirling of hope and love and fear as it related to Hannah, that I'm not sure I even knew where the other kids were from day to day. If I stopped and thought about it, sure, I could see Kyle in Costa Rica and Luke coming and going between Costa Rica and wherever the three of us were staying, and Beka in Newnan and going to school, but truthfully, it was all a maze of confusion.

Soon, we established a fairly standard regimen of nutritional intake for Hannah, with fresh, organic, homemade vegetable juices, all full of antioxidants to try to fight the cancer. We also purchased a significant amount of various supplements, all of which had provided varying degrees of success in fighting cancer in other cases.

We hated forcing the juice and the capsules down Hannah's throat, especially since she had never been good at taking pills, but we worked hard to make it work. This might have been Hannah's least favorite thing to do throughout her illness, as she simply did not seem to have the room to consume all the juice we set before her, not to mention the lack of appetite; at times, taking even one capsule seemed a monumental task. But she never complained. She did throw up both the juice and capsules at times, scaring Meg and me because of our belief that her life depended on following every single protocol, but Hannah just couldn't help it.

Sometime during our first night together in the queen-sized bed, I felt Hannah's long, slender fingers tenderly touching my back. I was lying fetal style, with my back to her, awake and staring out the window into the dreary darkness. Her fingers began, slowly and ever so softly, to scratch a small area of my back. She was trying not to wake me up.

Her tenderness crushed my heart, and I silently cried as she continued. It didn't last long. I don't think she had the stamina. But I knew Hannah. I knew what she was doing, what she was saying. That touch meant more than I can say, as if her fingers upon my back were the dew of Heaven resting upon me. She was communicating with me on that level that she and I shared, where words were not necessary, telling me that she appreciated me, that she loved me, that she was thankful that I was her daddy, and that she was happy I was there with her. This was one of the many things—what I call *the little things*—that would hallmark those fateful days. And this would not be the last time her fingers caressed my back in the dark of night.

Of course, I would lightly touch Hannah during the night, too. But I had to be careful not to disturb her, which I did a time or two, each time breaking my heart. I did not want to steal even one second of her much-needed sleep. It was very difficult, though, lying beside her and not being able to absorb some of her pain.

A couple of days after we moved into the house up the hill, Sarah flew down from Virginia with her one-month-old daughter, Norah, and stayed with us until we left there. When she walked into the house with Norah, Hannah lit up. Never have I seen anyone love babies and little children more (though Hannah's little sister Beka might give her a run for her money), and so Hannah adored Norah immediately. Sarah and Hannah had a unique and special bond, plus she had also come with another gift. She was a licensed massage therapist and would lovingly give Hannah massages throughout her stay with us.

Early on in her illness, Hannah had begun to suffer from back pain. It seemed a godsend that Sarah was there and able to help allevi- ate some of Hannah's pain, but finding a position of comfort where the pain could be mitigated was difficult. I don't think it was on the first day that her struggle with the back pain commenced, but fairly soon afterwards, it occurred to me that maybe I could help in an unorthodox way. Trying to stack the pillows up behind her was not sufficient.

I suggested it might help if I sat behind her on the bed and some- times on the sofa so that she could lean back into me and I could adjust whenever and however she needed. She liked the idea, so we gave it a shot. I crawled up behind her and splayed my legs out to give her room, and she slid back into me, resting the back of her head on my chest, and sometimes on my shoulder. It seemed to help her immensely right off the bat, so I was delighted.

This became our go-to throughout most of the rest of her ill- ness. The back pain was here to stay, though it would ride up and down the pain scale, and I even held her forward at times and mas- saged it where it hurt.

"Would you play with my hair?" Hannah asked more than once.

"Sure," I said.

I instinctively spread my fingers and started at the base of her neck, slowly sliding my hand upwards and tugging gently. Sometimes I used both hands. Her hair was so thick! We obviously had a lot of time to talk as well, so of course we did, and about every subject you can imagine.

"Do you remember when I took you to the kids' petting zoo in Tallahassee when you were little?" I asked.

I noticed her smile. Though she was sitting between my legs, I could slide out to the side a little to see her face better.

She lowered her eyebrows, deep in thought.

"Maybe a little," she said.

"Do you remember peeing right there on the park bench?"

"No!" she laughed. "I did not do that!"

"Yes, you surely did!" I laughed, too. "It ran down your legs, and I just stood there helpless. I was pretty clueless how to clean you up and get us out of there."

We both had a good laugh, Hannah acknowledging that it must have been true. Which it was.

"I can't wait to walk the beaches of Costa Rica with you," I said.

"Me too, Daddy."

But there was something in her voice. It didn't convince me. I could tell she wanted to make me feel better, to give me hope, but I think deep inside she knew that the beaches of Costa Rica were not in her future.

I also broached the subject of Heaven a time or two during those intimate moments as my fingers massaged her head and teased her hair.

"Do you ever think about Heaven?"

She nodded, a faint but sweet smile forming on her lips.

"Yes."

That was about it on that subject. I didn't like to go there much since I was convinced her best hope of healing centered around

believing in healing. But occasionally, it would filter in, we would specu-
late, and it would bruise my heart.

I would continue to slip behind her a few times per day to
hold my daughter. My back would ache at times, but I couldn't and
wouldn't tell her that. It was minuscule in comparison to what she
was dealing with. *She* was the warrior! Those times together as I sat
behind her might be what I miss the most. The special moments we
shared, where God allowed me to simply hold her, smell her hair,
sense her courageous and loving spirit, share private moments, all
while trying to alleviate a little of her pain.

Not long after we had moved into the Tatums' main house, Meg
asked me to run an errand that, to be honest, I did not feel comfortable with, and one that would likely take at least seven or eight hours.
I said no. Not only was I not comfortable with the job she wanted me
to do (nor did I feel certain it needed to be done) but I abhorred the
thought of being away from Hannah for that long.

I suggested that if Meg wanted it done badly enough, she take
Luke with her to do it. She did, and upon entering the house on their
return, I immediately felt something was very wrong.

But I could have never guessed quite how wrong it was.

"When this is all over, whether she makes it or not, I'm leaving!"
Meg said rather forcefully.

"No, you ain't!" I said. I was stunned. In shock, really. I simply
could not believe her.

Meg then went on to explain that she was, in fact, going
to leave me.

I went outside and sat on the porch, in even more pain than
before, if that were possible. My daughter was dying, the very
thought of which tore through me. And now? Now my wife was telling me she was going to leave me, too. The one person that I thought
I would be able to lean on in the wake of our daughter's probable
death was now letting me know that would not be happening.

PART THREE

As I sat there, looking out over the mountains near the property, I wondered how I would ever scale the emotional mountain that stood before me.

I hurt too bad to cry.

I determined that I would do whatever it took to get Meg to change her mind (and a bit over a week later, it seemed I had done just that), but I knew deep inside that it would be very difficult for me to ever overcome such a debilitating rejection from the woman I thought was my forever love.

Of course, I knew she, too, was hurting from the situation we found ourselves in, but I did not have the capacity at that time to see how much her pain had affected her to suggest such a thing. The prior years of selling our home, becoming nomads, disrupting the lives of others—all of that and more had simply been avalanched by the coming death of our daughter. She was in a deep, dark place, crying out.

But I could not hear the cry.

All I could do was cry myself ... even if it was only on the inside.

A CHANGE OF SCENERY

"It was the best hug of my life."

We stayed at the Tatums' property for about a month, and maybe halfway through our time there, Meg decided to call an old friend, Annie Hambsch, to let her know about Hannah's situation. They had been best friends in high school, down in Largo, Florida, and then roommates at Florida State. Quite a few years earlier, Annie and her husband, Eric, had lost their beautiful daughter, Erica, to an automobile accident when she was sixteen years old. As tough as it had been for Meg to hear of Annie's loss at that time, the memory suddenly poured in, and with Hannah so sick, Meg suddenly felt that it was very important to speak with Annie.

She couldn't connect with her at first, unable to locate her phone number, so she messaged Mary-Lynn, Annie's sister, on Facebook, who ended up calling her promptly after. What she asked next broke Meg down again.

"Did you hear about Kenny, Annie's only son and only other child?"

He had died, too, a couple of years back. Deeply emotional, Meg had to step outside to finish that call. She wondered if she should even call Annie, but Mary-Lynn assured her that she should.

Meg and Annie spoke soon after, and the tears flowed freely. Broken hearts merged together. Before we knew it, Annie called Meg back to say she had spoken with Eric and that they wanted to host us in their home outside of Tampa. They even wanted to—*wanted to!*—drive their RV up to Georgia to pick Hannah up so she could travel down in comfort. Meg and I had been considering relocating to a place by the coast anyway since Hannah was struggling with edema and there was the slightest hope that spending time in seawater could provide an advantage or two, even if it was only a degree of comfort. We jumped on the offer with tears in our eyes, hearts overflowing with gratitude, and a sense of renewed hope.

We agreed to meet Eric and Annie back at Buddy and Dina's home in a few days. After dropping Sarah and Norah off at the Atlanta airport and spending the night with the Dennises, we arose the next day to a beautiful RV pulling into the driveway in rural Georgia, about forty-five minutes south of Atlanta.

I really didn't know Eric. We had spent a small amount of time together, maybe twenty-five years earlier, but had not gotten to know each other well. It almost felt to me as if a stranger was coming to pick us up. I walked out onto the driveway, luggage already in tow, and watched as Eric exited the driver's side of the RV and walked my way.

You know, men can act pretty tough sometimes, especially as they try to figure each other out. The truth is that my mind was so consumed with pain and fear that I had not thought much about Eric and Annie, or the trip ahead of us. The only thing on my mind was Hannah. But when Eric reached me and opened his arms without any words, so did I. As we hugged, I heard a slight groan. This man understood. Within an instant, we were more than two men greeting each other. He embraced me from a deep place—a place of knowing, a place of empathy, a place where words were unnecessary, and, in some ways, a place outside of the physical realm.

It was the best hug of my life.

Eric knew pain—that was clear—and he instinctively embraced mine. I never told him this, but that hug gave me a boost. It spoke to me on a level I needed to know still existed and told me that there were those who not only cared but who could convey it in a way that sustained the desperate ones. Like me.

By late afternoon, we pulled into their beautiful place on the northern side of Tampa and sighed, another leg on the journey begun. Though the location was fresh and new and somehow hopeful, I observed Hannah and knew that we were fighting time. I began to see time as my enemy, taunting us as it ticked on by, stealing Hannah's life along with it.

Others seemed aware, too, that we were running out of time. During Hannah's last weeks, many visitors came to see her. Cornell Green, my former client who had once said, "Hannah could turn piss into lemonade!" was one of them. I knew he lived in Tampa, only a few miles down the road from Eric and Annie's home, so I called and gave him the news that Hannah was very sick and that we were very close by. That's when he let me know that Teri, his wife and the mother of his boys, also had cancer, and though it was not nearly as advanced as Hannah's was at the time, it had spread and was, of course, very serious. Cornell and I shared the same birthday and, as mentioned earlier, an occasional orneriness. Now, we also shared something no one would ever wish to share: watching our very special loved ones deal with life-threatening diseases.

It was very disheartening for Cornell to hear how perilous Hannah's situation was, partly because he loved her and she held a special place in his heart already but also because it scared him. If Hannah was on the verge of dying, as it appeared she may very well be, what did that mean for Teri? Cornell wondered how long it would be before Teri ended up just as ill.

Cornell brought Teri over for a visit a week or so after we arrived at Annie and Eric's house. It was already becoming difficult for Hannah to see visitors. For several reasons. First, she would exude energy and awareness whenever friends or family came to see her, which would inevitably leave her exhausted upon their departure. Also, unbeknownst to us (perhaps because we tried not to see it at the time), she was dying, and we later learned that those who are dying tend to go inward. On top of that, she was under a great deal of pain at times and could not gauge the level of the pain ahead of time. Yet, despite all that, she would always gather herself and put on a good face for the visitors. She was an extrovert and had always enjoyed being with people, so she insisted on meeting with who- ever took the time to come see her.

When we told Hannah of Teri's fight with colon cancer, she was determined to spend some time with her, especially with Cornell coming. Looking back on that visit, and on all of the special visits those last months, I was able to see something I had missed at that time: Hannah was honoring others above herself, giving life and love to everyone she could for as long as she could.

I saw Cornell and Teri pull up in the driveway and went to get Hannah. She waddled out with a smile on her face and a glow in her eyes and greeted them. It is difficult to convey the grace that filled the air within the vicinity of these two beautiful souls as they embraced. There was an instant physical and spiritual connection.

"We are going to get through this together," Hannah said to Teri. And Teri cried.

There were a good many more tears shed before Cornell and Teri left, mainly springing forth from a sweet, sisterly love born out of their mutual struggle. Their connection put them together on a platform from which to see the world more clearly, through a lens that most of us are oblivious to. They both now witnessed life with a deeper spiritual perspective than before, eternity in their minds and in their midst. In some ways, when they were together, though they had just met for the first time, it was almost as if the rest of us were not even there. They laughed and cried and laughed some more. And cried some more. You would have thought they were lifetime friends. When the time came, it was tough for them to say goodbye.

Teri left knowing that Hannah was much sicker than she was at that juncture, but the fact that Hannah had taken the time and expended the energy for her left a deep impression. Teri had a new strength now. She felt that she had a buddy for life and was so thankful that Hannah had simply loved her.

Cornell knew that feeling well.

As they got in the car to drive away, Teri began to cry. She was very emotional, repeating again and again how priceless those moments were to her, how priceless her new relationship was to her. She would frequently ask Cornell about Hannah over the coming weeks. Two young women with very different pasts had become as one as they forged a bond in those precious moments together. Less than two years later, Teri would join Hannah forever.

A couple of times during our stay with Eric and Annie, Eric's father, Josef Hambsch, joined us for dinner. He, too, was ill with cancer, though not quite as far along as Hannah. It was special to sit at that table with two people who saw life in a different context than the rest of us. Hannah and Mr. Hambsch would look at each other, talk, smile, laugh. There was an intimacy in their verbal and nonverbal communication, much like there had been with Teri. They loved each other on a different level. To call it sweet would almost be to belittle what they shared. It was heavenly. Literally. A quiet knowing. He would pass on a couple of months after Hannah did.

The disease continued on its relentless march, but Hannah remained as positive and sweet as one could. Meg and I did our best to take a deep breath, raise our chins, and establish a new routine, and then pursue it with as much love and passion as we knew how to. Eric and Annie stuck with us, side by side. They let us know that not only were they opening their home to us, but they were also there to provide meals, emotional support, and anything else they could.

The routine included the same protocols of juices and supplements, but now it also included a daily trip to a little spot called Sunset Beach, a tiny dot of land that somehow jutted out into the Gulf of Mexico, just west of Tarpon Springs. Again, we were trying whatever seemed to offer even the slightest hope, and this was an attempt to alleviate some of the swelling in Hannah's legs and abdomen, and hopefully aid in her comfort. Though we first enjoyed the waters, the trip soon became tedious and even painful for Hannah, so we only made it a few times.

PART THREE

As we were preparing to leave for our first trip to the beach—when we still had hope it could help her some—I walked outside to go get the car and bring it around the circular driveway so as to shorten the necessary steps Hannah would have to take (walking was already quite difficult for her, forty days or so in). As I wheeled the car around, ready to jump out and go help her, I saw the front door open. I stood up from the seat and peered over the roof of the car, and I saw Eric and Hannah, arm in arm, walking slowly down the front steps.

Hannah was smiling.

It was Eric's face, though, that caught my attention. He wasn't just doing us a favor. He wasn't just walking Hannah out the door. He wasn't just escorting a dying girl to the car. He was, as far as I could tell, loving her as if she were his own. Maybe he even felt, in a strange sort of way, as if he were being given a chance to love on his own daughter, Erica, one more time. Of course, I can't be sure of that. I would have to ask him, and I never did. But it did do something inside of *my* heart to watch this man, who had lost both of his children in just a few short years, allow some of that awful pain to trickle back in by giving his heart to my dying daughter.

From that time on, Eric would walk around the corner at just the instant we were about to head out the door in order to usher Hannah out as I would get the car. It was special for all of us.

Hannah had always been an avid book reader like her daddy, but now she didn't seem to have the energy to do the reading herself, so Meg had been reading to her from a book both of them really liked, a historical fiction titled *Outlander*. We would hang out in the shallow waters of the Gulf, Hannah floating delicately on a circular float, me galavanting here and there and snorkeling a little. To be honest, I got a bit bored at times, so when Meg asked me to read a little for her, I thought, *Sure. Why not?*

"This is porn," I said after only a couple pages in a mockingly judgmental tone. "What the heck are you guys doing, reading this smut?"

"I swear," Meg said, chuckling. "That's the worst part I've ever heard. Are you making this up?"

"No!"

Hannah laughed.

There we were, a dying twenty-six-year-old woman and her two emotionally fractured parents, hovering around a little tube in the ocean, reading, laughing, and doing our damnedest to try to enjoy the moments we had left together.

I continued to take on my reading duties—still with a few more X-rated scenes—which provided a bit of comic relief, a moment or two of lightheartedness. It probably cannot be underestimated how important these times of levity were for our sanity.

Soon, though, the trips to Sunset Beach ended, and on the way home from our last one, we stopped at a drugstore. Meg went in to get something as I sat in the driver's seat with Hannah beside me. As we waited, Hannah began to breathe in short nasal pulses, straining to take in oxygen. Her eyes widened.

"Daddy, I can't breathe," she managed to softly blurt out.

The panic I felt was immediate and intense. Oh dear God, don't let her die!

I really had no idea what to do. I felt sick, nauseated. I reached over and touched her hand.

"Relax. Just relax."

I felt so stupid, so inept, so very, very scared.

And then, just like that, her normal breathing resumed.

We did not tell Meg.

The rest of the drive back to Eric and Annie's home, the thought of my baby struggling to breathe haunted me. I couldn't shake it.

Couldn't we have just one day of peace?

GOING HOME

"It just don't matter."

I can be a man of action, a doer, a *take-the-reins* kind of guy, but as I look back on those one hundred days, I seem to remember Meg being the one to suggest almost everything and me rubber-stamping her suggestions and just going along for the ride. After about three weeks in Florida, Meg proposed we head back to where Hannah had been raised, the Peachtree City area. The thought of it pierced my heart.

Though we would both pray and hold out hope for healing until the bitter end (which at this point could only have occurred by miracle), the writing on the wall was formed with pretty big letters. My heart sank again, for maybe the ten thousandth time.

Meg scoured the internet for a suitable rental, and upon finding one that might work, Beka went and took a look for us. Within hours, we agreed to a little place outside of Senoia, Georgia—monthly, sight unseen.

Every day, Hannah looked physically worse. And every day was a struggle. To be honest, if not for Hannah's cheery disposition and attitude of love, I'm not sure Meg or I could have adequately hung in there. Hannah was racing toward her destiny with a peace beyond words. A peace beyond this world. While Meg and I were sinking toward ours, a numbing, unwordable pain.

One morning, maybe a couple days before the trip back to

Georgia, all three of us were in the bedroom Hannah and I had been sleeping in. Hannah, sitting on the bed, shared something with us.

"Earlier, I felt as if my spirit was prepared to leave my body," she said, Meg and I suddenly alert. "I could feel a movement within me, as if my very life was preparing to escape through my fingertips." She raised her hands gently and fluttered her fingers about.

Meg and I both instantly became a two-person rescue team, thrust into a mode of desperation by her calm acknowledgement.

"No, no, no," we echoed each other. "We can't think like that."

"God is healing you even as we speak."

"Let's keep our hopes up." And so on.

I raced around to the side of the bed and grabbed one of our computers, frantically searching for something—*anything*—to change the direction of the mood Meg and I found ourselves in. Hannah, on the other hand, seemed at peace about it. I clicked on iTunes, and my eyes settled on "Carry Me Through" by Dave Barnes, a favorite of all of ours by now. Well, we damn sure needed some *carrying through* in that moment!

As the words began to hover in the air in their soothing, crying-out-to-God kind of way, both Meg and I tended to Hannah, reinforcing the theme from the song. We wanted to make sure she did not give up. Looking back, I can see that the gist of what we were doing was trying to keep *ourselves* from absorbing any more pain than we already felt, while Hannah was clearly in acceptance with transcending into pure beauty and love.

Perhaps she was testing the waters, floating her true emotions out for us, revealing her yearning to let go of the pain and find rest. Perhaps she was hoping that she might find some form of acceptance from us.

But we were simply not ready to let go.

I can still see myself in that room, watching her fingers softly flutter, her beautiful eyes searching ours. Witnessing our frantic, almost chaotic frenzy to nip that in the bud. Despite her own wishes, she decided to tap into the reservoir of love and compassion she had for us by continuing to fight what she knew was inevitable.

Despite now being aware that I should have simply honored Hannah where she was and allowed her to go on if she was ready, I do not have regrets. We parents could beat ourselves up every second for the rest of our lives if we chose to do so, rehashing an endless list of situations that we would correct if given the chance. No. I see it all as what became a necessary journey for each of us: Hannah continuing to reveal an unearthly grace that very few could have (certainly not me!), a lesson in love under the most trying circumstances, and me clinging to a fragile father's hope for healing.

Who could blame me?

Eric and Annie offered to transport us back to Georgia in the RV, and we humbly accepted. As with every other leg of this journey, this one had its moments.

We stopped in Gainesville, Florida, a couple of hours into the trip to meet with one of Hannah's good friends, Meg Fanelli. Of course, this was partly because Meg's four little children, who adored Hannah, wanted to see her. Their entire family had become very close to Hannah during her time in Gainesville as a nurse. Meg and her kids came to meet us and spent an hour or so in the RV as we hung out in a parking lot on the outskirts of town.

Taking the time to meet with as many friends as possible was a blessing to both parties. Always. Even though it could be extremely taxing for Hannah, she still chose to meet with whoever wanted to see her. Though I did not know it yet—or let myself see it—she was doing all she could to drum up the energy to see and love all of her friends and family for possibly the last time; I believe she knew inside that her time remaining on Earth was short. So it was worth it to her, no matter the effort that it took. And if children were involved, it was somehow exponentially more important to Hannah.

So Meg Fanelli brought her four kids—Robby, Lena, Jane, and

Mary—ranging in age from ten to two, for the visit, and Hannah was in Heaven, so in love with those kids. I looked at her face as she gazed upon and gently played with them, my mind suddenly tracing back to a decade before and my heart seized with melancholic grief.

As I watched her with Meg Fanelli's kids, I could barely contain myself. It reminded me of Hannah's love for the kids at Camp Sunshine. It was the exact same, in fact, only in reverse. Though Hannah was still loving on kids, now the kids were loving on her, as *she* was the one dying. Full circle. The picture of this cut deep inside of me, and it was difficult for me to keep myself together. In addition, Meg Fanelli gave me a knowing look, her eyes revealing that she knew she would never see Hannah alive again. This tore at my heart.

"Hannah opened my eyes to see that age is timeless," Meg later told me. "That it was really about connecting on a soul level. Age was simply irrelevant to her. She exuded an aura that said, *'We are all here to love each other.'* She saw from the soul to the soul. I've never known anyone else who could do that. There really are no words that work in describing it. She was love."

She still is.

A few hours later, while driving through South Georgia on our way up to our old stomping grounds to find the rental home in Senoia, I made a call that I hated to make. Meg had received a phone call while riding in the RV notifying us of the test results from Hannah's last blood panel, taken shortly before leaving the Tampa area. She needed a blood transfusion as soon as possible.

Hannah had already received one blood transfusion a week earlier, and now another would be required to keep her alive. In my desperation, I called the Newnan, Georgia, location of the Cancer Treatment Centers of America to see if they could do the transfusion. I had a friend who worked there, a naturopathic doctor named David Oster, a wonderful man whom I had spoken with early on in Hannah's illness during my frantic search for help and advice.

The young woman in charge of financial matters called me back after I had left a message of inquiry. We had actually spoken a couple of months earlier at David's request. She kindly said that, yes, they did do transfusions, explaining she would have to check to see if the center was available to see Hannah that day, and then told me the price. The invoice would be somewhere between twenty and thirty thousand dollars if paid in cash. Hannah's situation was serious and complicated.

Already having spent tens of thousands of dollars in what seemed like futile attempts to save Hannah, or at least stave off the disease long enough for God to come through, everything about this was beginning to drag us down. In a very real sense, the money part was irrelevant. If there was any to be used, how could you not use it in an attempt to save your child? But it felt hopeless at the same time, draining your savings to buy a week or so, wondering if that was even what she really wanted. Confusion reigned.

I remember gripping the steering wheel just a little tighter and trying to speak.

"I'll do it," I somehow managed, tears streaming down my face, my voice cracking. I took a couple of deep breaths. "I'll do whatever it takes to give my daughter a chance." It took a while to get those words out. I wasn't sure she was still there.

Then I heard her say, "Mr. Williams, I'll call you back in a few minutes."

The truth is that money *does* mean close to nothing. It's crazy how we grab and fight after it, sometimes even destroying each other for it. If I could have shoveled out every goddamn digit I had at that moment to give her even a twenty-five percent shot, I would have done so without a second thought. I almost certainly would have robbed a bank. Or worse. I reckon many parents would do just about anything.

The road blurred on ahead of me. I really didn't know why she hung up. Was it something I said?

About thirty minutes later, my cell phone rang. The center's number showed on caller ID.

"Hello," I said.

"Mr. Williams?"

"Yes?"

"I have some information for you. I've checked, and, unfortunately, we don't have the availability for today to do the transfusion that she needs."

"Okay."

"But the hospital has decided to take your daughter's case pro bono."

I knew what pro bono meant, but in that second, that phrase kind of sat in my mind like an unopened gift from a stranger, with me clueless as to what it was.

"Huh?"

"We will take care of your daughter for free."

She waited for me to speak. It took a minute to process it.

"Mr. Williams?" she finally said.

My mind was sending the words to my tongue, but my tongue wouldn't move. I honestly don't remember much that came out of my mouth after that, though I'm certain most of it was unintelligible. I croaked a little, wept some, and somehow managed a weak, "Thanks."

"I'm so sorry we can't help today. You'll need to take her to another hospital for that, and when she is ready, we will be happy to see her for the rest of her needs."

I was extremely thankful that they decided to take Hannah on, though I knew it did not mean they could save her. In fact, I saw it for what it was—a loving gesture of care for a dying woman. To this day, I still don't know why they offered or who pulled the trigger to make it happen.

When we reached the rental house, we said emotional goodbyes to Annie and Eric, dropped off our luggage, and sped to the emergency room at Piedmont Fayette County Hospital, probably about a twenty-minute drive or so from the Senoia rental. It took me fourteen, I think. They looked at her and pretty much ushered us right on in.

Up until this point, we had visited various medical facilities—hospitals, walk-in clinics, doctors' offices, emergency rooms, holistic options—but we had rarely had to stay the night in any of them (except once for a blood transfusion in Florida). This was now changing. The stay at Piedmont was for several days, and shortly after leaving there, she would stay on and off at the Cancer Treatment Centers of America in Newnan, usually for days at a time.

From day to day, I did not know where Hannah was going to be staying and, therefore, where I was going to be staying. It was extremely difficult for me not to be with her for more than a couple hours at a time—I wanted to be there for her if she needed me. Though I think it was as much that *I* needed to spend as much time with her as I could. Deep inside, I knew there wasn't much time left.

I stood outside of the Senoia rental home after bringing Hannah back from our trip to Piedmont Fayette County Hospital. The stay had been for about a week. The home was cute, out in the country, with horses nearby and a small neighborhood within shouting distance. I just stood there looking at it.

It sunk in. Unless God reaches down and touches her on what would have to be His best day, this was where my baby would live out the rest of hers. It was a cute house, but it hurt to look at it.

I really didn't have the slightest clue how I was going to navigate the coming weeks. I was holding onto a razor-sharp thread that was cutting so deep I was bleeding out. The thought of survival beyond what seemed to be the inevitable—Hannah dying—was a foggy dream that was best kept hidden for the moment. All of our energy was dedicated to trying to save Hannah while maintaining our own sanity in the process. Could it be done? I didn't know. I only knew that I had to try to take one moment at a time. Nothing else would work. Besides, I figured that awful day was coming.

No, I was beginning to *know* that day was coming. And soon.

Meg and I would take turns wearing out the road in front of that little house, walking up and down, up and down, trying to get away from something and get *to* something else, never succeeding. I even lay down in the middle of the road a couple of times, squirming and crying, maybe hoping a big truck would come along. I think I was trying to bury myself.

As always, Hannah remained the sensible, mature one of the group. Maybe a week or two after arriving in Senoia, I found myself agitated at an email that had come in for her, sent for her to read. But she had not been on her computer or phone for weeks at this point, so it was my responsibility to relay messages to her. The email was from someone quoting scriptures and such, biblical mandates and the like, hints of judgment, even. Those who sent this obviously thought they were offering profound insights. It was painful to me and upsetting. I had a hard time deciding whether or not to even present it to her. I decided to let her be the judge of whether she wanted to hear it or not.

I stood before her and mumbled a line or two related to the email. I think Hannah sensed the irritation and even desperation in my voice. Before I could get very far, she raised her right hand and waved it slowly in front of her face without looking up.

"That stuff don't matter, Daddy," she said, still wagging her hand. "It just don't matter."

My God. I just stood there. Hannah was not judging anyone; she had simply reached a place where she recognized how unnecessary it was to worry about or even consider some of the observations and judgments people throw at each other. I felt ignorant and ashamed for even bringing it to her.

"It's okay, Daddy. It's okay." And she dropped her hand.

Hannah knew she was dying, and she had accepted that fact well before we were able to. She also knew (even more than we did) what was important and what wasn't. She realized that so much of what we bicker about is not only useless but potentially harmful. She knew that people usually meant well but that much of the *wisdom* we bestow upon each other is better left stuffed versus shared. When dying, that perspective often comes a bit easier.

Hannah was teaching her father.

Once more.

HER MAIN CONCERN

"Nothing more I would rather do."

Upon finding out that she was dying, Hannah's first words were, "I'm so sorry for you and Momma." This sentiment was not just for her parents, though; she voiced concern for others, too, over the duration of her illness, and in many different ways.

Of course, we had hope early on that God would provide a miracle and she would be healed. But as the weeks trudged on unmercifully and her condition deteriorated, we all sensed the inevitable. Hannah somehow became more and more concerned for others, rarely mentioning her own pain or fears. None of us can remember her complaining—not even once. As the end drew near, it was as if her heart felt the fear of those she was closest to. She could see the pain etched upon our weary faces and deep within our eyes and sense from our body language that we were all searching for something to hold onto.

Hannah hurt for us.

She knew that Kyle, in particular, had been devastated in the past, as two of his best friends had died by the time he was twenty years old. Josh Robertson, his best friend since they were five or six years old, the type of friend you tend to grow old with—sitting on a couple of rocking chairs somewhere with only a few teeth left, laughing-and-making-up-stories type of friends—had died in a rock climbing accident when they were both nineteen years old. This had left Kyle reeling, and Hannah had been the only person with the capacity to speak to him, to somehow meet him where he hurt back during that painful period, the only one who could help him with his grief. She somehow knew how to just be with him and shoulder some of his pain, like she had done for me during my shoulder pain agonies all of those years earlier. Within a year of Josh's death, another close friend committed suicide. Both of these deaths had obviously left an indelible impression upon Kyle.

Hannah wanted to assuage Kyle of his fears and protect him if she could. She hated that he would have to deal with death once more at such an early age, and from someone whom he loved so dearly. She expressed to Meg one day that she was concerned about him. She was worried about the impact of her death on Luke and Beka, too—just probably a little more pronounced with Kyle, under the circumstances.

Kyle, in fact, was the last one in the immediate family to see her during her illness. Upon returning from Costa Rica, maybe two to three weeks before she died, Kyle saw what we had been seeing the whole time: that a ravaging disease was mercilessly and rapidly progressing. He looked at her and his heart fell.

"Dad," he turned to me once we were far enough from her that she could not hear. "I had no idea it was this bad. You've been telling me all along that we are gonna beat this."

Tears fell from his eyes.

I looked to the floor and shook my head. "We need hope, son. If I had told you what things have really looked like, I'm not sure I could handle it myself."

Kyle was devastated. He is the sensitive type, with an air of calmness in whatever situation he finds himself in, and I believe that during those last weeks, he was a calm and loving source for Hannah, just being there and loving on her.

But she knew how tough it was for him. For all of us.

As the days were winding down in Senoia, Hannah would take hot showers to help alleviate the pain in her back. Meg and Sarah, who had returned with baby Norah to be with Hannah during her last weeks, would help her in and out of the tub as well as lend her a steadying hand.

"I'm sorry you guys have to look after me like this," Hannah said.

Meg's heart broke as she heard her firstborn lament the fact that she needed to be taken care of.

"There is nothing more I would rather do," Meg replied, and Sarah echoed the sentiment.

Now that we were back in the general area where Hannah had been raised, even more visitors began to pour in, mainly those who had known Hannah while she had lived there. To be honest, I think I sort of secluded myself, garnering up all of my energy just to *be* with Hannah. Other than Cornell and Tony, I barely called any of my former clients or friends to let them know what was going on. I guess I figured they could hear it through the grapevine, if at all. But Tony had to know. He was just too much a part of the family—had been so since the very beginning of our relationship—and was very close to all of the kids, though perhaps he felt a special bond with Hannah. She was the oldest, for one, and very mature. I think he recognized the old soul in her, and as the years passed, they became close friends. She was so grounded, an attribute he had never fully developed and yet yearned for. So I think he sort of clung to her in his own way, hoping that her maturity and her way of relating to the world might rub off on him.

Often, I would be sitting behind her, especially during those last weeks. Whatever thoughts the visitors might have had before entering her room, perhaps holding out hope for healing, would instantly vanish from their faces when they looked at her.

I did not blame anyone for looking downcast in her presence, not in the least. It was almost impossible not to, as Hannah's physical appearance screamed that she was not much longer for this world. The disease was not pretty. But things would almost always uptick as the conversation would unfold, as Hannah would bring out the best in them with her special kindness. Many of their faces would visibly change as she engaged them, as she loved them. It was painful for me to observe the faces of the people as they entered, but I could not have been more proud as Hannah smiled and asked them questions about what was going on in their lives, miraculously distracting them from the disease that was ravaging her body. And, yes, at times she would laugh.

I cannot help but smile when I think about Natalie Leak's visit in particular.

I had called Natalie in early October to let her know of Hannah's illness and that if she wanted to see her, she'd better visit soon. So in mid-October, she drove down to Senoia, aware that she would likely never see her good friend after this visit.

I greeted her outside, partly to let her know what she was about to walk into, that Hannah's appearance might be difficult to take.

We hugged. Then, nostalgia hit me.

"You know, Natalie," I said. "I don't even know how you guys met, or how you came to be so close."

"Well," she said. "I'll tell you."

A few years earlier, Natalie had walked into the Georgia State University campus library to get a little studying done between classes. Then, she saw something she had never seen before. There was a girl with an open Bible and what looked like a journal, scribbling away. Natalie paused just long enough for the girl to look up. Natalie would always remember those eyes and the smile, "both radiating a purity she didn't normally see."

Hannah invited her to sit with her, and the next thing you knew, they were fast friends. Just like that. Over the coming year or so, the friendship would deepen, and along with another friend named Kate Black, they became a somewhat inseparable trio, all graduating together and becoming nurses. Natalie and Kate remained in Atlanta while Hannah journeyed to Gainesville, Florida, to begin her nursing career in the trauma unit at UF Health Hospital.

"Thanks for sharing," I said, and then escorted her into the house and into the room where Hannah was. I could tell she was a bit anxious and, of course, heartbroken, simply not sure how to handle such an emotional, delicate encounter.

I watched Hannah light up as Natalie entered the room, and I left them alone to share this special time together.

Natalie stayed for quite a while, and soon I heard a great deal of laughter coming from both of them. This was so sweet to me.

When the door opened and Natalie stepped out, I walked her to her car.

"That was so beautiful," I said. "Listening to her laugh … "

And I cried and hugged her.

"Please tell me what happened."

She told me that when she first looked at Hannah, she could tell she was very ill—you couldn't miss that—but what settled her down immediately was Hannah's eyes, those same eyes that had so warmly greeted her years earlier.

They were still so beautiful!

Then, she shared with me the highlights of their time together.

Natalie sat down next to Hannah, and they held hands. She could feel a strength from Hannah's hands that pleasantly surprised her, given the progression of the disease. Natalie would later remember that their hands remained clasped together for the entire duration of her visit.

"How's Zoe?" Hannah had asked about Natalie's daughter, whom she had babysat several times while they were both nursing students to help Natalie out. Hannah and Zoe had become close, as well.

Then Hannah apologized for not staying in touch as much as she should have.

"You keep apologizing," Natalie said, "and I'm going to have to leave." They both broke out laughing.

They reminisced and laughed, laughed and reminisced.

Things turned a tad bit serious as Natalie, sensing that Hannah needed to be able to *go on*, said, "It's okay to go, Hannah. You don't have to fight anymore."

Hannah smiled and took a slow breath in, looking toward the door. "I'm afraid to leave them."

Natalie knew she meant she was afraid for *us*, her family, and what might become of us.

"God's got them. They'll be okay," she assured Hannah.

It seemed that something might have changed, that a slight bit of Hannah's burden may have been lifted. Natalie couldn't be sure, but it seemed so to her.

They prayed, talked some more, laughed a lot more, and hugged goodbye. Forever. At least on this earthly plane.

I could tell that Natalie left that day with the most amazing mixture of emotions: deeply sad and yet also with a heart aglow, almost joyful. Hannah's spirit had transcended the effects of the awful disease, and Natalie had been able to be with Hannah—just Hannah, and not the disease—as Hannah had been radiant, alive, and joyful herself, displaying the demeanor of a fully healthy woman. Natalie was at peace knowing that her friend would be okay and, more than likely, somehow better off than the rest of us.

It is extremely difficult to walk in and see someone you care about in such physical distress. Hannah's features were such that you knew she was near death, and most people simply did not know how to handle such a thing. I fully understand this. But Natalie somehow found the capacity to walk into Hannah's room and see her as she truly is, a beautiful spirit.

I will always be thankful that another soul was able to see past the physical and love my baby girl with joy and laughter at such a trying time. A lesson to me, and perhaps others, is to see life in the midst of what appears to be darkness.

We knew we were running short on time, and that if a miracle was to take place, it needed to happen soon. It had been well over two months since Hannah and I had received the news from Dr. Bergstrom at Beef O'Brady's on that fateful July day. We were desperate, and that desperation translated into a willingness to do whatever it took to give Hannah a chance at living. So we took the advice of Dr. David Oster, the naturopathic doctor at the Cancer Treatment Centers of America, where Hannah had spent a decent amount of time, and called Dr. Winston Cardwell of Atlanta Integrative Medicine, located in Roswell on the north side of Atlanta. His practice offered various intravenous therapies, including natural vitamin C protocols you couldn't get at normal hospitals, some of which had shown promise in helping others with cancer. What could it hurt?

This meant we would be traveling back and forth through Atlanta for however long we deemed necessary or helpful. Rush hour around Atlanta can be brutal, so we asked for whatever hours they could give us that would help avoid as much of the traffic as possible.

I could tell when we walked in for Hannah's first visit that things didn't look promising. I had gotten pretty good at reading the eyes and body language of medical professionals, and it sort of looked as if they were wondering why we were there. I didn't care. Anything that had any possibility of working was worth a shot.

Usually it would be just Hannah and me, but others tagged along at times. I remember, on one of the trips up, Kyle went with us. On the way back down to Senoia, on the south side of Atlanta, chugging along on I-285 near the I-20 exit, Hannah asked me a very unexpected question.

"Daddy, is it okay if I scream?"

My heart broke for the millionth time.

"Of course," I said.

I braced myself a little, knowing that I was obviously pretty messed up at this time and that loud or shrill noises could potentially set me off, especially with the traffic jam.

She screamed.

But that wouldn't be telling it just right. Hannah was so tired, so weary, so beaten down, that what to her was a scream to acknowledge her pain came out more like a whimper. It sounded more like someone having a nightmare, where they might be screaming in their dream, but whoever is nearby barely hears it. Kyle would later make the point, even years later as we reminisced, that Hannah simply did not have the energy to make a loud noise.

On what would end up being the last visit to Roswell, I loitered about in the hallway as the nurse was working with Hannah. Truthfully, I was bouncing off the walls, trying to work out some of my tension and fear, when one of the doctors who worked at the office came out and saw me. We hadn't ever spoken before, but because I was so desperate, I asked her a question.

"Have you ever seen anybody as far along as my daughter get healed?"

She looked at me for a few seconds. Then she stepped closer and said, "You need to lay her at the feet of Jesus. You need to let her go."

Just like that.

I looked at her without speaking. I could lay her at Jesus' feet, sure I could—because there might be healing there, right? But let her go? That I could not do.

At the same time, I found out later, Hannah was asking the nurse administering the IV to her whether or not she had ever seen anyone as far along in the dying process come in for treatments.

"No, honey," the nurse said.

"I want to keep trying as long as I can," she replied, looking toward the door and beyond, where she knew I was waiting.

"I understand, honey."

I did not tell Hannah about my conversation with the doctor, but sometimes the Universe brings two and two together. As we were heading back through Atlanta, this time on I-75, around four or so in the afternoon, the cars crawling along like they were in no hurry at all, I asked Hannah a question.

"Would you like me to pray?"

"Yes," she said.

I took a couple of deep breaths, wondering how to start.

"Dear God," Hannah broke the silence.

I looked over at her.

The next words to come out of her mouth pretty much did me in. She continued. "Please help my daddy let me go … "

I don't remember another word she said, not sure I even heard any more of it. She had her head bowed and her eyes closed, and she was going to God with all of her heart. All I remembered was that she had finally reached a point where she voiced out loud her need for me to let her go.

But as fate would have it, her prayers were as effective as my own prayers had been up until this point—useless, or so it seemed. I certainly did not, and could not, let her go. I couldn't do it yet. I just couldn't.

As we reached the final week of Hannah's life, still hoping for a miracle, my sanity was teetering on the edge. I could usually gather myself for a conversation if need be, but I'm pretty sure my faculties were lacking. "Um" came out of my mouth a lot. I was a step away from full-on zombie mode.

The doctors at the hospital had sent her home a few days earlier to die. *Palliative care*, they called it. I did not like that damned phrase at all. I refused to accept their beliefs, praying feverishly and fearfully, hoping against hope that an all-powerful and loving God might reach down and save one of His most beautiful creations *and* save Meg and me from a life of grief and sorrow. I did a lot of pacing, mainly outside of the rental house, up and down the street and all over the back yard, sometimes just from room to room. Nothing helped much. It was impossible to get my mind off the fact that my daughter was days away from dying, maybe less.

Almost all hope was beginning to bleed out. I felt a sense of panic, my mind incapable of relaxing or finding any peace. Sure, I was still negotiating with God—begging, really—and crying out to make any kind of deal. But all signs pointed downward.

God was deaf.

I was trying not to get too mad at Him yet, though, afraid He might turn His back at the last moment. But, oh, was the anger beginning to boil inside of me!

The last week or so of her life, I spent each night in the room with Hannah. The pain in my heart and the paralyzing fear grew each evening as I lay down to try to make it through the night. It was becoming unbearable. I was desperate for any help I could get during the middle of those heart-wrenching nights, especially when I simply couldn't meet all of Hannah's needs.

Several times, usually around two or three in the morning, I would arise and wake Sarah, sleeping on the den sofa with her baby, Norah, somehow securely snuggled in there with her. Sarah would softly get up—I could see the pain in her eyes through the dim lighting—and go in to Hannah, lovingly massaging her back and wherever else she asked.

While Sarah was with Hannah, I would sit out on the sofa with Norah to make sure she was safe and, to be honest, to garner up the strength to go back in when Sarah returned. All of the attributes of death were hanging in that room, and it was traumatic for me to remain in there all the time. My heart was bruising up in layers, and yet there was no way I couldn't keep doing it. I had to. I had to be in that room for her.

Sitting there with Norah, I could hear Hannah.

"I love you, Sarah. I love you. Thank you for loving me and being my friend."

And I would weep.

Once it became apparent that Hannah might not last much longer, I called Tony to fill him in on how difficult things had become. I knew Hannah would love to see him one last time, and so he hopped on a plane in St. Louis not long after the conversation and headed down to Atlanta on Saturday, October 17. As soon as it was confirmed that he was on that flight making his way to us, I walked into Hannah's bedroom and let her know he would be arriving in the late afternoon. She looked up at me when I told her and nodded slowly. Everything was starting to move in slow motion for her, all movements becoming more and more difficult.

"I heard a voice in my ear," she said. "It told me to wait." She nodded her head again. "I think this is why. Tony is supposed to be here." She seemed certain, matter-of-fact.

I knew what she probably meant, that he was supposed to be there for her last days, but I held out the slightest hope that maybe, just maybe—"Lord Jesus, let it be so!"—that he would be arriving with God's healing touch.

Hannah was the epitome of integrity. If she said something, you could bypass the damn bank and take it straight to God Himself. When she told me that she had heard a voice, I knew it was fact, simple as that. God had spoken to her. I was just hoping that it meant healing was on the way.

Tony had said, after his battle with drugs, that I was instrumental in saving his life. Was it now possible that the amazingly special relationship Tony had with our family, and with Hannah, would result in a miracle from God? That God would use him to pay it forward? I was scared to death and full of doubt, but I felt my hope edge up a little once Hannah told me she'd heard the voice.

While Luke was picking Tony up at the airport, we moved Hannah out to sit on the sofa. Little did I know it would be her last trip to the den. Her movements had slowed down during the day between the time I'd told her Tony was coming and those moments spent waiting for Luke to bring him to the house.

I heard the car doors shut outside. Tony opened the front door, and his eyes went straight to Hannah. He walked into that little rental house, dusk blanketing the countryside, an almost eerie glow seeping in through the windows. I kept looking at Tony's eyes as he looked over at her beside me on the sofa.

PART THREE

I have seen Tony cry many times, but never had I seen his eyes with the look they took on. He instantly saw she was near death. I could see that in his eyes, and it hurt me to see it.

I got to watch Hannah rise up in excitement.

One last time.

Her eyes got big as she exclaimed, "*Tony!*"

He walked over, looking only at her, as if none of the rest of us existed, and leaned over to where she sat.

They hugged. For a long time. It was heartachingly beautiful.

"I love you, Tony," Hannah said sweetly. Oh, so very sweetly.

That was Saturday night.

THE SUMMONS

"I love you."

The next day, Sunday, October 18, will always be etched in my memory as a day that blesses and haunts me at the same time. Along with Tony and Sarah, Hannah's nursing friend and mentor, Mary Oliver-Marney, was there along with her husband, Lou.

Due to a sometimes debilitating back injury, Mary was not able to work in the fall of 2015. This coincided with the latter part of Hannah's illness, which allowed her to travel and be with Hannah during some of her last three weeks. Mary was in a lot of pain, but Hannah let her know how special she was to her and that she wanted her by her side. How could Mary decline?

Especially after the memory of what Hannah had said to Mary almost two years earlier.

"I want you there with me and my family."

I sat in the living room of that quaint Senoia, Georgia, rental house, secure in knowing that Mary and Lou were keeping a tender and loving eye on Hannah. They spoke words of love over her, and I believe with all of my heart that she could feel their presence like a sweet fragrance.

By this point, it had become hard for me to be with Hannah all the time. Watching her deteriorate had taken a toll. I had slept either in bed or in the same room with her almost every night for over three months now, each time a little more difficult than the one before. I sank deeper into post-traumatic stress disorder (PTSD) without knowing it, without allowing myself to know it. I felt tremendous guilt about not being with her twenty-four seven, and yet I had to find a way to maintain my capacity to function. In snatches of time, I spoke with others about life outside of the walls of that house, a world I still held a glimmer of hope that I would experience once more with Hannah.

I sat and spoke in random snatches of time with Sarah. I'm not usually much of a stutterer, but I was still throwing out a bunch of *ums*, pretty much butchering the English language. Trying to speak to fill the aching void and yet not knowing what to say. Somehow, the distraction of speaking with Sarah helped a little, or at least it seemed to.

"Hannah wants her daddy!" I heard from the bedroom, where Hannah was propped up in a sort of laid-back sitting position on her bed, a special foam pillow helping her do so. Mary called again with a sense of urgency.

"Dad! She wants her dad!"

Hannah was not yet fully in a comatose state, but as of October 18, 2015, she seemed to have lost the ability to speak, an occasional "no" the only word that came out. *How was it that she could ask for me?*

I jumped up from the sofa and quickly walked into the room. When I arrived at the foot of her bed, I bent over to look into her eyes, the beautiful blues already glossing over. I did not want her to have to look up; she was already struggling with various movements. Yet she did ever so slightly, finding a way to meet my gaze.

That moment, those few seconds, will forever be burned into my memory. It would elicit a plethora of questions over the coming days and weeks and, yes, years. Some continue to race through my mind as I write this.

Her speech was slow, deliberate.

"I ... love ... you ... "

In many ways, this was the most complicated experience of my life. My beautiful firstborn, as sweet a human being as I have ever met, had spoken her last sentence on this Earth.

I said a thing or two back to her, several frantic "*I love yous*" mixed in.

That was it. "I love you." The three most beautiful words in the English language, when put together, and so humbly, by my daughter. Why did she call me in for *that*? Why just me? Why then? We had said this to each other a million times over the past three months.

But *this*? *This* was different, and I could not put my finger on it.

I still can't.

With Tony now in the house, it seemed that Hannah was finally beginning to let go.

He had arrived on Saturday, and by Tuesday, she was effectively comatose. This father's heart and mind—and entire being—were broken and shattered. I was not sure I would survive another night alone in the room with my dying daughter. Being in there with her, the oxygen machine droning on and the somber lights casting an eerie glow across the room, was emotionally crushing. I was actually scared I might lose my mind, glancing over at Hannah (we were in separate single beds in Senoia), with sleep coming in nightmarish snatches of time. I was beginning to beg God to either heal her or take her home. I longed for some relief. For her *and* me. I approached Tony and asked him if he would be willing to stay in there with her for a night.

With tears in his eyes, he said, "Yes. I would be honored to."

So on Tuesday night, he did so, and Luke actually joined him. I assume Hannah knew what was going on and approved. The next morning, he told me that it meant the world for him to be in there with her.

"Can you do it again tonight?" I asked.

Wednesday night, he slept in there by himself. It would be her last night.

PART THREE

Hannah had heard a voice.

"Wait," it had said.

Though I had hoped, with all of my being and against all reason, that the voice meant, "Wait—healing is on the way," it was obviously not so. The voice had simply assured her that one last person—Tony—needed to be there with us for her spirit to finally leave her body. For her, for me, and for the rest of us.

LETTING GO

"I'll be with you soon."

What I am about to share comes from the deepest place within me, a place so raw that I can only visit there in my most healed moments, those periods where I know that the world is not as I see it through my body's eyes but truly a place of eternal love, aglow with the spirits who have gone before us. It is in these moments that I am able to pluck the brutally painful memories and images from my mind and peruse their greater meaning. Here, I am forced to reckon with the razor-sharp pendulum that swings between life and death, beauty and horror, love and fear. Here, if love undergirds me enough, I allow the depth of life's deepest sorrows to run their course through my being, to sit a while, to hopefully do their part in transforming me into the man I came here to learn to be. To do so, I must not let my fears and grief dictate the direction of my life. Yet they do have their place in shaping me, hopefully for the best, *if* I can see them for what they are. It is not easy.

On October 22, 2015, Hannah slipped into a stage of dying that no parent can take without losing some grip on their sanity. Already in the throes of PTSD, I staggered around the rental cottage in Senoia, Georgia, feebly crying out to God to heal her. To say that my faith had weakened would be a grave understatement. One hundred straight days of deterioration had taken a toll. On all of us.

But Thursday, October 22, things changed. Late in the morning, *it* came. Hannah began to experience what is known as the death rattle. The fluids in her body were simply doing what they do when death is inevitable.

The sound is beyond awful to a father. Indescribable. Unwordable. The nurse from hospice warned that it can sometimes last for days, the thought of which tore through my very soul, a fearful agony and despair enveloping me. To be in the room with her was close to unbearable. Not only watching my baby die but being forced to listen to the hideous gurgling sound her body was making was like slicing open my heart and slowly pouring acid onto the wound. I wanted to beat my head against the hardest surface I could find. I wanted to run as fast and as far away as I could.

Truthfully, it was now painfully difficult for anyone, including both me and Meg, to be in the room with her. In fact, for a few moments, no one was. It was simply too difficult to take.

But this was my baby, my daughter, my Hannah, my love. I begged God to help me. Then, I walked to her room, stood in the doorway, and knew I had to be with her, no matter how brutally it ruptured my soul, no matter how damaged it left me, even if I never recovered from it.

I remembered her holding that precious space for me all those years earlier, when I was in such pain, when no one else could do so.

I walked in and sat by her bed, well aware of what the nurse had said, that this could go on for days. To say that I somehow was bestowed with a breath from Heaven, a calming presence, would be a bald-faced lie. I was devastated as I sat there. Trembling, delirious, heartbroken, without consolation.

What to do? What to do? God, I needed help.

Maybe it was an instinct from deep inside of me that snatched me out of my stupor, or perhaps it was simply desperation escaping in the only form it knew how, but I began to sing. I guarantee you, if there had been a recording of those few moments, anyone who listened would have wanted to destroy it. Never had I sounded so awful. My voice broke every rule of singing, I am sure. Except that

I have to believe it was somehow transformed, transmuted from the pitiful cryings of a wounded father into an angel's soothing voice, perhaps. What did I sing, you ask? The truth is that I was so frantic, I simply began to *remember* ... remember Hannah and me together when she was a little girl. I found myself making up the most ridiculous little ditties about Hannah and her daddy walking down memory lane through the beauty of childhood when all was innocent. I don't remember much about what words came out, mainly that we loved to be together.

Before I started to sing, I had softly taken her right hand and interlaced it with my left hand, placing them both on my left thigh. Due to her comatose state, I wondered if she could tell, if she knew we were holding hands. It had been a favorite pastime of ours over the years, simply sitting and holding hands in silence, even when she was older.

Describing the mindset I had is not easy. Maybe the words that somehow sprung from my lips in whispers between the sweet and silly verses give a clue. I would lean over and say ...

"It's okay, baby, you can let go ...

"I'll be with you soon ...

"Please, don't be afraid, all is gonna be beautiful ...

"Don't hang on anymore, baby, relax ...

"You can stop breathing now, it'll be okay ...

"I love you, I love you, I love you ... "

Think about that for a minute, if you will. Imagine you are with the one person in your life you cannot bear to lose, the very soul that reaches deep into your essence and loves as no one else can, who graces your thoughts with the realization that you will always have comfort as long as she is in your life. Someone to go to who can truly share your deepest pains and assuage your soul's deepest hurts. That very one who *knows* you, a depth of which you cannot explain to anyone else, for they could never understand. In some ways, this person embodies the incarnation of beauty and love that has enabled you to see the world you live in as a place that is worth experiencing.

PART THREE

And for those fathers who have felt their worlds change forever in that very second when they first held their baby girls in their hands and stared into their sweet faces as the tears unashamedly fell, you are with *your baby girl*. And you are now asking her to cease the very function that maintains her life. To stop breathing. *To stop being alive*. I can only ask you to picture it, for I myself can certainly not even begin to convey the depth of anguish that engulfed my soul.

But I loved her enough to finally let her know it was okay to let go. I finally knew I had to.

There is no way I can be sure, not with the state of hysteria I was in, but I'm pretty sure her last breath was within only a couple of minutes from when I first told her it was okay to let go. Her breathing slowed down, as if she were relaxing, allowing peace to flow in. It seemed that all she needed was for her daddy to tell her it was okay to go on, for me to do what she had prayed for me to do.

The moment she had found out she was dying, she had said how sorry she was "for you and Momma." Oh, how she hated to leave us! Oh, how she knew the pain we all felt! Oh, how she wanted to fight to live for us! It seemed all she needed, after all, was for me to let her know it was okay.

And that was all it took. With her beautiful, long fingers interlaced with my stubby ones, in that rental house in Senoia, Georgia, in the early afternoon of October 22, 2015, she breathed her last.

In a very real sense, Phil Williams died that day, too.

PART
FOUR

The Journey

A SIGN

"Do you see that?"

When the two men dressed in dark suits came to take my baby's body away—in subdued respectful tones, of course—the sky was cramped with gray clouds elbowing each other for space. No blue anywhere.

Meg and I stood in the front yard, numb, hollow, bewildered, angry. How could those guys just cover her up like that and take her? Just place her in the back of a fucking ambulatory van for her final ride on Earth?

Beka arrived just before they got in the van to leave. I couldn't bear to look in it. I had seen Hannah a million times over the past hundred days. Why once more, and like this? I paced behind the open door at the back of the van and shot a glance or two in her direction. Meg and Beka somehow found some scissors and leaned inside to cut off a lock of hair. It felt to me like they were violating her.

I knew my life was over, that there was no more meaning left. I stumbled around the little front yard, looking for relief. I couldn't go back in the house, the place where she had just died. But what could I find out here in the yard? Somewhere to sit down, maybe? Somewhere to hide? Somewhere to—God, somewhere to what? Nothing made any sense, and the aching in my heart and soul was unbearable. I wanted to scream so badly, but I was trying not to freak anybody out. Instead, I shook my head from side to side, as if it might be possible to shake it all out—the agony of it all, the excruciating memories of the past one hundred days, the terrible, hollowing hurt in my heart, everything.

Nothing, absolutely nothing made any sense; the realization kept hammering away at me. I wanted to get out of my body and leave the pain behind. I kept staring at the ground, the pathetically puny patches of grass struggling to cover parts of the front yard of the miserable little rental where my baby died.

I knew I had to scream. I had such anger boiling in my chest; maybe I could just lift my head and release a little bit of my venom toward the heavens. Toward *Him*. I raised my eyes upward. I took a deep breath, prepared to cry out, and then I saw it.

What the hell?

"Meg, do you see that?" I asked as she was walking back over to where I stood, the van revving its engine and preparing to back out of the gravel driveway.

"What?" she managed to say.

"Look up there." I pointed up into the sky.

She looked up but did not seem that interested. Quite frankly, I wasn't overly interested either. I'm not so sure that Jesus himself coming down from the clouds to console us would have impressed either of us much at that point. Meg came close, and we hugged once more, not really knowing what else to do. As her head lay on my shoulder, I looked back up.

How do I say this to her? I asked myself as my interest grew, ever so slightly. There was zero consolation in what I saw, but I had to admit to myself that it was at least … *unusual*.

"Do you think it might mean something?" I asked.

"I don't know."

"I've just never seen anything like that," I said. "Look at it again."

She kept her head buried into my neck and shoulder.

I kept staring at it. Maybe I was hoping. Hoping for what? A sign? What kind of sign? What could it mean? And whatever it meant, if anything, how could it matter? My baby was gone.

I was hesitant to say anything more about it, afraid if I said what I was thinking that it might sound trite, ridiculous. *But what if it did mean something?* What if it did hold out some kind of hope? How could I not make sure that she saw and understood?

"I don't know, baby, it's probably nothing. I know it's crazy. I'm probably losing my mind, but maybe Hannah is trying to tell us something. I mean, it's possible, ain't it?"

Meg pried her nose out of my neck and looked back up through her tear-filled eyes, wiping her face with the palm of her hand. Right above us, as if perched on the windowsill to Heaven—if, in fact, Heaven did exist—sat the smallest rainbow I had ever seen. There had been no rain that day, just a sky full of ornery-looking clouds, obviously there just to taunt us. So this little rainbow seemed very much out of place.

Meg peered at this rainbow with me. She didn't speak, but I knew she could see it now. It had another unique feature that I had never seen before. As the van pulled away and took Hannah's body, we both realized the rainbow was inverted.

An upside-down rainbow. The little rainbow, sitting up there in the midst of the depressing clouds, appeared to be smiling.

THE FUNERAL

"Carry me through."

We scheduled Hannah's funeral for October 26, four days after her last day on Earth, which also happened to be the anniversary of my dad's passing from prostate cancer.

Those days were not much more than a blur. They were surreal, as if I had been dropped into a horribly dismal and inescapable dream, one tinted with shadowy, gloomy blacks and grays. I don't remember any sunshine during that time; if there was any, I couldn't see or feel it. People came, people went. There was food, small talk, tears, offers of help—but no relief.

I have been to a few funerals, obviously to those of my grandparents, my dad, and a few others, and I never liked them. But walking into the church and seeing my daughter's blown-up photograph at the front almost did me in. The damned music that was playing, many of her favorite songs, got in my head and messed with me, whacking my heart out even more, taking me into my memories like a roller coaster ride from hell. I walked around the large narthex of the church, sort of like I did in that front yard of the Senoia rental as they had taken Hannah's body away, searching for somewhere to feel better and then somewhere else to hide as people started pouring in.

I'll never heal, I kept thinking. *The pain is too great and too permanent.* God, how I missed her.

Three of Hannah's favorite people in the world, Tony, Sarah, and Joelle (her roommate while living in Gainesville, Florida), all stood at the pulpit and spoke about her, how she loved her family, and how she had deeply affected each of them. It warmed my heart for a second or two. They played a slideshow on the big screen that someone was nice enough to put together. I watched from the front pew with my family and a couple of close friends. All of the pictures showed her smile, her joy, her aliveness.

I wanted out.

A long line of well-wishers and huggers queued up and did their best to convey their heartbreak to us. I said some rough stuff to a few of them, not at them, but in regards to our "loving" God, how He had basically fucked my baby and left the rest of us in shambles. There were some raised eyebrows and wide eyes, but I did not care.

One of the songs playing in the background was "Carry Me Through," the song we played in desperation over a month earlier in Florida as Hannah expressed that her spirit might be escaping through her fingers. The words seemed all sweet and hopeful. They spoke of a mountain to climb and a river to cross and of how the "heavenly hand" was gonna carry me through.

All I could think was *fuck that!*

I had bloodied myself, going up the Dave Barnes mountain. There had been no loving arms to greet me or console me, to bandage my wounds or carry me through. The river was deep and raging, its current was non-forgiving, and no life preservers were anywhere to be seen—not even a lone branch hanging over the rapids to lurch toward for safety.

No, this song was not doing it for me.

Be gentle, it said. *I'm just a man*, it said. *Kingdom love*, it said. I wanted to scream.

Gentle? More like a spiked hammer. His hand was a thousand tons as it crushed me. *Kingdom love?* I cursed under my breath.

I recognize that I am not the first person to lose a child, but I am the only *me* to lose my Hannah. How do you convey to others what that means, who she really was, how it hit me? No matter how hard

I try to come up with words and pictures to illuminate the truth of who she was or the effect it had upon me, the struggle remains. I was simply lost, lost as to knowing what to do, where to go, how to be, how to talk to people, how to love my wife, how to love my children, how to love, *period.*

Love had been ripped from me, and I was not totally sure I could find it again or if it had ever even existed at all. It felt distant, an unreality. Maybe it had just been an illusion all along, teasing me on until an opportune moment when, *bam!*, it could drop the hammer and destroy my world. Maybe. And if it had just been me, if I had not had to consider others, who knows what I would have done?

Meg, Kyle, Luke, Beka, and I wandered aimlessly around the Senoia rental house for a few more days, Meg and I clueless as to what to do next. We had no place to stay beyond the second weekend after the funeral. Thankfully, a longtime friend offered a temporary rental home in Fayetteville that could buy us a little time as we tried to figure things out. It was inexpensive, month-to-month, flexible. And then a former client of mine also offered his condo at the beach in Destin, Florida, to us if we wanted to get away. We jumped on that, not because the beach sounded appealing, per se, but because anywhere away from where Hannah had died and where the memories were most acute seemed a reasonable thing to consider. So Meg and I prepared to head down to Florida while the boys hauled our belongings over to Fayetteville. Beka was already back in her apartment in Newnan, Georgia, where she had been living before Hannah took ill.

Before we left for Florida, after starting the coffee one morning, I walked back into the bedroom and found Meg in the fetal position, an occurrence that was becoming more common. She was squirming back and forth as if on an invisible rocking chair that had fallen on its side, moaning and weeping.

"I want to die," she whimpered. It was not the first time she had said it, nor would it be the last. "I can't bear her not being here."

"I know." I nodded. "Me, too." I sat on the foot of the bed and gently touched her moving leg. "But we have to try to live. Hannah would want that for us."

"How do you know what she would want? She's gone. And I'm so afraid. Phil, I don't know where she is. How could she be in Heaven if God allowed that to happen to her?"

I understood what she meant. The deterioration of her body, the clouding over of the mind, the filling of her lungs with fluid that needed to be drained to keep her from drowning, the ungodly pain, and all the awful things that happened at the end.

She sat up, looking at me with wide, terror-stricken eyes.

"How could a loving God allow all of that and then bring her into Heaven? It doesn't make any sense. I don't know what to do!" She lay back down and resumed her rocking-chair movements.

"I just want to die."

I sighed. "Baby, if there is a Heaven, there is no way our baby is not there. You know that!"

"I don't know anything. Anything!"

I realized as I sat there that one of the things that *might* keep me going was my innate need to protect. True, I had failed with Hannah, a reality that haunted me, but now it was Meg who needed me. And I thought the kids and others might need me, too. We somehow made it through that morning and the next couple of days and then drove down to Florida, speaking very few words on the ride down.

Walks on the white sugar beaches of Destin in November were mainly quiet with very few tourists, which I was glad about, and we strolled along hand in hand, just staring at the ocean and the shore. We wore long blue jeans and jackets to fight the cool, blustery winds while walking barefoot on our long hikes up and down the beach in front of the dreary high-rise condominiums and hotels.

"Phil." Meg stopped and looked at me in the middle of one of our walks. I looked her in the eyes. "I don't want to be in the States during the holidays. I don't think I can take it. Besides, we don't really have a home here, anyway."

"What do you want to do?"

"Why don't we go down to Costa Rica before Thanksgiving and come back after the New Year? They don't do Thanksgiving, obviously, and I believe Christmas is less commercial down there. It might be good for us. Besides, it will give you a chance to spend some time there so we can make a decision as to whether it is still a possibility for us."

Georgia was unbearable at the moment, Hannah calling out to us from every grocery store, every park, every nook and cranny. I could see and feel her everywhere, every inch of Peachtree City and the surrounding area, but it was the Hannah of the last few days of her life that I saw. The skeletal face, the bulging abdomen from the cancer and fluids, the pulsating blood vessels on her head, the glazed-over eyes. I was having a very hard time shaking those images out, and I know Meg was, too. Maybe a change of scenery was not a bad idea. I had a fear that maybe it would be worse, though, and that I might even freak out, being away from all I knew—that the memories would make it hard to be away from where she grew up. But I figured we could fly right back if we needed to.

"Sure," I said. "Why not? Maybe it'll be good for us."

We looked at each other and smiled weakly. Grimaced, really. We both had our doubts that it would do a damn thing, but Meg was scared to death of being in the States for the holidays, so it was worth a go. I booked the flights that night for Meg, Kyle, and me, hoping that the other two kids could make it down for Christmas.

I have to credit Meg for starting me on my journey, or at least accidentally prompting me. For most people, I'm guessing, the fetal position is one step away from something worse, but for Meg, it was a place of deep contemplation. The yearning for death was there, for sure, but if Meg had shown me anything during our twenty-eight-plus years together, it was that she was what I would call a doer.

Her agonizing moments in full fetal position were accompanied by a pretty lucid thought or two, such as, "I need to learn more about Heaven" and "If I've been wrong about God, where am I wrong?" and "Is there really any hope for someone in as much pain as me, and if so, where can I find it?"

Like I said, Meg *does* things. Sitting around has never been her thing. For example, she never really learned how to operate a television remote control. Honest to God. But damned if she didn't master hitting those computer keys to order products from her Amazon account. Within days after Hannah's death, the books started pouring in—books on near-death experiences, on grief, on Heaven. Meg was also pretty adept at pulling up YouTube videos on what happens after death. Every time I looked, either her nose was in a book or she was fiddling with her computer or she was rocking away in full fetal. That was pretty much it.

I noticed the inflow of books right away. I picked one up and read it, or most of it, anyway. Something about a married couple, both counselors, who had lost their son years ago to cancer and had made it a life mission to interview bereaved parents from all walks of life and publish their results. The catch was that the loss had to have been at least five years in the rearview mirror in order to see how parents coped with the death of a child in the long run. Some of the children who died had been babies, some youngsters, others adults, and some even older adults, all leaving their parents in their own custom-made pits of despair.

To me, none of them had it as bad as I did. Their kid had not been Hannah. They were not in my shoes, or at least that is how it felt. And the impression I got from reading their stories was that most folks still struggled mightily, whether it was five years later or fifty. That depressed me.

The morning before heading to Florida, I noticed a book on the foot of the bed and picked it up. *Proof of Heaven* was the title. Meg looked up from her YouTube video and pulled out her earbuds.

"That one is very interesting," she said. "I'm not finished yet, but it's about a doctor who died and came back to life. It's his story about what happened while he was dead. I think you might like it."

"Do you believe him?"

"I think I do," she said, nodding. "It seems crazy, but he sounds legit to me."

"Hmmm," I murmured. I was not so sure. Stories about life after death and then life again … well, call me a skeptic. If it had not happened to me and it involved the spirit realm, then prove it. Then again, it was called *Proof of Heaven.*

Some of the information on the book jacket intrigued me as I perused it. Plus, I had been taught to follow the money. So if this very successful neurosurgeon had chosen to write a book about his near-death experience as opposed to returning to his far more lucrative career as a doctor—a book likely to be ridiculed, especially within the medical world—it at least gave me pause.

"I guess I'll check it out," I said. Meg didn't hear me, her earbuds firmly planted back in her ears, eyes glued to her computer screen, hoping for something to drag her out of her pit.

Over the next day or two, I finished the book.

DAMNED HOLIDAYS

"Let's go."

After arriving back in Fayetteville from Destin, we had less than two weeks to prepare for our trip to Costa Rica. There was much to be done. The flights were booked with a departure date of November 25, the day before Thanksgiving, and a return date of January 11. The departure date barely got us out of the country before the holiday season had been launched, a necessity at this point, with the return date somewhat arbitrary, the only requirement being that it had to be at least a few days after New Year's Day so there would be no signs of Christmas in the States upon our return. Meg had made it clear that the holidays would not exist in 2015, and I agreed.

We had already stacked four pallets to the ceiling in the Borsares' garage, which had been readied for the planned move to Costa Rica earlier that year. Terry and Linda had been kind enough to allow us to keep them there indefinitely until we could figure things out after Hannah's passing. Whatever else that was not tied up in the pallets had been hauled around with us during Hannah's illness, some of which we didn't want or need to take on our six-plus-week trip, including winter clothes, certain equipment, a 12-gauge shotgun my dad had owned, along with a few other miscellaneous articles.

I'm not sure if autumn is usually more overcast than summer, but it sure seemed that way. To top it off, there was very little natural light seeping into the rental house in Fayetteville, so that didn't help matters. All in all, everything was dreary. We couldn't wait to get out of the country, but we were not excited about what was waiting for us, either.

Damn, those days were dark and heavy. We spent most of the time packing and wondering what the hell could possibly matter in our lives anymore. Losing my daughter had numbed my capacity to be who I wanted to be for others, or at least it seemed so to me. Though I needed my other kids around me, for example, it would be a while before I could love them in a way that they probably felt I should. It's a strange thing, really. When a child dies, it is hard not to place them up on a pedestal—for a while, anyway. The mind does that, and I don't doubt the other kids might have felt the effects of that, too. But damn if I don't love them all with all my heart!

Luke drove Meg, Kyle, and me to the airport before the sun had a chance to rise on Wednesday, the 25th. Our flight time was 9:55 a.m., and we dutifully followed the airline's orders to be there at least three hours early. Hartsfield-Jackson Atlanta International Airport is larger than many cities, with enough passengers and employees on any given day to propel it into one of the top fifty populated cities in the country. Hence, you either get there early or you might not make it out. And getting stuck there was not high on our priority list.

Many times over the prior month, and really for weeks before that, my mind had played around with the thought of escaping, whatever that meant. No, I was not contemplating, nor had I ever contemplated suicide, but living was now painful, and the thought of something else—anything else—was appealing. I wanted out so very badly. Out of what, I couldn't really say, but my skin, or maybe my body, seemed to be restricting me. *Me*, the part inside that was struggling to breathe, to feel okay, was locked down, trapped. I really couldn't see a light of any sort, the proverbial tunnel feeling more like a cold, dark mausoleum. I instinctively felt, metaphorically speaking, that leaving the confines of the United States and crossing over the imaginary border might be my only hope of escape for the time being.

We checked in with Delta, boarded the plane, and, before noon, were somewhere out over the Gulf of Mexico, with the USA fading into the distance behind us.

Twelve hours later, after clearing customs and taking the long bus ride down to the Caribbean, we were dragging our luggage through the potholed *calles* (streets) of Puerto Viejo, searching for the hostel I had booked online for our first night. It took awhile; no one seemed to have heard of it. Eventually, we found it and slept fitfully for a few hours before the sun nudged us up around 5:30 or so and spit us back out into the calles of Puerto.

We had no idea what our next step would be, where to stay, what to do, or who to contact, if anybody. It sure as hell did not feel like a vacation, though the warm morning breeze and the pastel blue sky blended in nicely with the background music of soft waves breaking over the nearby corals. Enticing to most people, maybe, but not so much for me at the moment. Nothing really was.

We stood on one of the streets on the backside of Puerto Viejo and looked both ways. I looked at Meg and then at Kyle. We had pull-alongs by our side, backpacks on our backs, and no idea whether to go left or right or straight ahead. We eventually trudged forward and, after stumbling around for a couple blocks, noticed a sign that said *Hotel Guarana*, which rang a bell for Meg and me. We had stayed there years earlier while visiting. We checked in, and it became home for almost a week.

A few days later, we settled into a cabin in the jungle, about two miles from the beach, that was owned by some friends of ours who were not arriving in Costa Rica until New Year's Eve, so we had the place to ourselves for the month of December. We had no idea what to do other than sit around, staring at the jungle and listening to the howler monkeys that seemed to be spread out in patches here and there.

There was one other activity that interested us, though. And it was mainly Meg who insisted on it. Every day, we would hop into a barely functioning 1990 Toyota 4Runner, one she had purchased back in June and a friend had kept for us while we were in the States, and we would wobble across maybe a million and a half rocks strewn about the road known as Ole Caribe and make our way down to Punta Uva Beach. I really had no interest in doing anything but sitting in a hammock and staring at the jungle, but she would say, "Let's go," and off we would go. What else were we going to do with our time? The two-mile drive took about twelve minutes.

To picture Punta Uva Beach, think Robinson Crusoe with a bigger beach, palm trees swaying and lurching out over the waves in some places, especially at high tide, and corals sneaking up onto the golden sand as if they are trying to surprise you. A large stone outcropping like a miniature mountain sort of bookends the eastern end of *la playa,* with the beach crescenting around like a jagged quarter moon for a few hundred meters in the other direction. True, it was December, but this was the tropics, and it felt like late spring to us. The gentle breeze bid us welcome, coaxing us to sit, lie, or meander for a bit while teaming up with the sun and melodic waves to, if possible, ease our pains a little. Almost suggesting that it understood our grief.

We had no conception at that time that nature could care, that this living thing called Earth could actually speak to our ruptured hearts and assist in our healing journey if, in fact, we were on one. I would walk alone toward the western end of the crescent, find myself immersed in a jungly jutting point, and then continue onto a much smaller crescent beach with amazing corals, even more seclusion, and then on again to another one. All the while wondering if it would ever be possible to find any relief from the constant hurt oozing through the massive hole in my chest. Of course, sometimes Meg would tag along, but truthfully, I think she wanted to go inward as much as possible and let the soft rays of the Costa Rican sun bathe her in warmth while simply lying there.

Talking was at a minimum during our visits to the beach, each of us choosing instead to try to breathe and to breathe *in* what nature was giving us. Somehow, the combination of blue skies, warm sunshine, gentle breezes, swaying palm trees, azure waters, corals, and, of course, toes in the sand allowed for the slightest touch of what I will call *love* to embrace our wounded hearts, if only for a moment.

"Are you ready to leave?" one of us would ask the other.

"Not yet," was the standard response. "Maybe in a few."

I'm not suggesting that I thought we were being touched by the divine; it was a bit more subtle than that. It's just that we both started looking forward to *being* at the beach. And looking forward to *anything* was a start, an improvement, even if we didn't see it as such yet. Each trip to the beach obviously included a return to the jungle, as well, where we found ourselves bathed in quiet, or at least away from the noises of any type of civilization.

Though many of those first days in the Puerto Viejo area were, and are, a blur, we somehow put our minds together and pulled a pretty big trigger, one destined to greatly impact our lives.

We bought a home.

A NEW HOME

"Why did we buy this?"

Perhaps I should rephrase that.

What we had done was go and look at a piece of property wedged back in the jungle about half a mile from the beach, one that was part of a little community known as Cocles. When we pulled up to it, Meg and I looked at each other with wide eyes.

"You go first," I think we both said. "After you!"

The jungle can be a beautiful place, but when it has been disrupted and is fighting to renew itself, it can take on a rough appearance. The undergrowth and overgrowth were foreboding. I suspect most folks stayed in their cars when passing by this piece of property.

If you squinted your eyes from the road, you could see what resembled a small cabin sticking its neck up over the vegetation, as if it were trying to escape, stilted up almost ten feet above the ground. It looked awful, with no upkeep in quite a while. When you leave stuff to the elements in the jungle, with a thick cloud of humidity that clamps onto everything it can find, let's just say the stuff can change from its original appearance. What had been a pretty wooden structure, or so we were told, was now a graying, greening mess. A "Keep Out" sign was not necessary.

The fact that a snake had not yet slithered by as we tiptoed to the house told me they must have been hiding upstairs. I looked around for a machete. No luck. We pushed the door open and slowly stumbled around the 450-square-foot cabin; dust and dirt and muck and who the hell knows what else was everywhere. It looked like the last inhabitants had left in a hurry, lots of stuff lying around. I was beginning to think they might have been pretty smart.

But once we had given it a good look, taking into account the cost of cleaning off the land and sanding and refinishing the cabin, we made an offer on it. By the time we made our January 11 flight back to Atlanta, we were the proud owners of an acre of Costa Rican jungle with what presently looked like a haunted house on stilts standing in the middle of it.

Why did we buy this property so quickly? Besides our obvious brain damage? Well, not only was it a great price due to the shape it was in, but we felt we had found an element of healing, so far, in this magical area and simply decided we needed to stay for a while. It was inexpensive and ripe for a quick turnaround once cleaned up, so we basically said, *what the hell?* We even started a building project, adding two bedrooms and a bathroom below the stilted structure (my mother was coming to live with us), expanding the space to a whopping 900 square feet or so.

A few days later, we boarded our flight back to the States.

It felt odd, flying back to Atlanta, Meg and I both squirming in our seats a little. We didn't really talk about it, unsure what to say. Our hearts remained shattered, every day an attempt to just breathe a little more. One day at a time. But now, we were heading back to where it had all happened.

We arrived late at night and took the shuttle to a hotel near the airport and crashed. Someone had been nice enough to drop off our car for us, so we hopped in the next morning and headed down toward Fayetteville to go clear out the rental house we had leased after Hannah's passing. We pulled onto I-85 and headed south, not many words spoken.

I'm not sure how it happened or who went first or if we both lost it at the same time, but within a couple minutes of navigating I-85 South, both Meg and I began to weep. We both felt an overwhelming grief, pressing down hard and thick upon us by the cold, dreary winter that hovered over Atlanta. This is where we had raised her. This is where we had laughed and loved. This is where, on a hot, steamy day almost six months earlier, Hannah and I had learned that she was dying. This is where I had held her hand for the last time. This is where everything that had ever mattered seemed to have disappeared forever. This is where any semblance of the Phil Williams of the past had died. I'm sure it was the same for Meg.

In a sense, there was nothing special about it, just a couple of folks driving down a familiar road. But that's the thing, isn't it? There was no longer *anything* familiar, at least not the type of familiar that grounds you, that keeps you steady. That had now been destroyed. The sorrow that burrowed into our hearts on that old, familiar road was deep and brutal. I remember Meg and me looking at each other between the moans and wails and just continuing on, tears streaming down, our faces echoing each others' pain, our hearts freshly broken open again. We managed to calm down by the time we reached Fayetteville.

It took a few days to get everything loaded up in the house, and then at some point, I'm not sure when, I decided to take a ride by myself, one that Meg did not want to go on. For some reason, and one that is difficult to explain, I choose to revisit things from my past, to get face-to-face with my demons. I pointed the nose of the car toward Senoia, back to where I had last seen her alive. I was scared, to be honest. But something was drawing me back to that little house where I had last held her hand as she left her body.

I wasn't sure if my heart would make it all the way there, but I figured I could turn around or head in another direction at any time. I passed through Senoia and made all the requisite turns on the south side of town, at last taking the final left turn that put me on the road where the rental house sat. As it approached, my heart thumped rapidly and deeply within my chest, and I could barely breathe. I pushed the gas pedal down harder and sped on by, barely casting a slight glance toward the house.

What the hell had I been thinking?

I raced on down the road, eventually got my breath under control, and headed back a different way.

The next day, we were on our way back to Costa Rica.

A STRANGER

"He sighed..."

When we arrived back in Puerto Viejo in mid-January, the building project was in full swing, hopefully to be completed by Easter. The builder had been able to get a super quick jump on it because the footprint for the house was already in place. The current structure was on stilts, remember? And all we were doing in the first phase was adding stuff below what was already there. I'm not sure if they even had to pull any permits or not. In the meantime, I decided to go to what I will call a global economic-type conference in Acapulco, Mexico, in late February and then pick my mom up in San Jose, the capital city of Costa Rica, upon returning.

It had been approximately four months since Hannah had passed when I attended the conference, held in a hotel on the beach in Acapulco. To be honest, I had been scared to go there by myself, my grief still so fresh, at times suffocating. So far, I had always had Meg to hold onto when the fear and grief would manifest, so I wasn't sure how I would handle being alone. I had been encouraged to go, though, by both Meg and my mom.

During the conference, I was sitting in the back row, a favorite location of mine for just about any type of meeting (it also meant I could get out quickly!). We were actually in the middle of a prolonged break when I realized I was sitting next to one of the many speakers, a gentleman who exceeded me in years by maybe a decade, it appeared. We struck up a conversation.

To tell you the truth, I'm not sure what led into it, but somehow we reached a place where I felt the need to share the fact that I was a grieving dad, that my daughter had just recently died. What occurred next, I will always remember.

Something happened to his eyes. They changed. They conveyed compassion. I don't think this is something easily faked, and if it were, I believe most could tell. He sighed in a non-conjured-up way, feeling the pain of my soul. His eyes watered over.

I turned my head to look straight ahead, not that I was uncomfortable, but it seemed like the thing to do. As I did so, he reached his hand over and placed it on my shoulder. I'm not sure how long we sat there, both staring toward the front of the meeting room, neither of us speaking, both with tears flowing, his hand resting upon my shoulder, contracting at times. The human touch was incredibly real. I *felt* the compassion, possibly as much as I had from anyone else up until that point in time, and maybe since. He somehow *absorbed*, or shared, if you like, a little of my immense pain. My heart, my soul, my spirit were joined together for a moment in time with those of another who cared.

The gentleman didn't speak. But he loved. In that moment, I realized that even in the depths of my pain, I was able to witness a truth: as human beings, *this* is what we need from each other. A willingness to be vulnerable, to break down barriers, to allow ourselves to meld into the other person's world, even when the pain seems too intense. This man, this stranger, touched me. And though he may not have known it, he became part of my healing journey.

I returned to Costa Rica from Acapulco and picked my mother up at the airport before driving us both down to Puerto Viejo. Meg had found a rental home in Playa Chiquita, a couple of miles down the road from Cocles, a cute little place that worked great for the next month while waiting for the construction to be completed on our property.

Before sunrise the next morning, with Meg and me in one bedroom and my mom in the other, we were awakened by a shrill blast of noise. Evidently, the house we were staying in was snuggled up under the favorite hangout spot of a family of howler monkeys. It sounded like they were sitting on our window sills with megaphones in hand. When they open up their fairly small mouths, it sounds almost as powerful as a foghorn on an ocean freighter. *BOOM!* Meg and I lay there giggling, thinking about my mom in the next room. Welcome to the jungle, Marilyn! Mom actually thought it was pretty cool.

Maybe that is because she had been sleeping without her hearing aids.

As the days ticked off, we wondered if the construction would be finished in time. If not, we didn't know where we would be staying. It turned out that it was. Barely. Or at least enough for Meg, Mom, and me to join Kyle and Luke, who had more or less been camping out on the property since arriving to celebrate Christmas with us. So here we were, settling into a new way of life, whittling the days away as we struggled with our grief.

My mom likes things organized, especially in the spaces where she spends most of her time. When we moved into our new home, she quickly arranged her clothes, her books, and her photos—including one of Hannah, which she stood up with a couple of others on her bookshelf.

That probably lasted a few minutes or so because the first time I walked in there and saw it, I flipped it over. Face down.

I could not look at her yet. I didn't have to say anything to Mom. She understood.

At this point, most days were very difficult. I spent time reading different types of books and watching videos on healing while soaking up the beaches, breathing in the jungle, and trying to survive long enough to grab hold of something that might help. We had moments of hope, but at first, they were few and far between. We kept moving forward, or hoped that was the direction we were headed.

To be clear, if there is a manual on how to heal from losing a child, I haven't heard of it. If there was and it worked, the author would be a billionaire. Bereaved parents are some of the most desperate people on the planet. We will do almost anything to find a way to lessen the pain in our hearts and the torment in our minds. It can be difficult to even get out of bed for some.

Fortunately for me, I had a wife who was aggressive at going after what she wanted. And she wanted to heal, or at least find some relief. She was a tremendous influence and help for me in those early days, encouraging me to read books and look at videos. Nonetheless, we both remained somewhat paralyzed.

We were, in a sense, seeking healing together but, more so, on our own personal journeys. That's just the way it works. So I had to be proactive, take my own chances, work at figuring out my own stuff. And I was scared. Though the jungle and beach were wonderful, I was restless. So I began to plan trips and look at options that might be off the beaten path from my past routines and former belief system.

It should be noted that neither Meg nor I were gainfully employed at this point. We still had enough left over from my days working as an NFL agent to buy us a little time to hopefully figure out our next step. Grieving can be a full-time job in itself, and both of us were going at it pretty hard. Options for income would perhaps come later.

As the early months of 2016 slipped by, I realized that someone I was missing very badly at the time was my youngest child, Beka. She was still in nursing school at Georgia State University in Atlanta, following in the footsteps of her big sister. I managed to convince her to take a rather short vacation and arranged to fly her down to Fort Lauderdale, Florida, and meet me for four days in June.

There was no real plan—we were just winging it—but we had a blast, or at least I did. I rented a car, and we drove down to the Keys, the southernmost tip of Florida, spending special time together in Key West and a couple of other spots along the way. I cried a lot. I would often wonder how it felt for her to see her dad crying so much and talking about her older sister. Of course, it was painful for her, too. She loved Hannah very much, obviously. But sometimes, I would just ramble on incoherently about how much I missed Hannah. That said, I loved being with Beka more than words can say. When I dropped her off at the airport on the final morning, my heart ached.

I probably would have stayed there with her the rest of the summer if she had been able to do so. Just being with her was medicine to my soul. I couldn't help but smile at the mystery of life, at how, one second, a stranger can meet you in that secret place and, another, someone you love so deeply can do the same. Perhaps without either of them even knowing it.

By the time spring was sort of bleeding into summer, I was doing okay, progressing a little, and probably a lot better than I would have imagined I would be back in October. I was managing my pain for the most part, struggling at night but having some decent moments during the day. The journey was young, raw, confusing, and I had no idea if there was any chance at real life, whatever that was. I know people would see me laugh and even crack jokes, thinking Phil must be doing all right. But then I would go home and curl up into a ball, sometimes wanting to just fall asleep for good.

But, like I said, there were some good moments, too. We were trying to move along, have a life, do things that we felt were worthwhile. We started planting fruit trees on our little *finca*, getting involved in the community, making a few friends. We also began to develop our property here and there, adding a kitchen downstairs and a screened-in living area. Most of the wood for that project came from a tree in our yard, so that was cool.

Our house was an indoor/outdoor type of deal. Mainly outdoor. Before long, we had become quite amicable to sharing our living space with an array of creatures, including geckos, lizards, various types of ants, and more. You just kind of get used to them, almost befriending some of them. If you allow yourself, you could even have a little fun with it. For example, there's a place up in the corner of the bathroom that you can see from the bedroom (no ceilings between rooms, if you can picture that), so I would sometimes lie on the bed and watch three or four geckos triangulate around a buzzing fly or two, scheming and waiting, though mainly waiting—damn, those little fellows are patient!—and then, *zoom!*, striking out and nabbing a quick lunch. The wild kingdom from the comfort of bed. It's amazing how the geckos never seem to fall to the ground, even while Supermanning around after the flies. They also make this crazy sound like they're mimicking Curly from the old *Three Stooges* show. "*Nyuk, nyuk, nyuk.*" Laughing at each other, I think. Or perhaps at me.

One day, Meg said she thought we should get some marital counseling. Just like that. She was probably right—certainly after that episode in North Georgia—so I said okay, and for a few weeks, we met with a woman whom we would both eventually become good friends with, Eva Dalak, who has quite a background. She is Palestinian and was raised in Israel by Muslim parents while attending a Christian school. Talk about confusing! Perfect for counseling us, I thought.

So over the summer, while we were adding on to our house, planting fruit trees, making friends (mainly Meg), and starting to plan a trip or two, we also did a bit of therapy, something we'd never done before. Meg remembers me getting mad a few times. *Hmm.* That would probably be right. That did happen a few times after Hannah passed. In some ways, I was very mellow—passive, almost. But in others, there was a short fuse just waiting to be lit.

It got lit one day on the beach.

I had purchased a couple of young Rottweilers, Neo and Tank, who Meg nicknamed the Two Bumble-heads, and I fell in love with them both. I particularly loved Tank. One day, I was walking the lovable young brute on the beach in Cocles and passed by a spot where there were three men and two dogs, one of which was a German Shepherd. Well, Tank and I were just meandering by, minding our own business, when those dogs decided to attack. Once the German Shepherd had jumped on top of Tank's back in the shallow water of the Caribbean and started gnawing, I lost it. Tank was just a puppy, though a decent-sized one at that. Rage came over me, and I jumped on the German Shepherd's back and started kicking and punching and screaming at the top of my lungs, something like "Get your motherfucking dog off of my dog," up into the sky.

I was loud and delirious. I think the clouds began to darken. The dog slipped off of Tank and spun around and looked at me like it had never seen or heard anything like me. *What the hell is in this human?*

It was probably only a few seconds of activity, maybe five to ten, but I was out of control. By the time I looked up, two of the men were gone. *How did that happen so quickly?* I mean, who wants to be around a madman? I knew that if I hung around, I might do something I would regret. Maybe already had. I stared with anger for a minute at the one person remaining and then turned and left, Tank seemingly oblivious to everything, bopping along as if nothing had happened. The adrenaline stayed in me for a while. I eventually began to calm down and soon realized that something deep inside of me was very off. I was fucked up something awful. I wondered if I would ever make it out of the emotional mess I was in.

Tank and I passed by the same spot on the beach on the way back, maybe thirty minutes later. The fellow had the dog secure this time. I waved. Damn, I was trying.

So yeah, at counseling, I would probably scowl at Eva occasionally. Maybe not quite as ferociously as I did at the owners of those dogs, but still.

LAND OF ENCHANTMENT

"I'm trying to find me."

As summer progressed, Meg had begun teaching a Zumba Pilates combo class at CariBeans, a really cool rustic chocolate and coffee place. The owners are pretty cool, too. It was great for her on many levels, forcing her to commit to something that would get her involved in the community, help her make new friends, get in some exercise, have fun, and more. I eventually joined in, at times even teaching a Zumba song or two each class to give Meg a break. Meg laughed when she would hear me say that I was "teaching." She would lean in and correct me. "*Leading*," she would say. "Phil is *leading* a song or two."

We also began to be a part of a community event called Grateful Fridays, where anyone could come, bring a little food to share if they could, and basically just hang out. There would also be things to barter or give away, including books, clothes, bananas, et cetera. At least it was a good time to meet other people. My mom really enjoyed it. This went on for maybe a year.

Meg alerted me to an author and speaker named Gregg Braden, an interesting man someone in Puerto Viejo had recommended she check out. I listened to a podcast or two and then got a book, as well. He seemed to be a very knowledgeable guy with a science background and a way of seeing the world that was different from what I was used to. He began to open my mind to the world of quantum physics, among other things—an aspect of science that, from my perspective, gives a glimpse into the spirit realm.

He enamored me enough that I decided to do a little research and discovered he was going to be speaking at a grief conference in Santa Fe, New Mexico, in a few weeks' time. I have always loved the enchanted lands of New Mexico; plus, I was definitely grieving. Before you knew it, Meg and I had purchased event tickets and roundtrip airfare. The Transformation and Healing Conference hosted by Southwestern College was beautiful to both Meg and me for several reasons. We met so many sweet and beautiful and interesting people, many of whom were as loving as anyone we had ever met and with different spiritual perspectives than we had been used to in our previous lives. Of course, this was fast becoming a norm, a lot of our new friends on the Caribbean coast of Costa Rica marching to the beat of a different drum than we were used to in the past, as well.

Things were getting interesting. Our belief systems had been shelved, allowing for open minds and open hearts, eschewing the authoritative mandates of the past and simply exploring. It was refreshing. We were finding that our preconceived notions from our prior lives might need some adjusting, or at least that we were open to that possibility.

I cried a lot in Santa Fe, too. I mean, it *was* a grief conference. It's funny, though—while everyone else at the conference was earning credits for their respective careers, Meg and I were there to find healing. But you could tell it went deeper than that. In a sense, we were all looking for healing.

One interesting thing we noticed while in New Mexico was that we didn't sense Hannah's presence quite as much. Neither of us had been in Santa Fe with her in the past, and wherever you have been with someone you have lost, you can kind of feel it in the air. It's not that we weren't thinking about her all the time; it just felt a little different. And that was good.

We had barely made it back to Costa Rica before I made the decision to return to New Mexico, this time with the intent to head to Taos, a quirky, artsy, spiritual kind of place where many of the conference attendees lived. The only caveat for going was to make sure that Ted Wiard, one of the speakers at the grief conference, could spend a little time with me. I emailed him to ask that question, and he responded quickly, blessing my possible visit with open arms, even offering to host me in his home for a couple of days. I needed to meet with this man.

Ted was a native of the Taos area, and it is where he married his high school sweetheart, Leslie, who gave him two daughters, Amy and Keri. He was living the dream. But, in 1989, his brother died in a shipwreck in Alaska, then Leslie died after a two-year battle with cancer, and finally, both daughters died along with Ted's mother-in-law in an automobile accident. The dream had officially become a nightmare.

He fled Taos and found himself sitting on a beach in Hawaii, not soaking in the rays like the rest of the people there but contemplating swimming past the waves and never coming back. "If this agony is what the rest of my life is going to be, then I need to be done with my life," he said, recalling his thoughts on Maui beach. "Every day, I contemplated if I should die. All I wanted to do was kill myself."

Thankfully, his story did not end there, as he did end up finding healing and joy, which nurtured a growing compassion within his soul that, over time, led him to try to impart such gifts to others.

So I booked my flight and headed back to New Mexico only a couple of weeks or so after leaving the grief conference. The Land of Enchantment was calling me.

After spending my first night in Santa Fe on August 21, 2016, I arose early, grabbed a coffee to go, and headed up toward Taos. It felt a bit strange traveling without Meg, as so much of our time had been spent seeking healing together, but I was beginning to feel that if I was to truly find healing, it would be *my* journey and *my* choices. The desert and reddish cliff formations of Northern New Mexico spoke to my spirit as I drove, the raw and rough beauty somehow calming me. It felt right, my childhood fascination with the western mountains coaxing me along State Road 76.

It surprised me that there were a few extremely fertile areas along the route. I even took a few photos to show Meg that the desert had its oases here and there; a picture of life and beauty in the midst of what was known as desert—to offer us hope that we, too, might find life in our own personal deserts. I began to climb a small mountain, the road essing back and forth, forcing me to keep a slower pace than I wanted.

Shortly thereafter, I noticed the first sunflower.

Sunflowers were one of Hannah's things. For us, they represented her in a fashion. Whenever we came across them, whether in photos or in real life, they tended to grab our attention and elicit a strong emotion. I was very pleasantly surprised to see Northern New Mexico, and Taos County in particular, inundated with a stunning array of the most gorgeous sunflowers I had ever seen. I stopped a time or two to take photos. It felt like Hannah was paving the way for me, directing me along on this leg of my journey. In fact, the sunflowers pretty much ushered me all the way into Taos. By the time I arrived at Ted Wiard's home, which is also set up to facilitate the Golden Willow retreats that he offers, I was no longer surprised to find his lovely domicile surrounded by, and bathed in, a sea of beautiful sunflowers swaying in the breeze. I sensed that Hannah was saying hello. *Welcome, Daddy! This is where you need to be right now ...*

Upon settling in at Golden Willow Retreat, his healing center, and after receiving a tour of the facilities, I mentioned to Ted that I had an urge to explore as much as possible. This interest included a desire to experience the Great Outdoors and the mystical beauty of Northern New Mexico in addition to my obvious need to dive into my inner world, where I was hoping that Ted and some of his affiliates might be able to prove themselves worthy guides on my healing journey.

I sat in the den area by myself for a bit and noticed a book that boasted of the top fifty or so hikes within a few miles of Taos. I picked it up, perused the cover, and took a deep breath. The truth is that I had been dreaming for months about a particular scene, a vision I could not shake from my mind, almost as if a painting had been placed in my soul. The scene was one of a mountain lake, not so big, but perched up high in the mountains with clear pristine waters and hugged on a couple of sides by mountain ridges merging with a blue sky above, the only sounds being those of rushing waters, maybe, with the call of native birds echoing between the mountain walls. Meg and I had visited such a spot in Colorado many years earlier, and it had left a lasting impression.

I thought about that visual as I opened the book—not expecting anything, of course, just dreaming a little. I kid you not; the first page I came to in the book, a random choice near the middle, revealed a photo of a stunningly beautiful lake with mountain peaks on two sides. My mouth hung open. But that's not all; as my heart picked up speed in my chest, I read the name of the hike, or rather the name of the lake: *Williams Lake*. I began to cry softly, certain that I had been directed to this page, in this book, in this home, in this place called Taos, in this, my journey of healing. I immediately decided to make the trip the next day, weather permitting.

Taos is already approximately seven thousand feet above sea level, and Taos Ski Valley, the village where the trailhead to *my* lake was located, was another couple thousand-plus feet up into the sky. In fact, the hiking book reported it to be the highest municipality in the USA. That meant I would begin my hike over nine thousand feet above what my body was used to, as I currently lived maybe twenty feet above sea level, just a hop, skip, and a jump from the ocean itself. This information did not matter to me at first.

I drove up to the trailhead from Ted's home early the next morning, maybe a twenty-five-minute jaunt, and anxiously began the hike, enchanted with the beauty and peace of the forest on the initial leg of the three-mile trek. I barely made it a few hundred feet before this old athlete, who could jog the Caribbean beaches of Costa Rica at a decent clip, had to start slowing down to catch his breath. It wasn't even very steep at this point, yet I think a grandma or two might have passed me, giving me that knowing smile. I decided I would take it easy, make sure I could finish what was shaping up to be a very important journey for me. Eventually, I figured out a pace I could work with, and a couple of hours later, Williams Lake opened up in front of me.

I ended up spending maybe three hours there, a long time for this hurry-up-and-get-there and, once-conquered, get-back type of guy. I breathed it in from every angle I could, thinking that maybe it was speaking to my soul with whispers of healing, or at least that's what I was hoping for. I climbed the mountainside at the back of the lake, perhaps another hundred feet up or so, intent on finding the mouth of the waterfall that fed the lake, certain that I needed to spend a moment or two there. Its melodic humming echoed throughout the area.

Once I made it to the source, I sat down and opened my backpack to withdraw a pen and journal-sized notebook. I closed my eyes for a few moments and allowed myself to be absorbed by the whoosh of the water rushing by and cascading downward, which synced in with the even more painfully beautiful memories of Hannah. Together, they led me to a deep place.

I forced myself to wait, to try to accept whatever emotions and thoughts came up, to feel whatever the universe might want to share with me. After a short period of time, a torrent of emotion began to flood into my being and erupted into a deep, guttural moan, the sobs of a truly wounded soul. I wailed as I sat on a large boulder lodged into the side of the cliff next to the thunderous roar of the waterfall, oblivious to how it might have sounded below where a few hikers hung out around the lake, hundreds of feet away. I took the deepest pain and screamed it out into the New Mexico sky, nowhere else for it to go. It had been almost exactly ten months since Hannah had passed away, and I had yet to scream. Until Williams Lake. That day, it was a lake of tears.

After a few minutes of screaming and shouting and shedding my own waterfall, I began to write and speak to my baby girl.

To be honest, I'm trying to find me. I seek TRUTH, LIGHT, and LIVING WATER, and so much more. I want to see my baby so very badly … I miss you, Hannah. As you know, my heart has been broken. I believe you want it healed. I do, too.

I long to feel you joyous in your "new" real world, to have a taste myself, to know that all is okay. I ask you, Hannah, to implore on my behalf with God to help your daddy let go of all that encumbers me, to set me free from my "mind," to free me up to KNOW that you are free, that He is love, and how to love and not fear. And how to allow my eternal purpose while "here" to blossom.

I don't like parts of me … but I want to love me nonetheless. I need to love me, and then I can love others.

I will love you forever, my first, my teacher (you taught me love just by being you), my baby. You prayed for me to let you go. Though I felt sure it was to let you pass to the next life, I also feel that you want or need me to "let you go" in the form of the tremendous pain in my heart, which in some ways tethers me to you (or is it you to me? or both?). I desire to love you the way that is best. I ask you and whoever else can to help me do so."

I finished writing, cried a bit more, and, when I felt I had done enough, exhausted, I made my way back down. Upon returning down to the lakeside, I found that you could almost hear people whispering while up near the waterfall, hundreds of feet away, as if it were a megaphone. It seemed like an acoustic masterpiece. I guess the hikers were meant to hear the inner pains flowing out of a fellow sojourner on that day.

SUNFLOWERS

"Pay attention."

The belief systems we have each constructed over our lifetimes, willingly or not, deeply affect the world we see and, in turn, how able we are to listen to and explore the stories of others. At this point in my journey in search of healing and in search of truth, I began to delve more so into certain realms that in my prior life might have been considered off-limits, perhaps even taboo, or worse.

I was determined to discover the basis of this story, this form of authoritative admonishment, that had previously been securely lodged within my mind and yet was now oozing out due to the pain of losing Hannah, of losing my foundation. If there was a God that truly loved me, how could He not understand my pain, my grief, my need to search under every stone, to push the boundaries? I felt certain that I would find Him, if he was to be found, if only I would open myself up to more. The former me scolded me for even trying, and yet I now heard that voice as an obstacle to be ignored, suffocating dust rising up from the ashes of a dead man. I trusted from deep inside of me that if there was a God and if this God was Love, exploring beyond my little world of former beliefs was not only acceptable but encouraged. I reminded myself that I was all in and that God would somehow meet me if I fought to find Him. And so I journeyed onward, ready to explore new worlds.

Spending time with Ted will always hold a special place in my heart, whether he knows it or not. He took the time to walk with me, eat with me, and give me insights on how to continue dealing with my grief, though mainly he just sat with me and walked beside me. Ted knows the deepest pain of loss, which gives him a special platform from which to reach out and truly love others. He saw and felt my pain and, in a sense, was willing to relive his own if it meant helping a fellow grieving father find his footing. He was *love* to me. And my time with him represented a perfect time and place to initiate myself into the realm of the mystical and discover those areas that I had shunned in the past.

The day after my Williams Lake hike, I drove over to meet with Jim Lengerich, a gentleman on Ted's staff, with the specific intent to do what is known as a drum journey. What it basically entailed was Jim beating on a specific type of drum in a very rhythmic beat, an undertone reverberating throughout the full twenty minutes or so. The resulting vibrational frequency had a tremendous effect on me as I lay still and allowed it to penetrate my being. I was extremely relaxed and, at one point, felt as if I was slipping and sliding into a vortex that seemed to be heading into my chest area, including my heart. It felt as if I was on the verge of going deeper into myself. Being Mr. Analytical, I mentally snatched my *self* up before I could spin away, disappointed in myself as soon as I did so. Still, the entire twenty or thirty minutes that Jim beat the drum, I felt some sort of release.

"How are you feeling?" he asked as soon as I was able to sit up.

"Good. But I don't know, Jim, it seems like I can't get out of my brain. I felt myself going somewhere, but I grabbed myself before I could get there. Does that make sense?"

He nodded. "Perfect sense. This is new for you, and sometimes these things take time."

I nodded back and smiled. "Yeah. But I don't like it. I want something more. I want to experience the mystical, the divine. And it seems like I'll never get past my mind messing with me." I sighed.

Jim, ever the gentle spirit guide, smiled softly and said, "I suggest you just pay attention over the next twenty-four hours or so. There are almost always some residual effects. Keep your mind attuned to the spiritual. Don't allow yourself to see things as coincidences. You might very well be pleasantly surprised as to what might happen."

"Thanks, Jim. I will."

By now, it was lunchtime, and I decided to go back to a spot I had become fond of, one of Ted and Marcella's (Ted's wife) recommendations, the Farmhouse Cafe and Bakery on the north side of Taos. I enjoyed my meal as I sat alone in deep contemplation. My time at Williams Lake was still fresh on my mind, and I almost felt a buzz in my body, as if the resonance of the drumbeat had burrowed inside of me somehow. I kept reminding myself that Jim had told me to *pay attention*. Though I was cognizant of others around me, I truly sensed that I was in my own little world, that maybe things were not quite as they seemed, that reality might reveal itself to me in a different form than I was used to if I could stay alert. Though, truthfully, it all seemed rather vague to me.

I noticed what appeared to be a batch of angry, dark clouds gathering to the west. I paid for my lunch and started back to my rental car along a gravel pathway. Still in contemplation, I walked slowly and with my head down, pondering as I went. A gust of wind sprang up out of nowhere, and from the corner of my eye, I noticed some object twist and tilt over into my path. I jerked my head up in time to find myself a few inches from an enormous sunflower, possibly the most gorgeous one I had ever seen, softly fluttering. Face to face. I instinctively thrust my head forward and kissed her right in her center, and then the wind abated and she softly moved back upwards into her normal place.

A warmth spread through my chest as I contemplated what had just happened: my baby's favorite flower swaying in the wind, a breath out of *nowhere,* bending my way at just the perfect second, as if she wanted to say hello, to be affectionate, to let me know she was nearby, and that she loved and cared for me.

Within fifteen seconds, I was back in the rental car. I sat there for a few seconds, trying to take in what had just happened. I then heard a metallic sound and felt a vibration by my right ear, which sent a shiver down my spine. Immediately, I knew it was not an insect, but looked around anyway. Nothing. I instantly remembered hearing that sometimes a buzzing, whirring, humming sound can appear out of the blue as an aspect of spiritual awakening or when a spiritual being is present. Well, I sure didn't feel like I was *awakening,* but after the sunflower encounter, it made sense to me that Hannah might be present. I heard the buzz again, this time a bit more softly and a tad more clear. No, it was not an insect. And though I could not be sure, I felt certain that Hannah was with me.

THE HUMMINGBIRD

"I just want to see her."

After I left Ted's home, I bounced around a couple of short-term rentals within the Taos area and explored a bit. At Ted's behest, I took a short hike along the Rio Grande, the deep ravine with its rushing waters, its lifeblood, far below. Less than a mile along the gorge, I came to the site Ted had wanted me to see. There was a bench Ted had placed there as a memorial to his girls, overlooking a majestic view into the gorge. I sat there for quite a while, contemplating the beauty … and the pain. His and mine. It sure seemed his had been redeemed; I was hoping mine could be, too. It's crazy how pain can grab you and shake you and make you feel that you have it worse than anyone else. I thought to myself that, sure, Ted had lost his daughters and wife, but that was a long time ago. Look how happy he is, how good life is for him now. Whereas I'm here, mired in my grief. That said, I was at least starting to feel some slivers of hope.

A couple days later, I decided to drive over to visit a dear new friend, Rosy Verdile, who worked at the Monastery of Christ in the Desert, a Catholic monastery near Abiquiu in the Chama Canyon, maybe a five-hour round trip from Taos. We had met a few weeks earlier at the grief conference in Santa Fe, where both Meg and I had become fast and close friends with her. She had lost her husband a few years earlier to suicide, and our hearts had been intertwined rather quickly upon meeting. Grief can do that.

I took the northern route to get to the monastery, determined to soak up as much of the mystical beauty as I could, stopping a few times along the way to breathe in the magic of those enchanted lands, a wide array of shifting terrain that captured my imagination. I felt like a little kid again, basking in the awe-inspiring nature of the desert, mountains, and forests, all beneath a crystal-clear, blue sky. As I neared the monastery, the turn onto Route 151 took me deeper into the desert and onto a dirt road that I'm sure was probably impassable at certain times of the year, promising quiet and solitude for the residents of the monastery. Within a mile or so after turning onto Route 151, a beautiful, flowing river sidled up next to the road and escorted me through the cliff-like facades, multi-colored and varied, that closed in around the dirt road like a protective guardian.

Rosy was waiting for me. It was so good to see her and meet her where she spent most of her time, including many years with her husband. Her eyes ran deep with compassion, born, I believe, from much time spent in contemplation and meditation as well as countless hours of the soul-searching that comes from traversing the deepest grief.

After a small tour of the monastery and the grounds, she led me over to a guest house where we could sit and talk. The serenity was just what the doctor ordered, a majestic cliff wall as our background and the river a stone's throw away. The only sounds were the songs of the birds and the gentle melody of the river washing over the boulders in its path.

"Thank you for inviting me," I said to Rosy as we settled into a couple of comfortable patio chairs on the covered outdoor porch.

"Of course," she said.

"This is so perfect, just what I need," I said. "Peaceful beyond words."

She smiled. "You know, I came out here a few decades ago, mired in confusion. I was in my twenties and had no idea what to do with my life. I somehow found this spot, actually a mile or two back down the road, and threw up a tent. I stayed for quite a few weeks, by myself, and meditated. I didn't even really know what I was doing, just that I was meant to be here and to connect with God. And so I stayed here by myself, in the tent, with very little food, and meditated day and night."

"Wow," I said. "That's amazing."

I could sense that this place—the desert, the canyon, all of it—could very well allow for the spirit to be deeply touched. The beauty alone was barely describable, the quiet almost deafening, and yet the sense that you were not alone was palpable.

I looked at Rosy, my eyes watering over as they did so often. "You know, Rosy, I just want to see her, to feel her. I want so bad to know she's here."

She nodded understandingly.

Within maybe three or four seconds, a hummingbird darted into my view. In fact, it settled in the space between Rosy and me, only a foot or so directly in front of my face, and hovered there. Looking at me. Time froze for me as that little gal—for I'm sure it was a she—locked eyes with me. I tingled inside as we stared at each other. Maybe it was only a few seconds, but it was enough time for me to know that the universe had heard my cry. Jim had told me to be open to God reaching us through His other creatures. The hummingbird, for example, symbolizes the sweetness of life, and there was none sweeter than Hannah. It was also a reminder to live in the present moment, an attribute I was keenly interested in cultivating in my life.

When the little gal flitted away, Rosy smiled knowingly. We really didn't even need to speak. Never before had a hummingbird entered my space, so close and intimate, so timely. I overflowed in that moment with emotion, gratitude, love, and a soft tear or two. I knew that Hannah had come to me in answer to my heart's cry. I'm not saying that she was the hummingbird, but in ways that we humans frequently dismiss, Hannah, in spirit, had transcended my reality and shown me that she was present.

The remaining conversation with Rosy was a blessing, I hope, for both of us. As much as I wanted to stay and breathe in more of the pristine setting and maybe even go sample some of the monastery's homemade brews, I figured I needed to get back to Taos before it got too late. I said my goodbyes and headed out, this time taking the southernly route. It had been a magical day.

MY BIRTHDAY GIFT

"You're so sweet."

I "celebrated" my birthday while in Taos, mainly with a random cry here and there. Not that I'm sentimental about such things as my own birthday—far from it. It's just that I was very emotional about the things I was experiencing, and though the mystical experiences were exhilarating, they also brought my memories of Hannah into sharper focus. Hence, there were times when I longed for her and missed her terribly.

While I was contemplating these things in Taos, Luke was in the country of Colombia. It had actually been our idea—Meg's and mine—to send him there. Why? Well, we had been doing lots of research into a wide array of healing modalities, including exploring the healing properties of certain plant medicines, one of which we were beginning to hear a lot more about than we had in the past: Ayahuasca. It had evidently been around for thousands of years and was held in very high esteem by many of the indigenous peoples of the world. After speaking with numerous people we had met in the Puerto Viejo area who had experienced Ayahuasca, we deemed it a worthwhile thing for Luke to try, due to an extreme depression he was suffering from since losing his big sister, and he agreed.

Luke then traveled down to Colombia to do a nine-day Ayahuasca ceremony with a well-known shaman.

As I wiped a tear from my eye, the thought of Luke on his

adventure crossed my mind, and I wondered if he had taken the medicine yet. At about that same time, an email came in from Meg. He had emailed her on the afternoon of the 25th about what had occurred in his first night of ceremony, which she forwarded to me:

Mom. Hannah came to me. Last night was our first ceremony, and she came. I had taken the drink, and an hour passed and nothing happened. Then came the purge. I puked hard … It was a struggle. Then, I lay down. The world grew dim, and then a light came. Like a candle burning a few feet away from my closed eyes. She took over my voice. She had several lines to say, and she had me repeat them. She started, "You're so sweet. You're so sweet. You're so sweet." Then, she shared with me her experience of dying. I saw what she saw behind her fading eyes. I saw lights grow dim. I felt her fear and hesitation. I heard encouragement she received as she was passing. From voices unknown to me. She had me say, "You've got to let me go," multiple times as the candle slowly burned out. And then she was gone. And I came back and there was such joy. She shared with me her experience of letting go so that I might let her go.

That was it. What a frigging birthday present, huh? I could not have asked for anything better.

Any grieving parent will instantly understand the depth of emotion I felt at that moment, except, of course, those whose belief systems inhibit their capacity to receive this type of information. Honestly, less than a year earlier, I would have had serious doubts myself. But no more. My journey had opened me up to a plethora of previously judged taboos and forced me to consider the value in many new things, including plant medicines such as Ayahuasca.

A couple days later, as Taos was fading behind me in my rearview mirror, I think my mind was fading, too, right along with the magical town. I was daydreaming as I gradually picked up speed and made my way south out of Taos. There was a pretty decent stretch of road in front of me when, all of a sudden, I saw a dark shadow crawl across the road, maybe a couple hundred feet ahead. My heart raced. I had no idea what it was, but it almost looked otherworldly. I was pretty sure it was a sign of some sort. It felt obvious to me. *Pay attention.*

PART FOUR

As the road led to a curve, the landscape opened up before me, a mountain on the left and an expanse of desert on the right, the Rio Grande slicing through the middle of it. But that wasn't the interesting part. A few nasty clouds had clustered together at the top of the mountain to the left while the rest of the sky was blue with a few scattered clouds. Out of the heart of the dark clouds sprouted a beautiful rainbow that arched outward and downward, smack dab *into* the desert.

For the first time in my life, I saw the end of a rainbow.

Had I not been reminded once again to pay attention by that mysterious, dancing shadow (I hadn't the slightest clue what it was), I would have probably missed the amazing beauty of the rainbow and been oblivious to what it represented. For, out of the darkness, the turmoil, the swirling clouds, sprang forth beauty: a rainbow that bridged the gap between the storm and a parched land in need of a special touch.

No longer accepting that everything is just a coincidence, I knew what this sight meant. Hannah, God, the universe, all were trying to get my attention to let me know that beauty beyond imagination could be found in the midst of storms, that its life-blessing splendor can reach the driest, most dreary places.

AYAHUASCA

"Deconstruct."

Upon my return to Costa Rica a few days later, exhausted and emotionally spent, I figured to rest and recuperate for a couple of days.

I figured wrong.

As soon as I walked in the door, Meg said, "By the way, there is an Ayahuasca ceremony tomorrow night. Do you want to go?"

It should be noted that attending an Ayahuasca ceremony is a pretty serious thing that requires preparation—mentally, physically, and spiritually. Some recommend at least a week of eating a certain way with a spirit of prayerfulness, for example. But after hearing about Luke's experience and not knowing when another ceremony would be available, I responded, "Okay. Let's do it."

Thirty hours later, I drank the medicine and lay down. After maybe an hour, I heard a couple of the other participants vomiting. I felt sorry for them. For a few more minutes, anyway. Then, it hit *me*.

In a few short hours, I would be revered as the man who purged all night. I felt so awful through much of the night, puking up whatever was inside of me and, I think, maybe a few things that weren't. And yet, despite all of that, the experience was worth it. I felt remarkably grounded, clear-headed, in touch with my surroundings. All around me looked normal—the facility, the people, et cetera—but the sky was different than I had ever seen. Half was black with maybe seven brightly shining stars, serenely set in their places. The other half was plastered with a thick blanket of clouds, uniformly spread out. Within its midst was a strange orb, brighter than the moon, a wisp of what resembled a cat's tail hanging below the orb. It hung over the town of Bribri, a few kilometers away. I wondered if any of its citizens knew what was overlooking them. I naturally assumed everyone else participating in the ceremony saw the sky as I did, but I figured I would wait until morning to speak with them about it.

During my many hikes into the jungle to purge, I became acutely aware that the earth was alive, breathing, pulsating, beautiful. I felt a moment of sadness as I realized I had never noticed this before.

Finally, and probably most importantly to me, as I was lying still on my mat, something I will call "a visual download" came to me, out of the blue and without warning. One second, everything seemed normal, and the next, I was watching a comic strip of six frames, three of them on top of the other three, all with movement inside of the frames. Each one had a head in it, and though it was not my head, I knew it represented me. They were all slightly different, and yet the same basic scene was playing out in each. The top of the head would open up, and out would fly something I sensed was information—opinions, patterns, ways of thinking, supposed knowledge. As I watched, one word was given to me.

Deconstruct.

Nothing else. Simply, deconstruct.

It was clear to me that I was being instructed to deconstruct my world, my worldview, my belief system, maybe everything, and that if I were to proceed in this life and find the reality I was in such desperate need of, I would need to deconstruct it all. And then the comic strip was gone.

At some point, I fell asleep. As the sun began to rise, Meg leaned over and asked if Hannah had come to me. I told her no. She said the same. And upon asking others if they had seen the orb and the seven stars, all I got was a few raised eyebrows. I was the only one who had seen it. That dimension had opened up specifically for me, to show me, I think, that maybe things are not always what they seem on the surface.

Where was I on my healing journey? And could I even call it a *healing* journey yet? I had somehow instinctively known very early in the grieving process that a journey was set before me, with healing as its goal and with something *beyond* healing as its ultimate goal. And yet the cloud of grief hovered over me, causing my mind to sink into pity and misery throughout.

It's not that I was not doing better. I was. Some days were actually decent, with plenty of good moments. The nights, however, were more difficult. I would often pray just to make it through, the painful memories attacking more fiercely as I dreamed and lay awake during those dark hours of the night.

Did I say praying? That is not necessarily accurate as far as most define praying. I'm thinking it took somewhere from one to two years before I even considered praying again, actually, so angry was I at the past recipient of my prayers. I just couldn't muster up the feeling to pray to the God who had taken my daughter, and with such cruel and brutal tactics. So it was a bit difficult to consciously pray, in that sense. Yet, as I look back, I believe my soul was indeed praying. Crying out to a Love I was not sure existed anymore and begging for relief, hoping It would somehow provide healing at some point. I wanted someone or something to prove to me that God was not how I had seen Him in the past.

By this time, Meg was making several great friends. I, on the other hand, was not. This was a reversal of what our time in the States had been like, where I was the extrovert and Meg the homebody. I was very happy she had found great friends to help her through her grief and who remain steadfast friends with her today. Of course, I did have my mother around for a great deal of time during my early periods of grieving. I needed someone to listen. To offer their presence. To absorb even an ounce of my pain. And that is what my mother did. I'd walk down to her room on the main floor, one of the two bedrooms we had quickly added after purchasing our little jungle bungalow, and plop myself down in a chair to process my grief. She listened to a lot of shit, crying when I cried and never interrupting my ramblings, which takes a kind of patience that only a mother has. Of course, she had deeply loved her granddaughter, too, but she knew how especially close I had been with her, and she felt my pain. She seemed to understand.

And now, after the grief conference, the journey to Taos, and my Ayahuasca experience, I was beginning to open up a bit. For many months after Hannah's death, it seemed all I could see when I pictured her was a memory of those last days when the disease had ravaged her so. Now, I was sensing that I might be able to remember how she appeared before that difficult time.

But one day shortly after the Ayahuasca ceremony, I walked into my mother's room, said hello, went over to the little shelf where the photos were displayed, turned the photo of Hannah back over, and stood it up so that it could be seen. I stared at it for a moment, the first time I had been able to do so since her death, and smiled.

Yes, I cried, too. But I smiled.

THE DREAM

"Keep on coming, Daddy."

After returning from my trip to Taos, I couldn't seem to get the Monroe Institute off my mind. Between Eben Alexander's book, *Proof of Heaven*, and Rosy Verdile's recommendation of the Institute, I decided to do some research of my own, which quickly convinced me that going there should be a part of my journey. So I booked the retreat and my flight, excited about giving binaural beats a shot at helping to connect me with Hannah in a hopefully more tangible way.

On the way, I stopped in Atlanta to visit with Beka. It was mid-October, almost a year after Hannah's death, and I spent a couple of days with her before heading on up to Charlottesville, Virginia, where the Institute was located.

That night, I fell asleep next to Beka, expecting to do what I normally did while sleeping—struggle a little in the middle of the night. But, sometime after I drifted off, the universe decided to play a little.

I found myself riding a train, bound for who the hell knows where, with my youngest son, Luke, as my sidekick. It was dark outside. The next thing I knew, the train was slowing down to nudge Luke and me out in front of a couple of one-story buildings, both of which looked like a cross between maybe a school building or a church complex. As dreams would have it, somehow Luke knew he was supposed to go into the one on the right, and I knew I was supposed to take the one on the left.

As I checked out the entrance and took a couple steps forward, it hit me: I was here for a game of hide-and-seek. No one else was around, at least as far as I could tell, but I felt a sense of urgency to get on in and find a place to hide. Usually, in these types of dreams, a touch of fear starts to trace up my spine, but surprisingly, I felt a tingle of excitement instead.

I looked around and found my hiding spot—not a very good one—but when you're dreaming ...

Fairly near the entrance on the left was an opening I could slide behind. It was really nothing more than a tiny, doorless room, much like a large closet—just an opening, really, pretty much exposing me to whoever may be coming to find me. I managed to scooch my back up to a wall and wait, trying to blend in with it. It wouldn't take long.

I felt her first, as if a soft spring breeze had gently floated around the wall and found me, embracing me with warmth and comforting me. Then, I saw a body out of the corner of my eye walking toward the opposite wall. I looked up, subtle-like, so I wouldn't be noticed, and saw it was a female, though I still did not grasp the specialness of the situation, the reality that I was being found. A strange anticipation gripped me as I looked her way, her hair falling down and covering her face, still sideways to me, almost nose to nose with the opposite wall.

And then it happened.

She began to chuckle. I felt an anticipatory excitement, as if something wonderful was about to happen. As she laughed, her body began to shake with obvious delight. Slowly, I was able to make out the lips and notice a radiant smile. That's when I knew.

It was Hannah.

On cue, she turned and ... I want to say *looked* at me, but that's not exactly right. It was more than looking at me. She was *seeing* me, *knowing* me—in a strange sense, almost *merging* with me. I felt euphoric. It was that place we all yearn for, where all is right. Peace and joy seem almost inadequate to describe the essence of the moment.

Hannah glowed, her smile and aliveness brightening the room. As dreams go, this was *not* a dream. I've read books about near-death experiences where the authors struggle to describe the depth of the *ultra*-reality they experience, the beauty that breaks out of all molds formed from prior norms, with colors that make even the most vibrant on Earth seem gray, communications that do not need to be spoken and yet are understood perfectly, a heart that beats to notes of wonder, and a spirit that dances to a new and wondrous tune.

For a second or two, that was where I was.

"Keep on coming, Daddy," Hannah whispered to me. "You're getting closer."

My heart leapt in my chest. I heard her voice, a heavenly, rapturous voice. My baby had spoken to me, the first words since she told me she loved me as she slipped away into a coma four days before her passing. For that glorious moment, in that sacred place, all the pain was forgotten, softly snatched away and replaced with love. And yet that seems inadequate, as well. It was heavenly.

But only for a few seconds.

Hannah began to back away, still smiling, still radiant, still beautiful beyond description. I did not say a word the entire time. Strange, huh? I think I was just too delighted to speak, choosing instead to absorb the best moment of my life, dream or not. But as she continued on, I could see it in her eyes. *I have to go now, Daddy. I love you. I'll see you again ...*

And then she was gone.

I began to awaken, tears flooding my eyes. My elation turned on a dime. I literally convulsed. Instantly, I felt the sorrow that she was still gone from my world. I wept and shook for a short time. The pendulum of emotion had swung forcefully, ripping me brutally from the heights of ecstasy, only to thrust me into a place darker than I had been in a while. After only a few seconds, though, the hurt started to subside, and my mind began to clear. I got my wits about me.

I lay there in that bed, staring up into nothingness, picturing her face, feeling her joy. She came to me—*for* me. Maybe others wouldn't believe it, but of this I was certain. She had chosen to come in that moment, in that place, to visit me, for that is what it was: a visitation. Born out of a little game of hide-and-seek between a daddy and his daughter.

SHE CAME TO ME

"Daddy, write our story."

The dream at Beka's apartment had been like a shot of adrenaline, pushing me to a state of heightened awareness but draining me a bit in the process. All I had to process it with was my fifty-something-year-old filter, finely honed by decades of the old Phil. I might in the past have even ignored the dream, as brilliant as it was, as a fantasy of some sort. The thing, though, is that I knew it was real. I knew deep inside that Hannah had come to me. And yet still, I felt subdued, lacking in absoluteness.

No matter how spiritual something seems, we tend to forget, or at least minimize, the events that seem to reach to us from other dimensions. And, as meaningful and real as Hannah's visitation had been, I knew I would not be able to carry the high of her visit with me forever.

I entered the Monroe Institute program facility, dropped my bag off at my room, and then made my way to the basement, where most of our meetings would take place. Glancing around, I noticed a whiteboard with a drawing and a few words written on it.

Love. Peace. Joy.

In that order. Simple words, wonderful words, and their impact on me was instantaneous. These had been the same words Hannah used as passwords to her different accounts. In that same order. I could sense her presence, smiling. I smiled. It was a good start.

PART FOUR

Almost all of our meetings, meals, sessions, and various other activities took place within the main building. I was assigned a bedroom with a man who had come all the way from China to experience the binaural beats program. Each bed was almost its own room, an enclosed space with three walls and parts of a fourth, so we did not interact that much. This partial wall included a cutout with plenty of space to crawl into your bed and then velcro a thick black curtain over the entryway, effectively sealing yourself in. This was where the private sessions took place, as well, where, at the appropriate time, we would put on our special earphones and await the session. This is what we were here for.

Pretty early on, I could tell there was something to this binaural beats and Hemi-Sync phenomenon, though I couldn't rightly put my finger on it. I occasionally had visions during the sessions, though nothing to get too excited about. After each private session, we would meet as a group and share our experiences if we chose to do so. I barely spoke, especially after hearing some of the exotic and exciting stories from some of the other participants. I was a bit intimidated, maybe even angry at myself for being so in my head, too much of a realist, not able to let myself go.

Coincidentally (or not), out of a group of maybe twenty-four folks, three of us were bereaved parents, me and a couple of ladies. As badly as I was hurting, my heart also ached for them. They had each lost their only child, a son. Though Hannah had been gone less than a year and each of their sons several years, the pain was still palpable, such that they could barely even talk about it. At any rate, the group was aware of our losses.

About midweek, I was eating lunch and sensed that someone across the room was looking at me. I soon looked up to see who it was, a thirty-something-year-old lady from New York of Japanese ethnicity. She had been a fascinating attendee if you went by what she seemed to be experiencing during the private sessions. She would nonchalantly relate stories of fantastic color, beauty, and love. I wasn't exactly jealous, but I yearned to *see* some of the scenes she was evidently privy to. Okay, maybe I was a bit jealous. If what she was saying in our meetings was true, and she apparently was not the only one, she was being given a glimpse into a dynamic dimension that so far had eluded me. Yes, there had been the uniqueness of the Ayahuasca experience and the incredible brilliance of the dream of Hannah, but what she was describing seemed to be something altogether different. The effect, I felt, could be eye-opening, or, better said, *soul*-opening if only I could join her and a few of the others who seemed to be more enlightened.

I was almost finished with my meal when I noticed she was sitting alone at her table, the others having already departed. I could still feel her stealing looks my way. I took my last bite and stood up to put away my plate and utensils. She stood up simultaneously, and as I turned around to leave, she walked up and asked if she could speak with me for a minute.

"Sure," I said.

She motioned over toward the door that led to the stairs. Everyone else was either gone or exiting through one of a couple of other doors in the other direction. We entered the stairwell, and the door closed behind us. She turned and looked at me.

"Are you your daughter's *only* father?" she asked.

I'm pretty sure I crinkled my brow on that one. An original question, for sure. How could someone have more than one father?

"What do you mean?"

She smiled. "I mean, did she have another father? A stepdad or something? Was there anyone else she would have called dad?"

Ah, now that she mentioned it, I guess someone could have more than one dad, or at least more than one that could be called dad in some form. I shook my head.

"Nope. I'm it. Why do you ask?"

The young Japanese lady from New York, though still with a heavy accent from her native land, shuffled her feet for a second or two, looking from side to side, then looked deep into my eyes.

"She came to me," she said.

My heart froze. My skin tingled. My breath got shallow.

"She came to me in the last session," she continued.

Did this lady have any idea what she was doing to me? I was swirling inside, my emotions on edge. Anticipatory. A million thoughts racing through my mind within the split second between her words.

It is important to know that, as far as I could tell, this young lady had zero interest in fabricating anything. She simply seemed to feel the need to tell me what she had experienced. I couldn't imagine there would be any ulterior motive. In fact, if she was making this up, which I certainly did not sense from her countenance, her voice, her eyes, or even her demeanor, I sure as hell couldn't tell. *Why would she?* We would probably never see each other again after the next three or four days.

"How did you know it was her?" I asked.

"Well, she was represented as a bright light. I knew something was happening, that someone was in my presence, but I did not know who it was. Then, you stepped into my vision, into the light. Sort of in front of it. She spoke and said, 'This is the best Dad!' And I knew it was your daughter."

My head was spinning, my heart exploding in my chest, my eyes tearing up. I softly shook my head and smiled.

"No," I said. "No other dad." Then I began to nod my head. "That is just what she would say. Yeah, that is exactly what she would say. We were very close. We loved each other very much."

She nodded and smiled. I asked if there was anything else. She hesitated but then shook her head and started to walk up the stairs. I touched her arm.

"Thank you," I managed. "Thank you for sharing this with me."

"You're welcome."

The next morning provided more fireworks, though it started meekly. I'm not sure how long the session was—they never really told you that, and I wasn't checking—but I mainly just stared into a thick blackness, waiting for something, anything, to reveal itself to me. I also got a little sleepy. Some folks would evidently doze here and there, but I never came that close. Too anxious, hopeful that Hannah might show up, I did not want to miss a thing.

This particular session produced only one little measly occurrence, and I wasn't even sure if I had dreamed it up. *Probably did*, I chided myself at lunch as I sat alone at a small table outside, feeling a bit underwhelmed at my pathetic spiritual acumen. Over to my left, I noticed, was my new Japanese acquaintance and another lady who seemed to be receiving revelations, visions, and other experiences. They were excitedly sharing stories. I sank a little lower in my seat.

Between bites, I managed to shoot them a look and mumble, "Y'alls' stories are amazing. The only thing I got," I rolled my eyes and paused for a second, "was what looked like a copper cheese grater pop into my line of vision for a couple of seconds and then disappear. A frigging cheese grater. Psshhh." Then I felt embarrassed for even mentioning it.

I turned back to my plate and forked another bite of food into my mouth.

"I have to tell you something," the Japanese lady quickly started, her voice ratcheting up a notch, almost in a rush. I looked at her, her eyes big. "There's something I didn't tell you yesterday. I didn't know what to tell you or how you would take it, so I let it go. But in my vision, your daughter showed me a piece of metal with a bunch of little holes in it. She said something about how you were trying so hard to reach her, and yet there was blockage. That a little was getting through, just not much yet, like strands running through the little holes in the piece of metal."

Again, *why on earth would she make that up?* In fact, other than taking a picture with her before we left from the retreat, that was probably our last conversation, and I have never communicated with her since then.

We tend to magnify the big things and give little credence to the little things because they mostly seem insignificant. It was becoming clear to me that the universe was trying to get through to me in bigger ways, like the dream, and in little ways, like the momentary vision of a cheese grater, combined with the young lady's vision, of course.

I smiled and thanked her once more for sharing.

On the last day of the retreat, I spent my entire session doing something I was still not very comfortable doing: praying. I found myself asking God to reveal to me what I was supposed to do for a living, or do at all, from here on out. Having been an NFL agent for most of my career and now living in Costa Rica on a tiny farm that we were working to make as sustainable as possible, what purpose was left for me? Trying to dig myself out of the hellhole of grief from Hannah's death had left me feeling somewhat debilitated for much of the prior year, but what was in store for me in the future? Could the universe oblige and throw at least a hint my way? Was there anything to look forward to? Anything else, perhaps, to assist me on my healing journey while also providing a potential source of income?

This session was almost identical to the one that had plopped the inane cheese grater into my line of vision for a second or two. Only, this time, all I saw was a stark, unending blackness with no clues whatsoever to the answer I was seeking. My frustration was beginning to grow.

Right as I was beginning to think I would come away empty-handed, as if on cue, a picture flashed in front of me, transposed against the black backdrop. I felt like I was peering at the negative of an old photograph, with coppery tones giving life to the image before me. Though I was hoping for a clearer view, I could see a desk of some sort with a book or two angling on the left side of it and a high-back chair on the other side of the desk. Behind the desk and the chair was a wall of books, a library. Instantly, I understood.

I was supposed to write.

With my interest piqued, I got excited and threw out a question—just in my mind, I think, but I might have even blurted it out loud.

"What am I supposed to write about? Please show me."

I scanned all of the books and found myself hoping that one of the spines would light up and reveal a title. Seriously. I was very intent on the universe providing that piece of information for me—and *right now would be good, please*. Alas, the library started to fade out of view, and I was once more left with a totally black background. But almost immediately, I heard the most beautiful music start to play. I don't remember what it was exactly, but tears flowed without hesitation as I felt Hannah's presence and heard her say to me: "Daddy, write our story. Write about us and the journey this has put you on."

And then, just like that, she was gone.

To this day, I do not know if the music was real or in my head, given to me by God to allow me to open up and hear from Hannah. It could have simply been the music the teachers used to end each session with, and if so, that's totally fine, too. But whatever the case, my question was answered. And Hannah had spoken to me in its midst.

AN ANNIVERSARY

"I began to weep."

As I lay in bed on October 18, 2017, my mind began to drift. I was not yet asleep, and Meg was still flitting about the room, preparing for bed herself. I almost went into a trance, sinking deep into a memory so painful that I had been consistently casting it out the very instant it would enter my mind. I had honed this "casting out" technique over the prior two years so that any memory that brought pain would only be allowed in if I felt it wouldn't rip my heart and mind to shreds. Only then would I watch the scene of whatever memory came to me, but I always prepared to stop the tape at a second's notice if it felt like too much.

This time, though, I did not seem to be in control.

The scene entered my mind, and the movie began to play. It was that of Hannah summoning me into her room in Senoia, Georgia, during her last week to tell me she loved me, her last sentence spoken. I watched it play out in my mind from the moment she called me until a few seconds after she peered deep into my eyes and uttered those heavenly words. "I love you."

As the trance slowly faded away, the scene along with it, I began to weep. Deep, deep within me. A rush of tears fell onto my pillow, and Meg, obviously unaware of the source of my weeping, sat down on her side of the bed and placed her hand on my back. She didn't say anything. We rarely ever did in these types of moments. The monster waves of emotion had lessened over time, coming less frequently and without as much "gusto" as before. But every now and then, they seemed to rise up out of the blue. This time, that familiar old fifty-foot wave had rolled in out of nowhere and pummeled me.

As the trancelike scene descended upon me, I recognized that this time, I had actually *chosen* to go back into the memory if for no other reason than to honor Hannah. I wanted to feel her heart, to gaze into her eyes again, to hear the last sentence she ever spoke, to know that I could face the pain. I guess I was finally ready.

As I pondered the memory, a light bulb flickered—today was *that* day. It had been exactly two years since that moment, one that I will always remember, cherish, and in some ways also be haunted by.

The fact that that memory had just naturally dropped into my mind like that on the same day it had happened two years ago could have been just a weird little quirk. In the past, I likely would have called it a coincidence. But I don't think it was. In fact, I am close to certain that that memory came rushing in to remind me there was something much deeper at work in my life and that I had better do my damnedest to pay attention and keep digging. As the sniffles ended, I lay in a state of melancholy, awaiting sleep, a touch more certain that Hannah and the universe were guiding me in the right direction.

A DIFFERENT KIND OF MOVIE

"I was taken back."

In the fall of 2018, something was happening inside of me, something different. For the first time in my life, I could feel changes occurring within me, exciting new paradigms forming, ones that were unlike anything I had ever experienced as the old Phil. I found myself rising before the howler monkeys and meditating, then practicing breathing techniques, and then grabbing a coffee, my pen, and my journal. After learning several years earlier that the world was not as I had always thought it was, and having staggered through the most life-altering event a parent can ever experience, I had come to a place where I was totally open, willing to free my mind to consider whatever God might reveal, regardless of what I had previously believed or what "authorities" deemed as the truth. I was all in, digging with all of my emotional and spiritual strength in pursuit of whatever God might have in store for me. In pursuit of life.

Or at least it felt that way. I was beginning to see life differently than I ever had, bolstered by my new understanding of the spiritual realm, more excited than I had been in a while.

Meg, although growing and healing in her own way, was beginning to edge away from me. By this point, I had come to strongly believe that we all create stories, born from illusions that are instigated by our security-seeking egos. It takes a lot for us to be able to look at the root causes of these stories, built like formidable fortresses and constructed to defend our egos and fragile landscapes. If we are lucky, we begin to realize that these stories never do the job we assign them, causing myriad problems along the way. And, in the process, we weave more stories as a result of our attempts to "fix" them. On and on goes the cycle. My personal stories of pain, with Meg at times the main culprit in my mind, had taken on a life of their own during much of the proceeding few years and left many a scar along the way in both of our hearts.

Sometimes, I talk too much. I admit it. I'm an outward processor, throwing words and thoughts out into the public domain probably a little more than I should. For example, in my belief that speaking *truth* was of the utmost importance, and with a heart that felt like it had been severely damaged, I would occasionally spew stuff out to Meg like:

"I feel like my heart died. I will always love you, but my heart has just been too beaten up. I hope that my heart returns, and I truly believe it will. But it has died. I just can't seem to feel it anymore. I want more than anything for us to love each other as we once did, even more so, and I believe it will come. But, right now, I feel like my heart has died."

I'm not sure how many times I recited this motif, but I'm afraid I might have lost Meg's heart little by little each time she heard it, my words dragging her along a ragged path. Losing a child is always brutal on relationships, maybe even more so when one of the partners has a big mouth. Like me. Though both of us had fought hard to get back on our feet and perhaps stretch further than before in our quest for reality, truth, and life, we still recognized that losing a child would almost certainly require a lifetime of healing.

Meg was reaching out for her own rock to cling to, her own needs for security. And I guess if I had been in her shoes, I would have been concerned after listening to the "my heart is dead" quips. So she was doing what she needed to do for her, which likely meant that fully trusting me and my commitment to our relationship was becoming more difficult. I started to notice she had stopped being warm toward me, but I simply and naively assumed, like I always did, that things would just sort of work themselves out. Especially since I knew I was changing.

In relationships, though, as I was soon to learn, watching the other person change is often fraught with challenges, certainly more so when there are so many questions afloat, some of which point to a pretty deep crack or two. Meg felt she needed to be cautious with me. Her heart had been affected, too, and I did not blame her. Yet I still figured that the changes in me would be noticed and eventually remedy all of our issues. At least that's what I was hoping for.

In late October, Meg's sister, Amy, flew down to Costa Rica for a week or so, with plans for Meg to fly back to the States with her and spend a couple of weeks in Florida with her family and a few days with Beka in Georgia. By the end of the visit, Meg's edging away had become much more obvious. So much so that on the Saturday morning that Meg and Amy were set to leave, I decided to address the issue.

"So what's up?" I asked. "I can tell something's on your mind— something different. You want to talk about it?"

She seemed a bit nonchalant. "Yeah. But it can wait." She shuffled her feet. Then, almost immediately, she said, "I guess we can talk about it now."

"Okay," I said.

"Well," she said, "When I get back from the States, I was thinking maybe in January after the holidays, you could go somewhere for about six weeks, and then I could go somewhere for about six weeks. That would give us three months apart, time for me to better hear my voice."

Meg and I had been around each other, day in and day out, for over thirty-one years, probably more than anybody I had ever known, so on the one hand, time apart actually sounded good. But, on the other ...

"So you want a separation?" I asked.

She shook her head. "No. Just time alone. Time to think. Time to hear my voice."

Yeah, a time of separation.

"Okay," I said.

And that was pretty much it. I drove them to the bus stop in Puerto Viejo and hugged her goodbye, both of us throwing out an "I love you," fully knowing that we were diving into uncharted waters. Sad waters. Scary waters, perhaps. They left, and I drove home to ponder.

Over the next couple of weeks, I continued to immerse myself into meditation, breathing exercises, and a book called *A Course in Miracles*. Meg had ordered the book almost immediately upon learning of Hannah's illness, no doubt seduced by the title, but upon picking it up at that time, I had almost immediately tossed it aside. I could barely even read the first page, frustrated by almost every line. I just couldn't grasp what it was trying to say, coming across to me as if it were Yoda speaking in parables. But now, a little over three years later, it seemed that everywhere I turned, I heard the book calling out for me to open it again. I began reading it again, and for the first time in my life, I felt an energy flow into me that I knew was from the divine. Instantly.

I also began to receive downloads from somewhere. *Downloads*, you ask? Yes, downloads. As if my mind had been pried open by some unseen hand and a multitude of stories began to pour in. I had recently started writing short stories, mainly about grief, healing, and the realm of the mystical, but now they began to burst into my mind like an angry ocean through the walls of a rickety dam. So I wrote. And wrote. And continued to do so.

A few days before Meg was due to arrive back from the States, I had an extraordinary experience. My best guess is that the modalities I was practicing—the meditations (guided and unguided) and breathing exercises—and the reading and studying I was doing were all beginning to affect me on a subconscious level. I awoke in the middle of the night, and instantly, a movie began to play in my mind. I could tell I was awake, and yet, without warning, it was as if a DVD had been inserted into a slot in my brain and the video began to play. This was not *thinking*. It was *watching*.

I was transported back in time to revisit several events from my first seven or eight years. I was like old Ebenezer Scrooge in *A Christmas Carol*, invisible and simply observing the action. With one caveat: I could watch myself as a little boy while feeling the *emotions* of that little boy.

First, I was taken back to the time my mother had dropped me off at the church nursery when I was almost three years old and I felt utterly abandoned. I was terrified! This time, though, I watched as little Phil freaked out and screamed, feeling it within my own being as older Phil lay in bed in Costa Rica.

Next, I saw myself at six years old, jumping down off of my bicycle and looking down into a large culvert, back in the day when our parents trusted us to ride just about anywhere and make it home safely. I had gone to the culvert to find my older brother, Steve, who was down next to the water with a friend. As I stood by my bicycle, he reached down, picked something up, cocked his arm, and launched whatever it was in my direction. I felt a sharp pain on my left shin and quickly looked down. Blood was spurting from my leg, and a sharp piece of glass was lying on the ground beside my foot, the bottom part of an old Coca-Cola bottle. I looked down at my brother, and he was laughing. I jumped on my bike and sped home, blood flying everywhere, stunned and upset that he could be so mean. I still have the scar.

I knew that I could shut the video down whenever I wanted to, but I let it keep rolling.

Next, I was on an elementary school swing in Dawson, Georgia, where we had moved after Macon. It was my first day of third grade in our new town, and I was scared to death. School was already out for the day, and I was waiting for my mom, my face digging into the chains that held up the swing, crying, terrified. I was somehow convinced, I think, that this new place, and the new way they did school, was going to be my downfall. I saw the tears erupt from my young eyes and, at the same time, felt the fear as if it were happening all over again.

Many more scenes began to rush through my mind, staccato style, with just enough of a visual from each one to remind me that I was a deeply wounded human being. I eventually halted the projector.

I continued to lie in my bed, confused about what had just happened. *What the hell was that? And why now? What the frig is happening to me?* As I relaxed and processed it all, it came to me that I was being shown why I behaved the way I had, and felt the way I did, during many of the difficult episodes of my life. It was obvious to me, for example, that the mere possibility of abandonment could leave me in a state of panic, especially if it was of a foundational nature.

Abandonment. Though I was not aware of it at that moment, it would only be a few more days before I discovered I was teetering on the edge of an abyss of loneliness and abandonment so horrifying that I would have no hope of survival.

HELL... AND THEN HEAVEN

"Thank you, thank you, thank you."

On Thanksgiving Day, Meg returned home to Costa Rica and informed me that she was no longer in love with me. Though there had been many rocky periods in our relationship since early in Hannah's illness, this proclamation from the woman I had thought I would always be married to—"until death do us part"—shocked my system. The downward spiral that had been initiated right before she left for the States was now going full throttle. Clearly, I had experienced some of life's more difficult moments up until this revelation, but I was not prepared for what would come next.

Throughout my life, I had never experienced what is called a panic attack, and I didn't have one at that moment. During Hannah's illness and death, I had been delirious, fragmented, sorrowful beyond words, agonizingly distraught, and more, but never had I gone through the irrational terror of a panic attack. That changed on Thanksgiving night 2018. That night, I was confronted with the gates of hell.

I abruptly woke up in the middle of the night in sheer terror, my mind entombed in a state of heightened anxiety and despair, as if my entire world had fallen apart and there was nothing I could do about it. Somehow, I came out of it and eventually fell back asleep.

It happened again on Friday night, November 23, basically a carbon copy of the night before.

And then there was Saturday.

My Rottweiler, Tank, died early in the day, and until the moment I closed my eyes for sleep, I was in a state of high agitation. I had never really felt anything quite like it. Total instability, erratic thought patterns, extreme fear.

But, somehow, I fell asleep.

I awoke in abject terror in the middle of the night, with no hope of relief, a voice suggesting I find a way to end it all. Demanding I end it all.

It was at that very moment, when I felt I had run out of options, that another voice spoke.

Breathe. Become present. Do it.

I did.

In ... out ... in ...

What happened next is impossible to truly share in a fully coherent way and, certainly, to do so with words.

One second, I was buried deep within a more horrifying hell than I could have ever imagined. The next, a peace this world knows not of enveloped my absolute being.

Time no longer existed. I had entered eternity, and I was more wide awake than I had ever been during any instant of my time upon Earth. I was submerged within a timelessness that is, and always has been, untouched by the linear time that governs the world of men and women. I woke up from the dream of life on Earth and realized that I was in Heaven, in eternity, in reality, the likes of which made all that I had previously experienced as life seem as if it were little more than a blurry nothing. Everything just was.

It was in that very instant that I knew I needed nobody, that I was fully accepted forever by all that mattered (God, Creator, Source). I was intensely aware that our perceived need for something or someone to complete us is absolute, one hundred percent illusion. We are already complete and whole.

PART FOUR

Never had I felt so certain of anything in my life. I was given the perfect knowledge that the Creator of the Universe accepted me and that nothing could ever change that. Nothing! The peace that now enveloped me was far beyond what I had ever thought possible. A stunning, mind-blowing sea of tranquility softly buoyed me within its life force of love, pulsating all around me and within me. I was cocooned inside, and yet it was also within my being.

As far as I know, I barely moved. There was no reason to do so. I lay there still, with Meg's hand on my heart, floating in a sea of an amazing combination of peace and love and acceptance so ecstatic that it simply cannot be imagined. Not a single other highlight, including the birth of my children, nor any other experience I could offer can begin to touch the hem of the garment of beauty that I touched (or that dropped down and touched me). I began to speak audibly, into the ears of God, as it were, saying, "Thank you, thank you, thank you, thank you ..." On and on I went, a heart overflowing with gratitude that far exceeded what I thought possible. For the first time in my life, I truly understood what a thankful heart really was, what gratitude really meant. I'm not sure how many times I spoke it—maybe ten or so, maybe fifty. Maybe more.

I was humbled, not the slightest bit proud. Quite the opposite, in fact, marveling at the love of God that had allowed me to receive such a divine taste of our eternal inheritance. This knowledge has not left me for even a second since then; it matters not the least what anyone might say to counter this from a religious or anti-religious perspective. This realization erased my fear of abandonment, for I now knew that abandonment was simply impossible. Not impossible from a physical body standpoint—from that sticky, emotional place we seem to inhabit in our three-dimensional world—but from an ultimate reality standpoint, which is, well, reality.

Why did this happen to me? Why was this experience of Heaven given to me? And why did it come on the heels of such a painful, humbling, hellacious event—the extreme panic attack?

Who knows the answers to such things? No one. For whatever

reason, though, God had touched me, embraced me, enveloped me in love because ... it was what I needed. Perhaps it was spurred on by my desperation, the depth of which led to complete surrender. I just can't say for sure. And I can never be the same. The experience has given me an anchor within the turbulent ocean of life, an understanding that this world we see with our body's eyes is illusionary.

The experience of Heaven differed in one profound way from all that this life offers. The energy of the peace, the vibrational quality of the love, the frequency of the joy—all of it—was what might be called *constant*. It did not waver and could not waver. It was knowledge itself, with a realization that it could never deviate from its essence.

As I lay there orally expressing my deep gratitude to my Creator, I was certain I would experience this bliss for as long as I remained awake. I knew it. Though I'm not sure how long it lasted, I rested in that spirit of love and peace and knowing, soaking it all up. But I also knew—you could say that the information was given to me—that it would all be gone once I fell back asleep. As I lay there in that state, I recalled—or again, was given—a story I had read of someone who experienced the same thing and that it had lasted for months afterward. I didn't envy that person, but I knew it would not be the same for me. I knew I was going to be right back in the egoic dance, with lessons to learn.

And a purpose to fulfill.

The only thing constant on Earth is change. But now, I knew that one day this would end and that all of the shifting and changing and confusion of this world would be swallowed up by Heaven. And time will be no more.

POST-REVELATION

"Back to Earth..."

Inow knew deep inside that my journey had shifted. All of what had happened over the prior three years had led me to a place in life I could never have expected nor even dreamed possible. The revelation had given me a taste of that something beyond. I had heard others talk of such things, such beauty beyond conception, but truthfully, I wasn't sure I even believed them. I mean, where was the proof?

Well, now I understood.

I have tried to share the story of what happened that night with a few people and am often met with a change of subject. I understand. It's not normal and is difficult to process for many, entirely alien to others. I get it.

I also knew from the moment of Hannah's death that I was to write this story (as well as many other things), though I was clueless as to where it would end up. I was frustrated as I chronicled the journey, navigating the ebbs and flows of grief, clinging fiercely to the moments of relief. I wanted to know what the end of it would look like. How would things work out? Was there really a final chapter out there somewhere? A proper ending?

I have come to realize that, rather than an actual ending, the so-called final chapter is more like a first verse of a new story. In fact, there is no ending, at least within the context of how we think of them. But this is truly the beauty and wonder of it all, the "aha!" moment, the realization that the fabric of reality is not found in our future or our past but in our being, in the timeless aspect of who we are.

The physical world had taught me to protect Phil, to seek pleasure, to avoid pain. But I can now clearly see that all that exists in this tangible, physical world is merely a type of illusion, a game of shadows. It does not matter whether I am religious or not, whether I am conservative or liberal, whether I am a man or a woman, black or white, straight or gay, or any of the other countless criteria we use to separate ourselves from each other. None of this matters to me anymore. It is all a big, massive, convoluted ball of illusion.

Life is simply not what we think it is. The material physical world screams out at each of us: "Look out for me!" To buy this, have that, seek pleasure, leverage the future to have more now, protect my belief system, look down on others (for I am right and they are wrong), avoid pain for me while inflicting pain upon them (if need be), and on and on, a vicious cycle of misery that has played out through the ages.

That said, I am certain that this place of being, this experience of joy and peace and love and acceptance and gratitude awaits all of the Creator's children. All of us! I realize that many of our beliefs, religious and otherwise, suggest something different to many, but that does not make them true. This experience has confirmed to me what I was beginning to see as our destiny through my readings and meditations and such: that all creations of the loving Creator *of all* would eventually share a timeless bliss with their very Creator.

When I awoke the next morning, my first thought was, "Oh my gosh! Oh my gosh!"

Did I still feel Heaven? No. And I had known I would not. But I sensed a remnant lurking, as if the tiniest vibration of Heaven was still there. I knew that the truth of what had happened would never depart from me, from my memory, from my mind, and yet its consuming bliss had softly faded away. And that was okay!

The beautiful, the mystical, the essence of that which is real, I held within my grasp for those few moments, and for eternity.

But now, at this moment in time? Back to Earth I came. I even had one more panic attack the very next night. Then, little by little, I began to settle back into what I would call a place of growth. Morning and evening meditations (guided and unguided), breathing modalities, and a deeper dive into *A Course in Miracles*. At this point in my journey, I had become certain of one thing—things are not as we see them. I had been allowed to peek behind the veil and steal a glimpse of reality. Of Heaven. Of the fabric of the universe. And now my mind was forever open to a world far beyond that of the dream world or life on Earth as most of us experience it.

Look, we have all asked those questions, haven't we? "Why am I here? What is my purpose? Is there really any meaning to all of this insanity?" And a million more. But because we are so busy, so educated, so propagandized, so saturated with beliefs that we have learned somewhere along the way and subsequently honed to a razor's edge to protect our psyches, so fearful of losing our foundation, we trudge forward, trying to squeeze out as much pleasure as we can through whatever time we might have, all the while also trying to protect ourselves from the countless pains.

As I found out, no matter how hard I try, I simply do not have that type of control. No one does. In fact, the belief that we can control anything is an illusion. It is a forever losing game, yet one we keep fighting in the hope that the tides will change in our favor, that fortune might smile on us with a life of happiness and offer us at least some modicum of peace.

But now? Now, I knew. With my new way of seeing things spiritually, gleaned from my experiences of the prior three years, I now realized I was on a path that, to me, felt real and absolute. I was now on *the* path which I had instinctively known existed long before I found it yet which had been so elusive throughout my life.

Now, I have begun to hear another voice, one that's much more gentle than the maniacal screams of the material world. One that whispers the truth that is within us all.

The revelation of truth, coupled with an aggressive seeking after the Heaven I had experienced, was beginning to reveal many things to me:

We are all connected.

What we give, we receive.

The only real time is now.

Your pain is mine, as is your joy, and more.

I am here, as are you, to heal myself and others. And it is through this collective healing that we will remember the beauty of who we are as created beings.

We are perfect creations of God. No matter what we do or who we are, or what we have or do not have.

Seeking after this world's pleasures, sometimes at the expense of others, is a trap that will never lead to true happiness. This constant seeking only enslaves us.

We have all forgotten who we are, and if only a tiny spark of it can be ignited, a slight glimpse of our eternal beauty witnessed, our hearts and minds will be able to cross that threshold from death to life.

In many ways, it all boils down to the stories we tell ourselves about ourselves and others. These stories only have as much power as we give them. And if we give them too much power, we often become imprisoned within them, shackled into patterns of pain. Yet, if we choose to create new stories, those stories can point us toward that which finally liberates us.

Many of our stories are of judgment. And these always boomerang back upon us, keeping us stuck within the pain of our own judgments. Every. Single. Time.

Forgiveness is freedom. We learn to let go of our projection of judgment against the other and, most importantly, against ourselves. But only if we want peace.

Ultimately, we do two things, and two things only.

We either love or we call out for love. There is really nothing else.

EPILOGUE

Thank You, God!

When Hannah died, I believed that either God was who I had always thought He was—and hence worthy of the title—or that I had been wrong.

I wanted to be wrong.

I *begged* to be wrong.

My journey has revealed to me that I *was* wrong. Horribly wrong. Beautifully wrong.

Raised as a Christian, I lived much of my life under that banner, practically memorizing the life of Jesus (though at least partially formed by the interpretations of others). I spent many hours gazing through the pages of the New Testament at his life of Love. But I began to realize that many, myself included, had become masters at shaping scriptures to fit our lives, and our American lives at that. As Voltaire once said, "In the beginning, God created man in His own image, and man has been trying to repay the favor ever since."

Yes, I desperately wanted the depth of love that Jesus seemed to speak of; though, from my observation, that type of love is rarely seen within the walls of most churches or mosques or synagogues on Earth.

I had slung my prior belief system up onto the highest shelf after Hannah died, allowing me to pursue God on my own terms and not on those downloaded and programmed into me by others. Religious or not, I reckoned that if God loved me, He could and would meet me away from the physical, mental, and psychological structures built by man. That He would meet me where I was.

God's Love, I now know, exceeds our wildest imaginations, our highest hopes.

Picture, if you will, an all-encompassing Love. For me, it was when Hannah was born, the first time I felt what I consider *unconditional* love. I have now experienced, in an even more intense and beautiful way, that God created us into being in such beauty and love that even my love for Hannah and my other children could not begin to compare.

As I fought for healing, and for what might lie beyond, I began to see doors open up, and I experienced Beauty and Love unwordable. Love took on new meaning for me. I began to realize that the depth of God's Love for each of His creations, His extensions of Himself, was far beyond what we could ever dream of. With this realization, it became unfathomable to me that a Loving God could ever create with Love only to cast out His beloved. Love cannot destroy that which it creates.

Through forgiveness, I began to see the depth of this truth. I can now see how it was the stories I had made up in my mind to protect myself throughout my life that have led to almost all of my problems. As I have begun to learn to wipe those stories off the slate, to re-edit the story, I am now able to see me, and all of us, in a different light.

Relationships are tricky when we operate from an egoic frame of mind, hoping others can fill in our gaps. It is simply not their job to do so, and once I realized this truth and began to apply this insight to all my relationships, even if little by little, beauty began to emerge. Of course, this guarantees nothing for the future, no matter how much we would like to think so, but I am learning to live now, learning to love me, learning to find the truest form of Love within me. And, when this occurs, I am more at peace to let everything else take care of itself.

As I type these last thoughts out, I am filled with a deep sense of Love. One that is indescribable. I feel Hannah with me. She is now the one sitting behind me, holding me up, supporting me, whispering in my ear, pointing me toward truth, leading me forever to the Love we all seek. Her smile is radiant beyond words, her laughter resonating deep within my being, her eyes peering deep within me, touching my soul.

Hannah encouraged me to write this journey out, to share our love, to share the depths of my heart's pains and the agonies of my mind, to let others who are mired in grief know there is hope. Her first words upon finding out she was dying still echo faintly in my mind: "I'm so sorry for you and Momma." Though they have been ever softening under the beauty of her last words, which rest within my heart: "I. Love. You."

Hannah did love me so very much, yet her heart was big enough to love so many more with that same type of love. She loved from a different place—a place of knowing, a place of beauty. She saw each of us beyond our stuff, way past our silly, worldly prides and greeds and petty nothings. She somehow knew of Love's reality, that forgiveness is life, and she lived it out for us to witness.

I learned much from my daughter. I will always miss her. I long to be with her again.

But not yet.

She is now the one making up little songs, singing them with joy to me. Comforting me.

Once more, she slips her long, slender fingers into my short, stubby ones and sits with me. We don't have to say anything. We never did. We simply sit, our hearts connected. Comfortable.

I can hear her whisper that she loves me.

I whisper back.

"A hell of a journey you sent me on, baby!"

She smiles. A knowing smile.

"I love you, Daddy," she whispers.

Tears fill my eyes. Joy swells my heart. I look to the heavens and smile.

"Hannah, I love you …"

Acknowledgements

To acknowledge all those who have contributed to my story would require a volume longer than the book itself, so I'm going to limit my thanks to just a few folks.

But before I get to them, I would like to acknowledge the role of pain in shaping this memoir, in shaping me. Pain's sharp talons did what nothing else could do, opening my eyes to a world that I would have never known existed. And for that I am thankful. Though it may now feel free to get the hell out of here!

Now, onto a few more physically recognizable helpers, to whom I would like to express my gratitude.

First off …

My mom! Wow! I told her the day Hannah died that I was going to write this book and that it would be called *Fuck You, God!* My beautiful mother, a lifelong Christian, said, "I understand," as she had witnessed what I had been through, what we all had been through. And she did understand what I was saying. She has also been my greatest encouragement each step of the way and is always willing to listen. Always. And she is a hell of a writer herself.

My wife, Meg. What an amazing ride we have had, so many beautiful moments through the decades, raising not just Hannah but Kyle and Luke and Beka, an amazing group of kids as anyone could be blessed to have. Though the past few years have been more of a rollercoaster, I can never thank her enough for every last bit of the "good" and the "bad," each element instrumental on my healing journey. She was the catalyst in jumpstarting me on this journey of healing. I'm not sure I could have even begun without her.

Lara Blacklock, who came into my life at just the right moment and made it clear that this book needed to be finished, that everything else could wait. She was right! Her encouragement in this area and her foresight have proven invaluable.

Amanda Johnson and the team at Awaken Village Press, who I turned to when I needed someone to help me "see it through." Wow! What dedication, loving insights, and gentle corrections! Amanda has gone above and beyond in making sure this book shares my heart in the way I have intended it to be shared.

Phil Williams is a storyteller, merging the worlds of "normal" life, sports, grief, spirituality, and more—sometimes with a humorous touch and often with a knack for the whimsical. A former collegiate football star at Florida State University (two-time Academic All-American), he spent nearly three decades as an NFL agent before facing what many consider the most painful reality one can experience—the death of his daughter—and then stumbling through the brutal aftermath in search of healing and truth, open to exploring modalities that would have previously been taboo. For the past eight-plus years, he has enjoyed traversing what he calls the "Robinson Crusoe beaches of the Caribbean" in Costa Rica. Learn more or follow along at philwilliamswrites.com.